Using

Excel Visual Basic® for Applications

Using

Excel Visual Basic® for Applications

Elisabeth Boonin

Using Excel Visual Basic® for Applications

Composed in *ITC Century*, *ITC Highlander*, and *MCPdigital* by Que Corporation.

Credits

To my brother, Sam, for unflagging support and for proving it is possible to be even crankier than an author with a deadline.

About the Author

Elisabeth Boonin is a freelance writer and computer consultant. As a university lecturer and software designer, she has developed classes, seminars, and articles on many subjects. Her example-oriented, commonsense approach has built her a reputation as an effective teacher and writer.

Acknowledgments

The technical aspects of putting together a computer book are formidable, and I was fortunate to have many people available to help me. Nevet Basker at Microsoft worked long hours to help standardize the conventions I use. And thanks to my augur, Alonzo Gariepy, who foretold the outcome of this book through frequent evisceration and scrutiny of the entrails of Windows 95.

Thanks goes to many of the editors at Que—in particular to Deborah Abshier, for patience and persistence in pulling together the parts of this book, and to Fred Slone for getting me involved with the project. Lisa Gebken, Robin Drake, and Joe Risse were invaluable in transforming the book from my first draft to this, the final version.

Many people gave me personal encouragement and support while I wrote. My parents, Nancy and Joe Boonin, were instrumental in the conception of the project. They were always there for me (I was here). Susan Moretsky got me going in the mornings, kept me fed and watered, and distracted me when I needed it. Geoffrey, Vijnani, and Dharani helped to keep me going during slow days. Judy, Shawna, and Jon Dannhardt were always very patient with me and enthusiastic about my work.

A very special thanks goes to Steve Roti, for his encouragement and advice. As publisher, technical advisor, mentor, and friend, Steve stands out as the kind of guy who deserves to wind up in book acknowledgments.

Tell Us What You Think!

As the reader of this book, *you* are our most important critic and commentator. We value your opinion and want to know what we're doing right, what we could do better, what areas you'd like to see us publish in, and any other words of wisdom you're willing to pass our way.

As the Executive Editor for the Programming team at Macmillan Computer Publishing, I welcome your comments. You can fax, email, or write me directly to let me know what you did or didn't like about this book—as well as what we can do to make our books stronger.

Please note that I cannot help you with technical problems related to the topic of this book, and that due to the high volume of mail I receive, I might not be able to reply to every message.

When you write, please be sure to include this book's title and author as well as your name and phone or fax number. I will carefully review your comments and share them with the author and editors who worked on the book.

Mail: Executive Editor
          Programming
          Macmillan Computer Publishing
          201 W. 103rd Street
          Indianapolis, Indiana 46290
          USA

Fax: 317-817-7070

E-mail: vb@mcp.com

Contents at a Glance

Special Topics

Appendix

Help Index

Index

Table of Contents

"Hey, look at all those colors!"

see page 28

"Oops. That wasn't what I meant to do"

Don't know the keyboard? Learn from the macro recorder

5 A Little Bit of Programming Goes a Long Way

What happens when... If/Then and Else

Part II: VBA Programming Guide

6 VBA Information Online

"But I don't know what it's called!"

Expressions and operators give you more programming power!

Indenting code Makes it easier To read

Refer to objects by.using. names.like. this

see page 187

"What went wrong?"

12 Getting Information Into and Out of Worksheets

Loops and arrays work great together

see page 225

13 Working with Lists of Things

Part III: Changing the Face of Excel

Hold it right there! How to pause a procedure

see page 247

16 Using VBA to Work with Your Menus

*Tons of
toolbars!*

Add controls to make your dialog boxes easy to use

see page 320

Part IV: Special Topics

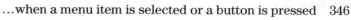
21 Integrate Your Program with Excel

*All kinds
of add-ins*

see page 356

22 Making Code Run Automatically

23 Making Your Programming User-Friendly

Appendix

How to make Excel look for an event

see page 372

Help Index

Index   411

Introduction

Did you study a foreign language in high school? If you did, chances are you probably got pretty good at conjugating verbs, memorizing vocabulary words, and maybe even conversing with your language teacher. I started German in the seventh grade. After four years of fairly diligent work, I met some real live Germans. Imagine my shock when I found out that I could barely communicate with them! Was I going to have to study the language for four more years before I could use it?

The following year I traveled to Sweden as an exchange student. When I arrived there, my Swedish was limited to *Smorgasbord* and *Volvo*. However, after just a couple of months of living with a Swedish family and attending a local school, I found that I was chattering along quite well in the language. Oh, I probably knew more German vocabulary and grammatical rules, but the Swedish I knew, I used. The words I knew were ones I needed to know, and if my grammar or pronunciation was slightly off, it didn't seem to matter. I was actually using the language and communicating with people.

If you want to become a professional programmer, you certainly need to learn the finer points of good programming style. If, however, your interest in programming is to make your Excel work more productive, there's no need to spend weeks learning about the different kinds of variables and procedures before you ever try to use what you've learned.

Excel's built-in programming language, VBA, doesn't require months of study. You can create simple and truly useful programs and macros from the very beginning. As your language power improves, you'll be able to generalize these techniques and use them as building blocks for more elaborate programs.

What makes this book different?

Most programming language books teach you to become a programmer. This one does not. Instead, it shows you how to do new things in Excel—things that are really useful and help you in your work. The funny thing is that with this book, you become a programmer along the way. The difference is that by using this book, you can get results before you know much about the VBA language. As you learn more of the language, you'll have the structure in place to be able to put what you learn to good use.

Think about how you learned Excel. You probably didn't know much about complicated formulas or tables when you began to enter numbers into rows and columns. You learned things as they became useful. As you found out more about Excel, you discovered more functionality. If you're like me, you're still learning how to do things in Excel. And, if you're like me, you don't want to know *everything* about Excel, just what helps you in your work.

When you want to learn how to do something with VBA, this book cuts right to the chase and tells you how. It's also a great source of new ideas for ways to improve your Excel spreadsheets and the way you work.

Above all else, this book is designed to help you understand and use VBA, without using a lot of fancy jargon and technical descriptions.

How do I use this book?

If you've never programmed or created Excel macros before, the first few chapters of this book are designed to give you a quick start in the world of Excel programming. You can read the chapters from beginning to end, or browse through some parts and focus on the topics that seem interesting and useful to you.

After this, you'll definitely want to start picking and choosing where to devote your attention. As much as possible, the topics are independent of each other. If the thing you need to know how to do is described on page 250, you don't have to read pages 1–249 to get there. When topics are related, there will be notes in the margins referring you to other parts of the book, so feel free to jump around.

The table of contents is very results-oriented. Chapter and section names describe what you can do, rather than listing obscure programming terms. If you're trying to figure out how to do something or you're looking for ideas, the table of contents is a great place to look. If you want information on a specific topic or VBA term, check the index for references.

How this book is put together

To help you find your way around, this book is divided into four parts. Each section encompasses a bit more of what is possible with VBA, although there's no need to read them in order.

In fact, you'll find that some of the later chapters will be very useful right away and are not difficult to read. For example, Chapter 19, "Using Dialog Box Controls," requires no special VBA knowledge to read. Without doing any programming, you can learn how to put buttons and other controls right on your worksheets and use them to affect the values of cells. Don't feel like you need to use the book sequentially, or that if you haven't quite mastered one chapter, you won't be able to read later chapters.

Here's how the sections are organized:

Part I: Getting Started

Brand new to the world of Excel programming? Spend some time with this section. You'll learn how to write complicated Excel programs without knowing a word of VBA by using the macro recorder. You'll also learn how to create simple programs from scratch. If you're familiar with programming or Excel macros, you may want to skim those parts.

If you're skeptical about how fast you can actually start writing useful programs, take a look at Chapter 4, "Write Your Own Worksheet Functions." You'll be able to convert your existing Excel skills into VBA programming skills right away.

Part II: VBA Programming Guide

Just like a foreign language, VBA has its vocabulary and grammar. This is your reference to the VBA language in a nutshell, giving you detailed descriptions of variables, statements, objects, properties, and control structures—all of the parts of speech for this language and rules for their use.

I recommend that you don't try to read this part of the book from beginning to end. The information provided in these chapters is abstract in places and is best digested one piece at time. Keep looking at other parts of the book and create lots of macros and worksheet functions without feeling like you need to know everything written here. You'll find these chapters useful as a reference and as a way to gradually expand on your programming skills.

Part III: Changing the Face of Excel

Using nothing but the tools that come with Excel, you can completely change the spreadsheet environment, with tricks like these:

- Create new menus and menu items

- Build custom toolbars

- Make dialog boxes that interact with the users and run your programs

Toolbars, menus, and dialog boxes can all be created and changed with very little programming required. Of course, when you've got extensive programming to go with them, they become even more useful. This part of the book contains a lot of information that's very easy to implement and can make your spreadsheets look fantastic.

Part IV: Special Topics

This section deals with several different subjects ranging from making code run automatically, to working with databases. They all fall into the general category of putting together various programming skills to create a unified whole.

Chapter 21, "Integrate Your Program with Excel," is non-technical and very useful. This chapter will be helpful to you if you want other people to be able to use your programs—even very simple ones. Once you're really cranking with VBA, Chapter 23, "Making Your Programming User-Friendly," will give you tips and tricks for designing front ends for Excel that replace the normal interface. You'll be turning Excel into your own application!

Special book elements

This book contains a number of special elements and conventions to help you find information quickly—or skip anything you don't want to read right now.

 TIP **Tips point out information often overlooked in the documenta-**
tion, or help you use your software more efficiently. Some tips help you
solve or avoid problems.

CAUTION   **Cautions alert you to potentially dangerous consequences of a** procedure or practice, such as loss or corruption of data.

Q&A   **What are Q&A notes?**

These are notes cast in a question-and-answer format. Some are just additional information. Others discuss solutions to common problems. Many of the problems are easy-to-make but hard-to-find coding mistakes.

❝ *Plain English, please!*

These notes explain the meanings of technical **terms** or computer **jargon**. **❞**

For references to other chapters with related information, look for this cross-reference in the margin.

The following is an example of program code:

```
Sub Greeting()
    user = InputBox("Who are you?")
    If user = "Sam" Then
        Beep
        MsgBox "Hi Sam"
    End If
End Sub
```

After each code listing, look for the magnifying glass to identify the text that explains the code listing. Everything you need to know about the preceding code listing is discussed here.

How do I use this in the real world?

These notes give you insight on how the subject at hand applies to real-life problems.

Catch the bug

Like a mini-quiz that you can use to test your knowledge, Catch the Bug elements show you programming code with a problem. Your job is to figure out what is wrong.

Speaking of VBA

Special words in the VBA language are presented here with a condensed description of how they are used. Words that appear in *italics* are sample terms that are to be replaced with text specific to a program. Text that appears in square brackets [like this] is optional.

This element is a mini-reference to the words and is generally followed by an easy-to-read description and examples of what the word is used for.

Throughout this book, I use a comma to separate the parts of a pull-down menu command. For example, to start a new document, you'll choose File, New. That means, "Pull down the File menu, and choose New from the list." The underlined characters in these words indicate the accelerator keys for a command. This means you can hold down the Alt key and type the letter as a keyboard alternative for the command. For example, since the F in File is underlined, you can type Alt+F to choose the file menu. And if you see two keys separated by a plus sign, such as Ctrl+X, that means to press and hold down the first key, press the second key, then release both keys.

In addition to these elements sprinkled throughout the chapter, at the end of each chapter you find a set of review questions and review exercises. The questions are designed to test your knowledge of the terms and concepts that you just covered. The exercises ask you to apply this understanding, often by modifying an existing code segment from the book or writing your own code from scratch. The exercises will give you some ideas for programs, but the best exercise of all is to use what you learn in your own work.

Also, throughout the book you'll run across text that is in a different typeface. **Bold** is for new terms or text that you type. Monospace is used to identify VBA code listings. Words written in monospace refer to words that appear in VBA programs.

1

Introducing Macros

● In this chapter:

- What is a macro and why would I want to use one?

- How to create and use macros

- Fast ways to run macros

- How do macros fit into the world of VBA programming?

The Excel macro recorder allows you to start writing really useful VBA programs right off the bat . . . . ▸

I have a favorite recipe for cheesecake that I got from my father. Every time I make it, I perform the same steps. I measure, combine, and bake the ingredients according to the written instructions. I could, if I had a personal chef, hand the instructions off and have the cake baked for me. Actually, though, I like baking things myself so there's not much chance I'll be hiring a personal chef anytime soon.

What I'm not too crazy about is doing the same work over and over again when I use my computer. When I have a task involving several different steps that I need to perform regularly in Excel, I hand the work off to a macro, one of Excel's personal chefs.

Macros can automate jobs such as formatting worksheets, entering data, creating charts, or drawing graphics. As you'll see in this chapter, anything that you can do in Excel using your mouse and keyboard, you can get a macro to do for you, as if you were actually performing the mouse and keyboard actions by hand.

 Plain English, please!

A **macro** is a list of instructions that Excel can carry out automatically. If this sounds suspiciously like a program to you, you're absolutely right. Macros are actually a special kind of VBA program.

How are macros created?

There are two distinct ways to create a macro:

- Perform the task you wish to automate, and let the computer record all of your actions for later playback

- Write a macro from scratch by using the VBA programming language

To learn how to program a macro in VBA, see Chapter 2, "Module Sheets: The Home of Macros and VBA."

This chapter focuses on the first method. By using the **macro recorder**, you can create extensive macros without knowing any VBA programming whatsoever.

 Plain English, please!

The **macro recorder** is a tool built into Excel that can watch you perform a task and later repeat these steps for you automatically.

The macro recorder

One day, I may actually hire a personal chef to bake my cheesecakes. If and when I do, I'll need to give him the recipe. I could do this by writing all the directions down on a piece of paper. A different solution would be to turn on a video recorder and then make the cake myself while being taped. Then all of the ingredients, measurements, and preparation instructions would show up on the video.

Creating macros with the macro recorder in Excel works much like videotaping yourself. The macro recorder keeps a record of your actions as you perform the task you wish to automate. Later, you can perform the same task by playing back the macro you recorded.

Recording a macro

The process of recording a macro can be broken down into six steps:

1 Alert Excel that you want to start recording a macro.

2 Name your macro.

3 Select options for your macro, such as its description and where it should be stored.

4 Start the macro recorder. (Once you do this, the camera is rolling. Every action you take after clicking on the OK button will be recorded by the macro recorder.)

5 Perform the task(s) you wish to automate.

6 Stop the macro recorder.

To see this process in action, let's record a macro that enters some text and formats the font. Start with a new worksheet in front of you:

1 Select Tools, Record Macro, Record New Macro. The Record New Macro dialog box appears.

2 Enter the name **ExpenseReport** (typed as one word with no space) and the description **writes and formats text** as shown in figure 1.1.

Fig. 1.1
How you name and
describe your macro
will help you to
identify it later.

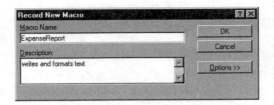

3 Click on the <u>O</u>ptions button. The dialog box expands to display more
options. In the lower left-hand corner are three option buttons grouped
together in a box called Store In. Make sure the button labeled This
<u>W</u>orkbook is selected. Later in this chapter, you'll learn what that
means.

4 Click OK. The Record New Macro dialog box closes and the Stop
Recording toolbar appears with the Stop button, as in figure 1.2.
The camera is now rolling.

Fig. 1.2
Once you start
recording your macro,
the Stop button
appears on your screen.

5 Here's where you perform the actions you wish to have recorded.
In cell A2, type **Expense Report**. Make it bold and change the size
to 18 points. Then, widen column A to accommodate the text.

6 Click on the Stop button or choose <u>T</u>ools, <u>R</u>ecord Macro, <u>S</u>top Recording. Your actions are no longer being recorded.

Q&A *Why is there no Stop button on my screen after I start
recording?*

The Stop button's toolbar may have been accidentally hidden. While
recording, choose <u>V</u>iew, <u>T</u>oolbars and then make sure that the Stop Recording box is checked.

Q&A *I see the Stop button, but why can't I click on it?*

You probably have not finished editing the current cell. You need to press
Enter or use some other method to accept the cell edits before the macro
can be stopped.

Using macros you've recorded

Once the macro is created, you never need to go through the process of performing the action again; just run the macro, and it will repeat the steps you took when the macro recorder was on.

 Plain English, please!

Running a macro is the act of using a macro that you've recorded previously. The same terminology applies to other kinds of VBA programs: to make them do their stuff, you **run** them. Outside this book, you may encounter the phrase **playing a macro**. This means exactly the same thing as running it.

To run the macro you created above:

1 Select an unused worksheet in the same workbook as the one where you created your macro.

2 Choose <u>T</u>ools, <u>M</u>acro. The Macro dialog box shown in figure 1.3 appears.

Fig. 1.3
Excel automatically adds any macros you record to the Macro dialog box.

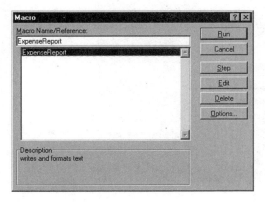

3 Click on the name ExpenseReport and then click the <u>R</u>un button.

It may have happened faster than you could follow, but the formatted text is now added to your worksheet, just as if you had typed it in and formatted it yourself. Your personal chef just prepared a meal for you.

Q&A *ExpenseReport doesn't appear on my list. Where did it go?*

You may have switched workbooks from the one where you created the ExpenseReport macro. Try recording it again and then run it from the same workbook.

If it seemed a little cumbersome to run the macro, don't worry. The next section in this chapter includes a number of ways to make running the macro very efficient.

Options available when recording macros

There are several different options available to you in the Record New Macro dialog box. Of the options described in the following sections, all except for the Macro Name and Description are accessed by clicking on the Options button. You can see this button in figure 1.1. Once you click on the button, the dialog box expands and looks like the one in figure 1.4.

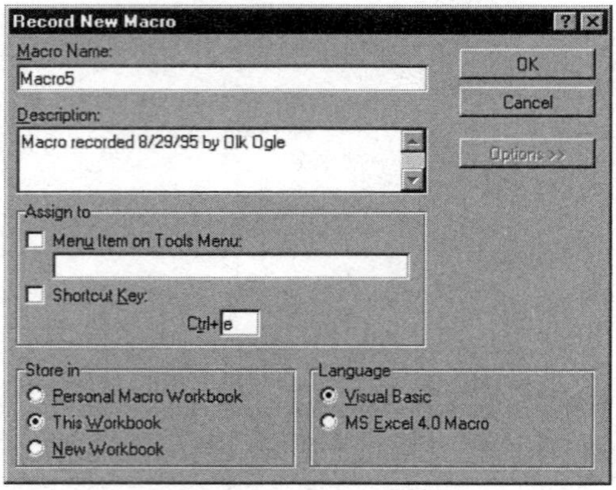

Fig. 1.4
In the expanded version of the Record New Macro dialog box, you can specify options for your macro including keyboard shortcuts and menu items.

Macro name and description

On the one hand, it doesn't really matter what you name your macro, because it will perform the same actions regardless of what you call it. On the other, you want to name your macro something that will help you remember what it does. If you're experimenting with macros and you don't care too much about telling one from another, go ahead and use the name that Excel provides automatically: the word Macro followed by a number.

There are a few rules that must be followed when naming macros:

- The name must start with a letter, although it can include numbers as well. You can also use the underscore character (_) if you wish to separate words. Thus, **Expense_Report3** is a valid name for a macro but **Expense Report** and **3rdReport** are not.

- There are several symbols that cannot be used when naming macros. If you just stick to using letters, numbers, and the underscore character in your macro names, you'll have no trouble.

To learn more about keywords, see Chapter 2, "Module Sheets: The Home of Macros and VBA."

- The words that VBA uses for special meaning, called **keywords**, should be avoided in macro names. Some of them are strictly forbidden and will create an error if you try to give that name to a macro.

The description field gives you a place to create a lengthier description of what your macro does. This description shows up later in the Macro dialog box when you select the name of the macro. You can write several lines of description here, but don't make it too long. The space in the Macro dialog box for displaying the description is somewhat smaller, so if your description is very long, not all of it will show up.

TIP **To change the description after you've created a macro, choose** Tools, Macro, and then click on the Options button. You can now edit the macro's Description box.

Two quick ways to run your macros

Since macros are supposed to help speed up your work, it makes sense to make them as convenient to use as possible. Thus, Excel provides you with two easy ways to provide quick access to your macros: shortcut keys and menu items. Both of these are found in the Assign To section of the Record New Macro dialog box.

Assign it to a shortcut key

A **shortcut key** is a key combination that runs a macro when you press it. To create a shortcut key for your macro, put a check in the Shortcut Key check box. You may use the key combination that Excel suggests or create one of your own. Be careful to pick something that isn't used in Excel for some other purpose. For example, the Ctrl+B key combination is used to set the font style of the selection to bold. If you assign it to your macro, you won't be able to use it for bold anymore. If other people will be using your workbooks, keep in mind that unexpected surprises like this may not be welcome.

To change the character that Excel suggests, delete it from the box and type your own.

TIP **You can also add the Shift key to your shortcut keys so that you** end up with Ctrl+Shift+*letter*. To do this, hold down the Shift key while typing in the character you wish to use.

Add it to the menu

Another way to get to your macros is through a menu item. By checking Menu Item on the Tools menu in the Record New Macro dialog box, and typing the name you wish to have appear on the menu, your macro automatically is added to that menu. In figure 1.5, the item Expense Report has been added to the Tools menu.

Fig. 1.5
The name on the menu doesn't have to be the same as the name of the macro. Here Expense Report appears as two words, unlike the macro name which was written as one word.

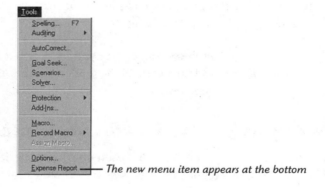

The new menu item appears at the bottom

If you want, you can add an accelerator key to your menu item. An **accelerator key** is an underlined letter in a menu item that can be selected with the keyboard. To add an accelerator key, type an ampersand (**&**) before the letter you wish to use. For example, typing **&Expense Report** produces the menu item Expense Report shown in figure 1.5. Check the Tools menu before creating an accelerator key. It's best to use one that hasn't been used in another menu item.

Deciding where the macro gets stored

To learn more about the personal macro workbook, see Chapter 2, "Module Sheets: The Home of Macros and VBA."

There are three different options for storing your macro in a workbook. You can keep a macro in the current workbook, a new workbook, or a special workbook called the Personal Macro Workbook.

In this chapter, you've stored all of your macros in the current workbook. Macros can be run from the workbook in which they are stored or from other open workbooks. For now, continue to store your macros with the This Workbook option selected in the Record New Macro dialog box.

What language should I use?

In older versions of Microsoft Excel, version 4.0 and lower, a different macro standard was in place. By selecting MS Excel 4.0 Macro, you record a macro that can be used with these old versions of Excel.

 **CAUTION** **This book does not cover any techniques for programming in the** MS Excel 4.0 macro programming language. Unless you have a specific need to do otherwise, record all of your macros with the Visual Basic option selected.

You control where the action takes place

Imagine that you're in a car with a friend. She tells you she's going to show you something interesting, but you can only see it from this particular spot. Which spot does she mean? Maybe it's a special vantage point from which you can see a mountain. In that case, "here" refers to where you've driven. On the other hand, she could mean that there's something in her car she wants to show you and you can only see it from the passenger seat. In that case, "here" refers to your position in the car. You might drive 100 miles away, but you'd still be in the same spot relative to the car.

The Excel macro recorder faces a similar dilemma when writing macros that affect certain cells. You specify that actions take place in a particular spot, but which spot do you mean? Here are three examples of macros where the cells in which you'd like the action to take place are different:

- A macro that writes your name in cell D1 of your spreadsheet, regardless of which cell is selected when you run the macro

- A macro that writes your name in whatever cell is selected

- A macro that writes your name in whatever cell is selected and the date in the cell immediately below it

When you record these macros, you tell Excel, "I want this macro to take place HERE," but what you mean by "here" varies from instance to instance.

Macros can run in selected cells...

Sometimes, you'll want to create a macro that will operate on a cell or cells that are already selected before running the macro. For instance, suppose you want a macro that will change the font in the selected cells to bold and italic with a border. This can be achieved with the following procedure:

1 Select one or several cells.

2 Choose Tools, Record Macro, Record New Macro.

3 Give the macro a name, and click OK.

4 Click on the Bold and Italic toolbar buttons.

5 Choose Format, Cells and click on the Border tab. Select Outline and the double border style.

6 Click OK to accept the border selection.

7 Stop the macro recorder by clicking on the Stop button.

Notice the order of steps 1 and 2. First, you selected a cell or cells, then you turned on the macro recorder. The selection of cells was not recorded as part of the macro. This has the great advantage of making no assumptions about which or how many cells you wish the macro to operate on. You may have recorded the macro on a single cell, but you can run it later on a range of cells or a different single cell.

To run this macro later, you simply select the cell or cells you want to format, then run the macro.

...or run in the same place every time

Sometimes, you want to create a macro that performs an action in the same cell or cells, regardless of what is selected when you run it. Perhaps you want a macro that writes Monthly Report and your name at the top of the current worksheet. By starting the macro recorder before you click in the desired cell, the instruction to select that cell is included as part of the macro.

Here's a macro that puts the title Monthly Report into Cell E1 and your name into cell E2. Before creating this macro, however, select Tools, Record Macro. In the Record Macro menu, there is an item called Use Relative References. For this example, make sure that there is no check mark next to Use Relative References. It should look like figure 1.6. Later in the chapter, you'll learn about creating macros with this option turned on.

Fig. 1.6

The missing check mark next to Use Relative References indicates that this feature is currently turned off.

Now you're ready to record the macro:

1 Choose Tools, Record Macro, Record New Macro.

2 Type the name **TitleMaker** and click OK.

3 Select cell E1 and type **Monthly Report**.

4 Select cell E2 and type your name. Press Enter.

5 Click on the Stop button.

Try running this macro in different worksheets with various cells selected. It should always run in cells E1 and E2.

Using relative references

Here's a puzzle: suppose you want to create a macro that writes your first name in whatever cell is selected and your last name in the cell directly below it. How can you record this macro?

Because you want the macro to operate on whatever the currently selected cell is, you'll choose the cell before turning on the macro recorder. Suppose this is cell C2. After typing your first name, you'll want to select cell C3. You can do this with the mouse, with the arrow keys, or by pressing Enter. No matter what you do, though, you're telling the macro recorder to select cell C3.

Why is that a problem? Suppose you want to run this macro later in another column. You select cell D5 and then run the macro. Your first name is written in cell D5, but then your last name gets put into cell C3. When you selected C3 during recording, it wasn't recorded as the cell below the one where you started, but specifically as cell C3. Instead, you'd like to record a macro to choose the one below where you started. If you're not convinced this is a problem, try recording a macro like this and see what happens.

Relative references provide the solution to this dilemma.

 Plain English, please!

> A **reference** is how you indicate a cell or group of cells to Excel. You can use an **absolute reference** to indicate a cell that is unvarying regardless of what is selected in the spreadsheet, or a **relative reference** when its position is based on the current selection. **"**

Activate relative references by choosing Tools, Record Macro and selecting the Use Relative References option in the menu (shown in fig. 1.6). A check mark should now appear by this menu item. Now, when you record your macro, all of your cell selections are recorded in relation to the starting place.

For many macros, it doesn't matter whether Use Relative References is checked or not. A macro that doesn't make changes to any individual cells or group of cells won't care whether or not relative references are being used. For example, a macro that turns off gridlines and changes the page layout will perform exactly the same whether it was written with Use Relative References checked or not.

What do macros have to do with programming and VBA?

Excel has a built-in programming language, called **VBA**. With VBA, you can create all kinds of additional functionality for your Excel spreadsheets.

 Plain English, please!

VBA is an acronym for **Visual Basic for Applications**. There is also a separate software package called Microsoft Visual Basic which is similar, but not identical, to VBA. If you own Excel 7, you already have the Excel version of VBA built in.

Q&A *If VBA is so great, what's the big deal about the macro recorder?*

The macro recorder actually *writes* VBA programs for you. When I say that it writes VBA programs, there is no metaphor intended. As you record macros, the steps are immediately translated into programming code and written on a special sheet in your workbook. You could create the identical macro by going to that sheet and typing in the programming code by hand.

To learn how to find the VBA code that the macro recorder writes for you, see Chapter 3, "Using the VBA Editor and the Macro Recorder Together."

So, by using the macro recorder, you write VBA programs without ever having to personally use the VBA programming language—the macro recorder translates it for you.

Why then, you might wonder, would anyone ever want to learn to create VBA programs without using the macro recorder? The answer is that the macro recorder only allows you to do a fraction of what is possible with VBA. The rest of this book explores various projects you can accomplish in VBA, much of which would be impossible with the macro recorder alone.

However, the macro recorder will continue to be a useful tool, even when you're much more familiar with VBA. Often, recording a macro is the first and easiest step to writing a program. It provides the program framework which you can supplement with VBA programming. It is also an amazing learning tool, because to find out how VBA works with much of the Excel environment, you can record a macro and then look at the VBA code that was automatically generated and learn a great deal by example.

Leveraging the very basic skills required to operate the macro recorder allows you to start writing really useful VBA programs right off the bat.

Summary

This chapter introduced you to macros and the macro recorder. You learned how to create new macros, including providing different options for running them. You also learned how to specify more precisely which cells your macros should run in.

Review questions

1 What is a macro?

2 What is VBA?

3 How can you write VBA programs without actually typing programming code?

4 Name three different ways to run a macro that you've written.

5 Name two things that affect which cells a macro runs in.

Exercises

1 In a new workbook, re-create the ExpenseReport macro from the "Recording a macro" section earlier, adding a border around the cell.

2 Create a macro that types your name and put a menu item for it in the Tools menu.

3 Without re-recording the macro, add a shortcut key to the macro you created in Exercise 2.

4 Find some text that you often enter in a worksheet cell and create a macro that will type it automatically in the currently selected cell.

5 Write a macro that puts your name in whatever cell is currently selected and writes your address in the cells below. (Hint: use relative references.)

Module Sheets: The Home of Macros and VBA

● **In this chapter:**

● **Where and how does the macro recorder save macros?**

● **Real programming! Write a macro without recording it**

● **What you need to know about the VBA editor**

● **Customize the editing environment so things are the way you like them**

Sometimes, you'll want to create a macro from the ground up by typing it directly into a module sheet . . . . ➤

In the previous chapter, I mentioned that when you record a macro, it's stored in your workbook. What I didn't explain was specifically where it was stored or in what form.

This chapter explains where and how the macro recorder stores your macros: as written instructions in a special kind of Excel sheet. It teaches you how to create macros there yourself, without the help of the macro recorder. While you're creating and running these macros, the Visual Basic toolbar can provide some handy shortcuts.

What's a module sheet?

You're already familiar with one kind of Excel sheet: the worksheet. Excel has other types of sheets, one of which is called a **module sheet**.

A module sheet, shown in figure 2.1, is more similar to a word processing document than a spreadsheet. There are no gridlines because its job is to handle text, not columns and rows of numeric information.

Fig. 2.1
Putting a module sheet into your workbook gives you a place to start programming.

Type in text just like in a word processor

The Module sheet tab

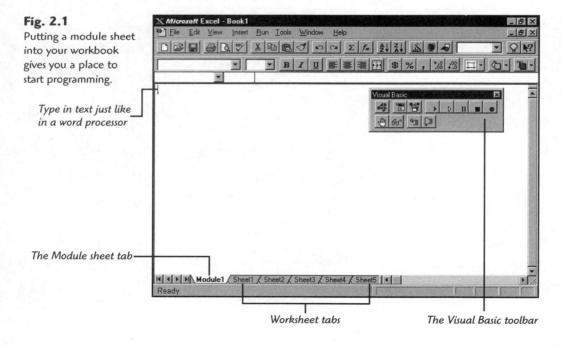

Worksheet tabs

The Visual Basic toolbar

To learn about dialog sheets—another type of Excel sheet— see Chapter 20, "Creating and Using Dialog Boxes."

 Plain English, please!

Module sheets are often simply called modules. A **module** is a programming term for a set of programming instructions that are stored together. In the case of VBA, a module consists of the contents of a single module sheet.

The text that you work with in module sheets is VBA code. It can get there in one of two ways. When you record macros with the macro recorder, code is automatically entered in a module sheet for you. Alternatively, you can type code directly into a module sheet.

 Plain English, please!

Code means instructions written in a programming language—in this case, the VBA programming language.

Create macros without the macro recorder

The macro recorder is a great administrative assistant that can automatically make macros for you. Why would you ever do anything else?

It turns out that there are many things that can be achieved in a macro that can't be recorded. The macro recorder is also not the last word in making macros as polished and efficient as they might be. Sometimes, you'll want to create a macro from the ground up. In other words, you want to write a VBA program.

Speaking of *Macros*

That's right. You create a macro by writing a VBA program because that's what macros are: a special kind of VBA program called a subroutine. Subroutines are discussed in greater detail in Chapter 8, "VBA Procedures."

How to add and remove module sheets

When you first open a new workbook, Excel automatically puts some new worksheets in it for you to use. Excel doesn't include any module sheets for you, however. You must add these yourself.

To add a module sheet to your workbook, choose Insert, Macro, Module. Alternatively, you can click on one of the existing worksheet tabs with the right mouse button and choose Insert from the pop-up menu that appears. Then, double-click on the Module icon in the Insert dialog box.

Q&A *If Excel doesn't add module sheets on startup, why does this workbook already have one?*

Whenever you record a macro using the macro recorder, Excel needs a module sheet to store it and adds one to your workbook if necessary. You probably recorded a macro in that workbook. Go ahead and add a new module sheet so you have a clean one to work with.

Once you've added a module sheet, you can find it listed among the worksheet tabs along the bottom of your workbook. You can delete module sheets by choosing Edit, Delete Sheet while the sheet you want to get rid of is on top. Or, you can click on the tab for the module sheet and select Delete from the pop-up menu that appears.

CAUTION   **When you delete a module sheet, you delete all of the macros** and other programs that are stored there as well. Before deleting a module sheet, look at the entire sheet to make sure that there's nothing in there that you want to save.

Typing a macro into your workbook

What goes into a module might well seem rather cryptic at first if you've never done any programming. But you only need to become familiar with a few key concepts, and it will all start to make sense.

If you haven't already, add a module sheet to your workbook by choosing Insert, Macro, Module. Type the following three lines of text on the sheet. The indent on the second line is achieved by putting a tab in front of the word Beep. Once you indent the second line, the third line may automatically indent as well. You can press the Backspace key to get rid of this indentation.

```
Sub MyProgram()
    Beep
End Sub
```

That's it. You've written a macro the "old-fashioned" way.

The first line of your macro, Sub MyProgram(), is its title. The word Sub tells VBA that this is a subroutine, a kind of VBA program. MyProgram is the name of your macro. The parentheses are a required part of every subroutine. Later, you'll learn more about them and what kinds of things you can put into them.

The second line, the word Beep, is the whole guts of the macro. This line is the VBA instruction to make the computer beep. The last line is merely notifying VBA that the program is at an end.

If the program seems confusing to you, bear this in mind: the first and last lines of a macro program are always just like the ones in this program (except with a different name in place of MyProgram). You don't need to understand exactly what the word Sub or the parentheses mean to start using VBA. The only part of this program that *does* anything is the line in the middle, the one word Beep, which tells the computer to beep.

How do I run it?

Although the way you created this macro is very different from the ones you created with the macro recorder, Excel can't tell the difference. You can run these macros in the same way:

- Choose <u>T</u>ools, <u>M</u>acro and select it from the list of Macros. (Excel has automatically added your macro to this list.)

- Define a shortcut key to run your macro

- Create a <u>T</u>ools menu item to run your macro

TIP **To define or change a shortcut key or menu for a macro that** already exists, choose <u>T</u>ools, <u>M</u>acro. After highlighting the name of the desired macro, click on the <u>O</u>ptions button to bring up the Macro Options dialog box. In this dialog box, you can create the shortcut key or menu item.

Try running your macro. If your computer speaker is working, you'll hear the beep.

Catch the bug

Type the following macro into a module. It writes `Hello` in the active worksheet cell. If you type it exactly as shown, then it is a perfectly functional macro, with no problems.

```
Sub Howdy()
    ActiveCell.Formula = "Hello"
End Sub
```

Without switching to a worksheet, choose <u>T</u>ools, <u>M</u>acro, and run the `Howdy` macro from the list. It produces the error message shown in the following figure. Now you have my word for it that this is a completely bug-free piece of code, so why isn't it working?

Answer: The Howdy macro is designed to be run in a worksheet. Its job is to put text into a cell, but there are no cells in your module sheet. To make this macro work properly, you need to be in a worksheet when you run it. The reason you didn't run into this problem with the MyProgram macro is because it didn't use anything specific to a worksheet, like a cell.

How can I use this in the real world?

A macro that beeps? You couldn't create it with the macro recorder, but is this really useful? In Chapter 20, you'll learn how to create your own dialog boxes and you can use the Beep statement to alert users to the fact that a dialog box has appeared.

Typing in module sheets

Entering text into module sheets is much like using any text editor or word processor. You can put text into a module sheet by:

- Typing it in, like you did for MyProgram

- Copying and pasting it from somewhere else (another module sheet, for example)

- Using the macro recorder. The macro you record will automatically enter text into a module sheet for you.

The set of editing tools that lets you type text into a module sheet is called the **VBA editor**. Unlike most word processors, though, the VBA editor monitors what you type and makes changes to your text. For example:

- Assuming you have a color monitor, you'll notice that some words turn blue or other colors as you type them.

- Some words, like Sub or Beep, are automatically capitalized if you type them in all lowercase letters.

- If you don't type things exactly the way they're written in this book, error messages may appear.

The VBA editor is set up to make programming as easy as possible. The liberties it takes with your text actually provides information about the code that VBA is figuring out for you on-the-fly. Once you learn what VBA is telling you, you may find this information quite useful.

You may want to experiment with writing text in module sheets to try out some of the things described in the following sections. Don't worry about trying to write programs—just get a feel for how the editor works. If the error messages are irritating, the section later in this chapter, "How do you want to handle syntax errors?" explains how to disable these temporarily.

VBA changes the capitalization

When VBA recognizes a word, like Beep or Sub, it makes the capitalization for that word uniform. Thus, Sub is always written with a capital S and lowercase u and b. Try typing **sUB MyProgram ()**. When you get to the next line, VBA will have changed it for you. Sometimes, the editor will also change the capitalization of things that you have named yourself.

Blue text marks special VBA words

Some words have a special meaning to VBA. In the MyProgram code, the words Sub and End are words that are set aside by VBA for specific purposes. You can't, for instance, name your program "End" instead of "MyProgram." You could, however, name it "EndZone" if you wanted, because EndZone is not a special VBA word.

The words that have predefined meaning to VBA are called **keywords**. Not all keywords turn blue when you type them, but everything that turns blue is a keyword. The keywords that turn blue are a special set of VBA words called **restricted keywords**. Restricted keywords can only be used for their special purpose. You cannot use a restricted keyword as the name of a macro, for instance.

There are also keywords that are not restricted. For example, Beep is a word that VBA recognizes as having a special meaning but will not prevent you from giving a macro this name. If you know a word is a VBA keyword, you should not use it to name your macros, because it will make the original meaning of the word unavailable.

Green text is for comments

Sometimes, you want to write things down in your code as notes to yourself. Maybe you want to write a reminder of what a program or a part of a program does. The problem is that VBA tries to run the things that you write. If you write

```
This program beeps at me
```

then VBA will try to run those words like a program and won't be able to.

To learn about viewing and editing the code created by the macro recorder, see Chapter 3, "Using the VBA Editor and the Macro Recorder Together."

The way around this is to put an apostrophe (') before your comment. The apostrophe tells VBA to ignore whatever is on the rest of that line. So, now you can write

```
'This program beeps at me
```

without causing errors. The apostrophe and the subsequent text turn green. Text like this is called **commented code**. When the macro recorder creates macros for you, it puts your description above the macro code as commented code.

Comments are an important feature of programming. Although they don't make the program behave differently, they can make it much easier to read. If you're looking at the code of a program at a later time, your comments will understand what you did and why.

 TIP **You can put a comment on the same line as programming code** that you want VBA to run. Just put the code first; VBA ignores everything to the right of the apostrophe.

Red indicates problems

Sometimes when you type a line, all of the characters turn red. This is probably accompanied by a dialog box giving a (usually incomprehensible) description of what's going on. A red line is one that contains a syntax error.

 Plain English, please!
A **syntax error** is a kind of violation of the VBA language. When you write a line of code that breaks some rule of VBA, you've made a syntax error. **"**

A red line requires further attention before VBA is able to run your code. Not all lines with problems turn red—only the ones that VBA can tell right off the bat have syntax errors. The line

```
Hi Mom
```

won't cause a syntax error. However, the line

```
End(MyProgram)
```

will. That's because VBA knows how the word End should be used and can spot immediately that it's being used incorrectly. The words Hi Mom might refer to some things named Hi and Mom that it just doesn't know about, like other programs that you've written. It won't be until VBA tries to run the program that it will encounter any problem with Hi Mom. Errors that VBA doesn't discover until it tries to run them are called **run-time errors**.

How can I write long lines of code without running off the screen?

One thing the VBA editor lacks that is present in virtually all other kinds of text editors is **word wrap**. When you reach the right side of the screen, rather than automatically starting a new line for you, VBA just keeps adding to the current line, scrolling the screen as far as it needs to. This seemingly perverse behavior has a good reason behind it. VBA treats each line of code as an individual entity. If a line got split into two, it would try to deal with each new line separately.

Here is a line of VBA code that assigns a numeric value to a variable:

```
Expenses = 2500
```

If instead, you wrote the code across two lines

```
Expenses =
2500
```

then VBA wouldn't know what to do with it. It would try to deal with the first line, get all ready to assign a value to `Expenses`, and then not find it. It wouldn't look down to the next line, because it must deal with each line completely before going to the next one.

Sometimes, though, a piece of code that all goes together is too long to fit on one line comfortably. You could put it on one line and use the scrollbar, but then you can't read all of it at once. The solution is to use the underscore (_) character.

The underscore character allows you to split what should be one line of code across two lines. Here, the underscore character is used to split the line from above:

```
Expenses = _
2500
```

Notice that a blank space is inserted between the equal sign (=) and the underscore (_). This is necessary to include so that VBA doesn't try to interpret the two characters together as some new symbol.

Keep your module sheets safe from harm

Programming code is a delicate thing. If you erase a crucial comma, an entire program may refuse to run. Also, to the uninitiated, VBA code looks like so much gibberish. A coworker coming across your macros might think this was some strange word processing document and unsuspectingly destroy some of your work.

It's a good idea to take precautions against this situation. You can do one of two things: hide your module sheets and/or protect them (or do both, for that matter).

Hiding the sheet

Hiding a module sheet makes it invisible. Choose Edit, Sheet, Hide, and the sheet simply vanishes. Other users need never even know it exists. To get the sheet back, you must unhide it. If a module sheet is the currently active sheet, you can unhide another module sheet by choosing Edit, Sheet, Unhide. A list of all the hidden sheets will appear. If a worksheet is the current sheet, then choose Format, Sheet, Unhide to bring up that same list.

Protecting the sheet

If you want to go a step further in safety, you can protect your sheets from being changed. Choose Tools, Protection, Protect Sheet, and the Protect Sheet dialog box appears, as shown in figure 2.2. You can create a password if you like; then the sheet cannot have the protection removed unless the password is entered. A protected sheet will not allow any editing changes to be made.

Fig. 2.2
You can use a password when you protect your sheets—just be sure not to forget it!

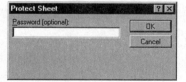

TIP **If you use a password to protect a sheet and then forget the** password, you can still copy and paste the information in that sheet into a new sheet that won't be protected.

How to make your programs available to all workbooks

You'd probably like to be able to use some programs in many different workbooks. To do this, you can copy the code from one workbook to another, but this can get pretty inconvenient if you want to use the code frequently.

Excel provides an easy way to make code available to all workbooks. By storing the code in a special file called the Personal Macro Workbook, you'll be able to use it from any workbook.

The Personal Macro Workbook (PERSONAL.XLS)

The Personal Macro Workbook is a workbook that is automatically loaded whenever you run Excel. However, it's normally hidden to keep it out of the way, so you might never notice that the Personal Macro Workbook is open, because it's invisible by default.

When you have several workbooks open, Excel allows you to run a macro from one of these workbooks while another workbook is active. Because the Personal Macro Workbook opens automatically when you run Excel, you always have access to its macros and other programs. And since it's hidden, it's less likely to be tampered with by clueless coworkers.

The Personal Macro Workbook is actually a file called PERSONAL.XLS, which is kept in the XLSTART directory. If you installed Excel with the default settings, this will be in your Excel directory. However, you don't actually need to know where it's stored to use it.

Q&A ***Why is there no PERSONAL.XLS workbook in my XLSTART directory?***

PERSONAL.XLS is automatically created when you first record a macro there. If you've never recorded a macro to the Personal Macro Workbook, it doesn't exist yet. To create PERSONAL.XLS, you must record a macro there. This process is described in the following section.

Storing macros in PERSONAL.XLS

To record a macro in the Personal Macro Workbook:

1 Choose Tools, Record Macro, Record New Macro.

2 Click on the Options button in the Record New Macro dialog box.

3 In the list of Store In options, click on the Personal Macro Workbook radio button, as shown in figure 2.3.

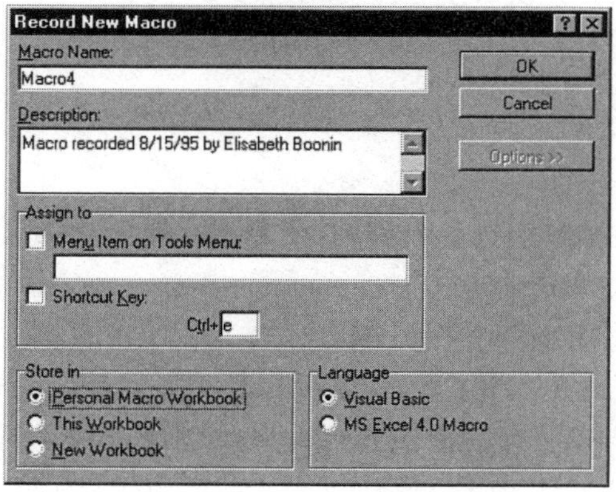

Fig. 2.3
Macros can be stored in the current workbook, in the Personal Macro Workbook, or in a new workbook.

4 Click OK to start recording.

The macro you record will now be stored in the Personal Macro Workbook.

Running a macro in PERSONAL.XLS

Macros stored in PERSONAL.XLS are available just like macros stored in a regular workbook. You can run them through the Macro dialog box, or with shortcut keys or menu items that you've defined.

When you bring up the Macro dialog box by choosing <u>T</u>ools, <u>M</u>acro, the macros that are stored in the Personal Macro Workbook are listed along with the macros stored in the current workbook and any other open workbooks. The ones stored in the Personal Macro Workbook can be identified by their names which are given as PERSONAL.XLS!*Name*, where *Name* is whatever name you gave to your macro. In figure 2.4, the first and third macros on the list are stored in PERSONAL.XLS and the second is stored in the current workbook.

Fig. 2.4

Macros stored in the Personal Macro Workbook appear with PERSONAL.XLS! before their names.

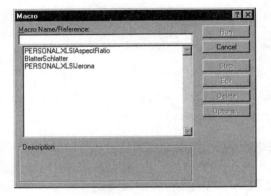

You can even edit PERSONAL.XLS

Until you record a macro there, PERSONAL.XLS doesn't exist and can't be edited. So, you'll have to record a macro to PERSONAL.XLS to get things started. Once you've stored macros to PERSONAL.XLS, it can be edited just like any other workbook once it's made visible. The macros and other programs there are stored in an ordinary module sheet.

To view PERSONAL.XLS, choose <u>U</u>nhide from the <u>W</u>indows menu. A dialog box appears, listing all of the hidden workbooks (probably only one). Select PERSONAL.XLS from the list and click OK. The PERSONAL.XLS workbook appears.

TIP **Don't forget to hide PERSONAL.XLS after you're done working with it.**

You can now write and edit macros and write any other programs in the PERSONAL.XLS file, just as you would in any other module in any other workbook.

If you close PERSONAL.XLS, the macros in it won't be available until you open it again. PERSONAL.XLS opens again automatically when you next run Excel. But, if you close it in the middle of an Excel session, you have to open it again to use its macros.

Customizing the editor

As with most parts of Excel, you can customize the editor to reflect your preferences while working in module sheets. The Options dialog box found by selecting Options in the Tools menu has two tabbed pages which affect module sheets: Module General, shown in figure 2.5, and Module Format, shown in figure 2.6.

Fig. 2.5
The Module General tab of the Options dialog box is where many of the settings for the VBA editor can be changed.

Fig. 2.6
The typeface, size, and color of fonts can be changed in the Module Format tab of the Options dialog box.

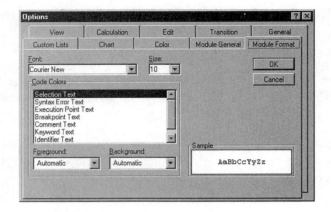

The Auto Indent Option

You could write your code entirely without indenting your text. VBA understands it just the same. However, indents play a big role in helping you to organize your programming. All of the programming examples in this book, as well as the code that the macro recorder generates, use indentation liberally. Indentation of programming code allows you to organize it into a kind of outline format.

Since you'll often want to follow one indented line with another one that is indented equally far, Excel provides the Auto Indent feature to automatically indent a new line as far as the previous one.

If you don't like this feature and choose to remove the default check mark, you can still indent different portions of your code with the Tab key as usual.

How do you want to handle syntax errors?

If the Display Syntax Errors box is checked, two things happen whenever VBA detects a syntax error:

- The line in which VBA detected the error turns red

- A dialog box explaining the error appears

Sometimes this seems like too much of a good thing; the dialog boxes can be annoying and less than helpful. By turning off this option, VBA continues to detect syntax errors and turns the corresponding lines of code red, but does not display the dialog box.

I have a love/hate relationship with this feature. Sometimes the information it gives is really useful. Other times, though, I've just made an obvious typo that I would have figured out immediately on seeing the text turn red. I tend to leave this feature turned off, and turn it on only when I'm having a hard time figuring out what's wrong with my code.

Set the width of the tabs

Unlike the tab character in most word processors, the VBA editor doesn't really use a tab at all. When you press the Tab key on your keyboard, it inserts spaces for you. The number of spaces it inserts is selected in the Tab Width field. You may want to increase or even decrease the width of your tabs, although the default setting of 4 seems to work for most people.

 TIP **Use an even number for your Tab Width setting. Then, to remove** indents from your code, you can select Edit, Replace and remove all instances of two consecutive spaces.

Font and color settings

Another of the tabbed pages of the Options dialog box is called Module Format; it's shown in figure 2.6.

On this page, you can change the font and color of text in module sheets. If you have a black-and-white monitor, you may want to use some different setting—such as using reverse text colors—for identifying syntax errors or comments.

The Visual Basic toolbar

To learn about debugging, see Chapter 14, "Fixing Your Code: VBA's Debugging Tools."

Among its multitude of toolbars, Excel includes one for VBA called the **Visual Basic toolbar**. It's a handy shortcut to several frequently used commands. Several of the buttons are used for purposes covered later in this book, such as debugging. The Visual Basic toolbar is shown in figure 2.7.

Fig. 2.7
The Visual Basic toolbar
provides a quick way
to access frequently
used programming
commands.

Q&A   ***Why is my Visual Basic toolbar missing?***

Excel can be configured to automatically display or hide the Visual Basic
toolbar. Choose <u>V</u>iew, <u>T</u>oolbars, and make sure there is a check mark next
to the Visual Basic option in the Toolbars dialog box.

Using the toolbar in a module sheet

The default behavior for the Visual Basic toolbar is to float over your Excel
macro sheets. You can also make it disappear by clicking its close box, or by
selecting <u>V</u>iew, <u>T</u>oolbars and then removing the check by the Visual Basic
entry.

TIP   **Dragging the Visual Basic toolbar to the top of the screen will turn**
it from a floating toolbar into a regular, "anchored" one.

Here's a description of what some of the toolbar buttons do:

    The Insert Module button works just like choosing <u>I</u>nsert,
<u>M</u>acro, <u>M</u>odule.

    The Run Macro button works in one of two ways. If your
cursor is located anywhere within the code for a certain
macro, the Run Macro button runs that macro. If your
cursor isn't located within a macro, the Run Macro button
opens the Macro dialog box.

    The Stop Macro button should really be named the Stop
Recording Macro button. It does exactly the same thing as
the Stop Macro button that appears when you begin
recording a macro.

    The Record Macro button works just like choosing
Tools, <u>M</u>acro, <u>R</u>ecord New Macro.

TIP **Pressing F5 on your keyboard has the same effect as clicking the** Run Macro button.

You can use it in a worksheet, too

The Visual Basic toolbar is useful from within an Excel worksheet, as well as from within a module sheet. If you like, you can display the Visual Basic toolbar in your worksheets by starting in a worksheet and selecting View, Toolbars and putting a check mark beside the Visual Basic entry.

Whether the Visual Basic toolbar is displayed depends on the type of sheet that is active. Displaying it in a module sheet will not make it appear in a worksheet; you need to display it in the worksheet separately. Similarly, if you hide it in a worksheet, it won't hide it in the module sheet unless you select that sheet and then hide it there, too.

You can use the Visual Basic toolbar from within a worksheet to run existing macros, insert module sheets, record new macros, or stop the macro recorder. The Run button automatically brings up the Macro dialog box. This is different from its behavior in a module sheet where it will run the macro in which the cursor is currently located.

TIP **If you're in a worksheet and want to find the code for a particular** macro, click the Run Macro button on the toolbar to display the Macro dialog box, select the macro from the list, and click the Edit button in the dialog box.

Summary

This chapter introduced module sheets—the place where Excel stores macros and other kinds of VBA programs. You learned how to enter and edit text in module sheets and how to customize the special features of the editor. You also learned about the Visual Basic toolbar and the uses for several of its buttons.

Review questions

1 What is a module sheet?

2 What is a syntax error?

3 What does the first line of a macro look like? The last?

4 What does red text indicate in a module sheet? What about green text? Blue?

5 What shortcuts does the Visual Basic toolbar provide?

Exercises

1 Re-create the MyProgram macro giving it a different name.

2 Add a description and shortcut key for the macro you created in Exercise 1.

3 The code

```
MsgBox "Hello"
```

creates a message box with the text Hello in it. Write a macro that includes this code.

4 Add a line as a comment to the same macro.

5 Turn off the Display Syntax Errors feature and type

```
Sub End
```

into a module sheet. Turn the Display Syntax Errors feature back on and try it again.

3

Using the VBA Editor and the Macro Recorder Together

● In this chapter:

- Where do my recorded macros wind up?

- Fine-tuning recorded macros

- Where do I put all these macros?

- Use the macro recorder as a VBA tutor!

By combining the features of the VBA editor and the macro recorder, you can make a little bit of VBA knowledge go a long way. . . . .

The macro recorder lets you create many useful automated programs. With the macro recorder, you're not limited by your level of fluency in VBA—all the programming is taken care of for you. However, VBA provides a great deal of functionality that is not available using the macro recorder alone. You can solicit user input, make decisions about which part of a program to run based on user preferences or numeric values, create custom dialog boxes, and much more. Functionality has its price, though. There's a lot of VBA out there, and who has time to learn all of it? You want to be productive immediately.

By *combining* the features of the VBA editor and the macro recorder, you can make a little bit of VBA knowledge go a long way. You'll be able to use the editor to create a framework for your programs, and the recorder to fill in the details. As you learn more VBA, you'll be able to increase the scope of your programs, but you'll always have at your disposal the full range of the macro recorder's capability.

Use the VBA editor to organize your macros

If you've been creating lots of macros with the macro recorder, you may find that things have gotten a little scattered. Macros are recorded into different workbooks or are in various sheets. Using the VBA editor, you can move your macros around, combine them, or delete ones you no longer use.

Arrange your macros into one module or several

When you create a macro with the macro recorder, it doesn't always put the macro where you want it to wind up. You may want all of your macros in one module sheet, or you may want to separate them into different module sheets.

Excel will run any macro from any module sheet in a workbook. Thus, you might want a separate sheet for each macro, or you might want to keep all of them on one sheet. If you have several macros that you use together and want to put in other workbooks, grouping them together on a sheet can make it easier for you to move them to another workbook later.

Q&A ***Within one particular workbook, how many module sheets should I use?***

Answering this question is like answering the question, "How many directories should I have on my hard drive?" It all depends on how much code you have and how you like to organize things. For example, you might want to have all of your formatting macros appear on one module sheet, and all of your calculating macros on another.

It's easy to reorganize your macros by copying and pasting them to other module sheets. Until you have enough macros that you're saving for the long haul, you can probably get by with one module per worksheet, but if you'd like to have several, go right ahead.

Using several module sheets in one workbook is pretty much a matter of personal preference. Excel treats the macros in a workbook as if they were stored on one sheet. However, putting macros in different workbooks affects when they are available.

A macro can only be used when the workbook it's stored on is open. For that reason, you should make sure that a macro you wish to use with a particular workbook is located in that workbook or in PERSONAL.XLS (which is always open).

TIP **If you want to be able to use a macro from any workbook, store it** in the Personal Macro Workbook.

Here's how you can move a macro from one sheet to another. You can use this technique to move a macro within a workbook or to another workbook entirely:

1 Select the text of the macro (including any comments that describe the macro).

2 Press Ctrl+X to cut the text.

3 If you are moving the macro to a different workbook, open this workbook.

4 Click on the sheet tab of the module sheet you wish to move the macro to, thereby activating this sheet.

5 Position your cursor where you want the macro to go, and press Ctrl+V to paste the macro.

Deleting macros

You may find yourself creating many macros that you won't need to keep around for posterity. Some macros become outdated, and some might just be VBA programs you were experimenting with and don't want to keep. It's good to get rid of the macros that you won't be using anymore. That keeps things better organized, and makes your workbooks and macros run faster.

There are two ways to delete a macro: in the module sheet where the macro is stored, or through the Macro dialog box:

- To delete a macro with the editor, select all of the text for the macro and press the Delete key, eliminating it as you would any text. Excel will take care of removing it from the Macro dialog box. The next time you look at this dialog box, your macro will be gone.

- To delete a macro from within the Macro dialog box, select its name and click the <u>D</u>elete button. When you check the module sheet where the macro was stored, it will be gone.

CAUTION   **When you delete a macro using the Macro dialog box, no** confirmation dialog box appears to check if you're sure. Furthermore, you can't undo this action! If you're going to delete a macro this way, be 100 percent sure that you want it gone.

On the other hand, if you remove a macro by selecting the text and pressing the Delete key, you can reverse your action by selecting <u>E</u>dit, <u>U</u>ndo Delete.

Creating a macro that rolls several macros into one

A macro can run another macro that's in the same workbook, even if they are in different modules. You run one macro from within another by **calling** it in a line of code.

Plain English, please!

The term for running a macro or other procedure is **call**. You **call** a procedure, in this case a macro; or, you make a procedure **call**. Both uses mean the same thing.

To call a macro from within another, you simply type the name of the macro you wish to run. Here's an example:

```
'creates a title for my reports
Sub Title()
    Range("E1").Select
    ActiveCell.FormulaR1C1 = "Report"
    Selection.Font.Bold = True
End Sub

'changes the margins and page orientation
Sub Layout()
    With ActiveSheet.PageSetup
        .TopMargin = Application.InchesToPoints(0.5)
        .BottomMargin = Application.InchesToPoints(0.5)
        .Orientation = xlLandscape
    End With
End Sub

'sets up my reports the way I like them
Sub MySetUp()
    Title
    Layout
End Sub
```

The first two macros perform simple formatting and text entry tasks. The third macro, MySetUp, is the one that calls the other two. When VBA runs MySetUp, the first piece of code it encounters is the line Title. VBA looks through the workbook for the Title program, finds it, and runs it from beginning to end before returning to MySetUp. The next line tells VBA to run Layout, which it does in the same manner.

Layout and Title could have been located anywhere in the workbook, even below the MySetUp macro or on a different module sheet.

Note that to run this combination of macros, you only need to run the MySetUp macro. VBA takes care of looking up the other two.

Changing recorded macros

There are many reasons why you might want to change a macro. You might come up with additional functionality that you want to include, or decide to remove some of what a macro does, or simply rename the macro. It's a good idea to take a look at your recorded macros, even if you don't intend to change them. You may be surprised at what the macro recorder has included.

To change a macro, you first need to find it. If you have many different workbooks and/or module sheets, this can be challenging. Several techniques for finding macros are discussed in the next section.

Once you've found the macro, you can edit it, add to it with the VBA editor, or even add to it with the macro recorder.

How do I find a macro that I've written?

Yesterday, you wrote a great macro, but where did you put it? Excel offers a number of different places to store your macros, in various workbooks and different module sheets within a workbook. It's not unusual for you to find that you have no idea where a particular macro is.

To learn how to choose where a recorded macro is stored, See Chapter 1, "Introducing Macros."

When you record a macro, it is stored in one of three places depending on which option was selected in the Record New Macro dialog box:

- The workbook that was active when you began recording the macro

How can I use this in the real world?

The benefit of writing smaller programs and combining them like this is that they are reusable. For example, you could create a macro that changes the page setup to prepare a document for a particular printer in your office.

This macro would be useful in many different situations. You could call it from other macros that create the titles and formatting for your Monthly Reports and Annual Reports. You could also run it as a stand-alone macro when you're putting together a new spreadsheet that you want to send to that specific printer.

- Another workbook that you specified in the Record New Macro dialog box

- The Personal Macro Workbook

Your macro will be stored as VBA code on a module sheet in one of these workbooks.

Likewise, macros that you write from scratch can be in any workbook. They're right where you left them, if you can remember where that is. If you can't, then take a look at the next two sections for help.

Finding a macro with the Macro dialog box

The quickest way to locate a macro in an open workbook is through the Macro dialog box. Choose Tools, Macro to view the Macro dialog box.

All of the macros in all open workbooks are shown in the Macro Name/ Reference drop-down list box. The ones in the current workbook are listed with just their name. Macros that are stored in other workbooks are prefaced with the file name of the workbook and an exclamation point (!). Thus, a macro called Expenses that's in the current workbook appears in the list simply as Expenses. If it's in the PERSONAL.XLS workbook, though, it appears as PERSONAL.XLS!Expenses.

To learn about PERSONAL.XLS, the Personal Macro Workbook, see Chapter 2, "Module Sheets: The Home of Macros and VBA."

Figure 3.1 shows the Macro dialog box. Three workbooks are open, and all contain macros: the current workbook contains one macro called TitleMaker; the worksheets CORGIS.XLS and PERSONAL.XLS each contain two macros.

Once you've selected the macro you wanted to find, click on the Edit button in the Macro dialog box. The workbook for that macro becomes active, and the appropriate module sheet appears on top, with the cursor positioned in the macro.

If you're trying to edit a macro that's located in a hidden workbook (such as PERSONAL.XLS), you'll have to unhide the workbook before you can edit it. Select Window, Unhide to see a list of hidden workbooks, and unhide the one you want to work with.

Fig. 3.1
The Edit button sends you right to the macro you're looking for.

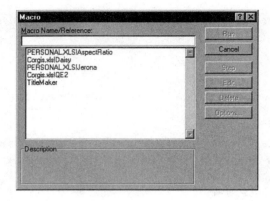

To learn about the Object Browser, see Chapter 11, "How VBA Refers to Things in Excel."

Note that only macros appear in the Macro dialog box. If you're looking for another kind of VBA procedure, like a function or a subroutine that is not a macro, you have to use other methods such as the Object Browser.

Finding a module sheet in a workbook

Perhaps you've forgotten the name of the macro and you want to browse through the different module sheets in your workbooks.

You may find that the workbook has more than one module sheet. If you inserted a module sheet into the workbook, the macro recorder will still create its own module sheet to store macros, so be sure to check all of the module sheets in your workbook.

One way to find a sheet within a given workbook is to look through the tabs along the bottom of the workbook. All sheets that are not hidden can be found here. Module sheets, like worksheets, can be renamed so your modules might not be obvious at first glance. Figure 3.2 shows a module sheet that has been renamed as `Formatting Macros`. Along the bottom of the screen, you can see several other sheets including worksheets and another module sheet called `Module1`.

TIP **To change the name of a sheet, double-click on its tab to bring up** the Rename Sheet dialog box.

Fig. 3.2
It can be hard to tell worksheets and module sheets apart by looking at their worksheet tabs, especially if you change the names.

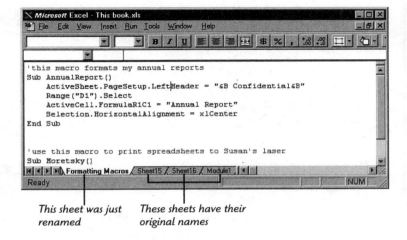

This sheet was just renamed

These sheets have their original names

Adding more to a macro with the macro recorder

You can use the macro recorder to add code to the middle of an existing procedure: one that you recorded earlier or one that you typed in. This is a great way to combine different features of Excel into one macro.

To add code to an existing macro, perform the following steps:

1 Position the cursor in an existing macro at the point where you'd like to insert new code.

2 Choose Tools, Record Macro, Mark Position for Recording. No apparent changes will take place, but the macro recorder has noted the location of the cursor.

3 Perform any actions necessary to *prepare* to add code to your macro. You aren't yet recording these actions, and you'll probably want to switch to a worksheet at this time to "catch up."

4 Choose Tools, Record Macro, Record at Mark. Now the macro recorder is running.

5 Perform the actions for the code you want to add, and then click the Stop button to halt the macro recorder.

Cleaning up after the overzealous macro recorder

I once had a children's book about a silly maid. Her problem was that she took all of her employer's instructions literally. When told to draw the curtains, for instance, she sat down with a sketch pad and made a drawing of them. She was always on the verge of being fired, and was saved only by her excellent cooking.

The Excel macro recorder suffers from a similar ailment. Try the following experiment:

1 Select a cell and choose Tools, Record Macro, Record New Macro. Name the macro **BoldMaker** and click OK.

2 Select Format, Cells. The Format Cells dialog box appears.

3 Click on the Font tab to bring up the tabbed page of the dialog box shown in figure 3.3.

4 Select Bold from the list of font styles, then click OK.

5 Click on the Stop button to stop the macro recorder.

How can I use this in the real world?

The Record at Mark feature is a great way to combine complicated macros with very basic programming structures. With very little programming knowledge, you'll be able to create highly functional, sophisticated programs.

In Chapter 18, you will learn how to create message boxes, which will present you with several buttons to choose from. You can write a program that will look at which button you select and then perform an action based on the button selected. The various actions could each be recorded with the macro recorder and inserted into the larger program using Record at Mark.

The programming required to achieve this kind of functionality is very limited, while the parts inserted by the macro recorder can be extremely complicated without taxing anything but your mouse and menu skills.

Fig. 3.3
Take a look at the various settings available in this dialog box. They'll all show up in the code of the macro you're recording.

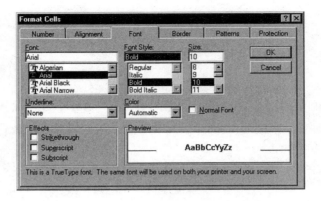

This is a very simple macro, right? All you did was change the font style to bold. Take a look at your module sheet, though, and see what was recorded. Here's how mine came out, but yours may differ slightly:

```
Sub BoldMaker()
    With Selection.Font
        .Name = "Arial"
        .FontStyle = "Bold"
        .Size = 10
        .Strikethrough = False
        .Superscript = False
        .Subscript = False
        .OutlineFont = False
        .Shadow = False
        .Underline = xlNone
        .ColorIndex = xlAutomatic
    End With
End Sub
```

Although you may not understand the exact syntax of the code, it should be clear that this macro is doing all sorts of things to your font: setting the font to Arial, the style to bold, the size to 10, and so on.

The line `With Selection.Font` is the beginning of a list of instructions that are to be carried out upon the font of the current selection. This structure is discussed in Chapter 5, and you'll often see it in the code of recorded macros.

You can use the editor to remove the extraneous lines of code that the macro recorder put in. If it is indeed the case that all you want the macro to do is to change the style to bold, the macro can be pared down to the following:

```
Sub BoldMaker()
    With Selection.Font
        .FontStyle = "Bold"
    End With
End Sub
```

Is it important for me to perform this cleanup?

Cleaning up your macros accomplishes several things. For one, your macros run faster and your code is easier to read. More significantly, however, by removing the code that you don't want in the macro, you prevent undesired actions from occurring.

To illustrate the problem, suppose you recorded Macro1 earlier as a way to change the font style to bold and didn't edit it. Now imagine that you have a title written in 18-point Times Roman to which you'd like to add bold. Running the original, unedited macro indeed puts the title in bold, but it also changes the font to 10-point Arial which is not at all what you had in mind.

It may be necessary to clean up after the macro recorder in order to get your macros to run correctly.

Why does it write all that extra code?

If you stretch your imagination a little, you can see why the macro recorder interprets things the way it does. While recording BoldMaker earlier, you brought up the Font tab of the Format Cells dialog box, made a change, and then clicked OK. By clicking on OK, you indicated that this was how you wanted your cell to look. You didn't say that you just wanted to change the style to bold (even though that is the only action you performed). Instead, you accepted the current font settings as they were, indicating that you were happy with the end result containing all of those settings. Since the dialog box deals with many different font settings, the macro recorder took note of each and every one of them.

Consider this: the fact that the font setting was already at 10 might have been a coincidence and you might want this to be a part of the macro. Excel can only guess at your intentions and errs on the side of including too much.

If you had recorded the macro instead by using the Bold button on the Formatting toolbar, you would have received the following macro which is much closer to what you had in mind.

```
Sub NewBoldMaker()
    Selection.Font.Bold = True
End Sub
```

In this case, there is no approving of a list of formatting settings, just a click on a single button whose sole purpose it is to set the font style to bold.

How do I know which parts to take out?

In the BoldMaker macro, it's pretty clear which lines performed which actions. Sometimes, though, it's not immediately clear what should be removed. You might, for instance, have edited BoldMaker down to the following:

```
Sub BoldMaker()
        .FontStyle = "Bold"
End Sub
```

As it turns out, this was just a little too much editing. The macro won't run anymore. Now, to re-create the macro, you either have to remember what the particular programming terms were that you deleted, or re-record the macro and edit it all over again.

To learn about comments, see Chapter 2, "Module Sheets: The Home of Macros and VBA."

A good way to experiment with what can be removed is to make it a comment rather than deleting it. You can do this by putting an apostrophe (') at the beginning of the line that you are considering getting rid of. Then the lines that begin with an apostrophe will be ignored as comments. This way you can test the macro without deleting the lines. If it works properly with the lines turned into comments, then you can remove them.

Let the macro recorder teach you to program

One of the best ways to learn how to do new things is to watch how others do them. By looking at the code written by the macro recorder, you can learn a great deal about programming.

Among the biggest challenges in learning VBA is figuring out how it refers to all the different parts of Excel. You can use VBA to affect almost any part of the Excel environment, but not unless you know what to write in the module sheets. By recording a macro that affects that part of the environment, you can usually figure out how various parts of Excel can be manipulated with VBA.

The following program was created when I started the macro recorder and then clicked on a worksheet tab for various worksheets.

```
Sub Macro2()
    Sheets("Sheet2").Select
    Sheets("Sheet5").Select
    Sheets("Module1").Select
End Sub
```

To learn about collections and methods, see Chapter 11, "How VBA Refers to Things in Excel."

It seems reasonable to assume that the way you select a sheet is with the line of code:

```
Sheets("SheetName").Select
```

where *SheetName* is the name of the sheet you want. You don't have to know that Sheets is a VBA **collection** or that Select is a **method**. There's nothing wrong with knowing about collections and methods—it's just not necessary to know all about them to use them.

If I record a macro and hide a sheet, I wind up with this line of code in my macro:

```
Sheets("Module1").Hide
```

Now things are starting to look even clearer. You write

```
Sheets("SheetName")
```

to specify the sheet you want to do something to, and then you put a period and a word that says what you want to do. You don't know all of the different words that could go there, but you might make some reasonable guesses, like Copy, Unhide, or Protect and check them out. All of these turn out to do exactly what you'd expect; they copy, unhide, or protect the sheet in question.

Summary

This chapter showed you how to perform a number of tasks using a combination of the macro recorder and VBA editor. You can use the editor to rearrange the location of macros or change the contents of the macros themselves. Often, it's necessary to edit macros that were created by the macro recorder to get them to run properly. The macro recorder turns out to be a great tutor for picking up new vocabulary and grammar in the VBA language.

Review questions

1 Why would you want to edit the macros you record?

2 What's a good way to test whether it's safe to remove a line of code or not?

3 If you want to call a macro from another macro, do they have to be in the same module sheet?

4 How do you add to an existing macro with the macro recorder?

Exercises

1 Record a macro that you'd like to have available in all worksheets, but store it in the current worksheet. After you've finished, move it to PERSONAL.XLS.

2 Using steps very similar to the ones used to create the BoldMaker macro, record a macro that adds the strikethrough effect to your text. Go to the module where this macro is stored and make every line a comment except for the following three: the first and last lines, and the one that mentions strikethrough. Try the macro to see if it runs.

3 Fix the macro you overedited in Exercise 2 by removing the apostrophes from the With lines. Test it. If it works properly, remove the commented code.

4 Record a macro that changes the margins using the Page Setup dialog box. Edit that macro so that no excess code appears.

5 Start the macro recorder and rename one of your worksheets by double-clicking on the worksheet tab and entering a new name. Find the macro code and determine what VBA code changes the name of a worksheet.

4

Write Your Own Worksheet Functions

● **In this chapter:**

● What's a function?

● How to create user-defined worksheet functions with VBA

● Using these functions in worksheet formulas

● What's the bare minimum I need to know about programming to start writing useful code?

Here's just enough programming to write functions that actually help you in your work . . . .

I've come up with a rating system for visiting the video store. If it takes longer to watch the video than it did to pick it out, I rate the trip a success. It's amazing that with so many movies to choose from, I can never quite find the one I want to watch. Of course the perfect movie may just be sitting there on the shelf, but who can tell what it will be like by glancing at the cover?

Scrolling through the list of predefined Excel worksheet functions can be just as bad. You know exactly what you need, and you'd like to find a function to perform the task for you. Of course, you could do it without a function. You could type in the whole formula, or set up a range of cells to do the calculation step-by-step using existing functions, but the best way would be if the exact function that you needed was there waiting for you.

In this chapter, you learn how to create your own worksheet functions using VBA. Then, if Excel doesn't seem to have a function that you'd like to use, you can tailor one to your exact specifications. That way, you'll only need to use one cell to get the job done, and you'll be sure that the function works the way you want.

What are user-defined worksheet functions?

Using VBA, you can create your own functions and use them the same way as the ones that come with Excel. Sure, it takes a little time to create the function, but once it's there you can use it at any time. Creating **user-defined worksheet functions** is one of the easiest and most useful ways of incorporating VBA programming into your spreadsheets.

You probably already have a function in mind that you've always wanted: perhaps it will perform a complicated calculation that you often type or paste into your spreadsheets. By the end of this chapter, you'll be able to write code to create your function and invoke it by name.

To learn about functions in a more general context, see Chapter 8, "VBA Procedures."

 Plain English, please!

What is a **function**, anyway? The answer depends on who you're asking. It turns out that Excel and VBA use the word *function* to mean different things. For Excel, a function is one of the special words like SUM or AVERAGE that will perform a calculation on your numbers when you put it into a spreadsheet formula. I'll call these **worksheet functions**.

A VBA function is a piece of programming code that gives you a value back whenever you use it. If it sounds similar to an Excel function, you're right: it is. But, VBA functions can do what Excel functions can do and more. In this chapter, you're going to use VBA functions to create Excel functions. I'll call these **user-defined worksheet functions**. 〞

Create a simple function

Let's try out a very simple VBA function to see how it's used. Before you start programming, choose Tools, Options to open the Options dialog box, and then click on the Module General tab. You'll see a check box that reads Require Variable Declaration. For now, you want to make sure this box is not checked. Otherwise, the examples in this chapter just won't work. In Chapter 9, you'll learn what it means to declare a variable, and you can decide whether you want to use this feature or not.

To learn how to enter code, see Chapter 2, "Module Sheets: The Home of Macros and VBA."

Just to keep things simple, let's reinvent the wheel. Here's a function called AddUp which will add two numbers together. Go ahead and type it into a module sheet to try it out.

```
Function AddUp(x, y)
    AddUp = x + y
End Function
```

Every function that you write in VBA includes a special first and last line. The first line always starts with the word Function to alert VBA that this is indeed a function that's happening. The next word is the name of the function, in this case AddUp.

The name of the function is then followed by parentheses. What goes inside the parentheses depends on your function. Do you want your function to do something with two values? With five? With none? What you put in your parentheses tells VBA what values are coming in. In this case, VBA is expecting to receive two values. Since you don't want to specify ahead of time which two values, you give them names for the time being. In this function, you named the values x and y, but you could just as well have named them Jekyll and Hyde. VBA takes the first value you send it and assigns it to x, then takes the second and assigns it to y.

In the middle of this function is the line `AddUp = x + y`. The whole purpose of a VBA function is for it to return a value when invoked. This line says to VBA, "Let the AddUp function return the value of x plus the value of y."

The last line, `End Function`, just tells VBA that it's done working on that function.

Suppose we used the AddUp function by sending it the values 2 and 5. Then, the first line assigns the value 2 to x and the value 5 to y. The second line tells AddUp to **return** the value 7, which means to send the answer somewhere. Where does the function return the value to? That depends on where the 2 and 5 came from. Wherever the function was called is where the value 7 will be returned. This is very similar to the same way you might use one of Excel's worksheet functions, like SUM. As you'll see in the next section, you can use AddUp in a similar way.

 Plain English, please!

> **Variables** are where programs store values. In the AddUp function, x and y are variables. A variable is created by giving it a name. Once created, it is a placeholder for whatever value you wish to store there. **"**

Trying it out

To try AddUp, click on a worksheet tab in the same workbook you just used to type the function. In any cell, type the formula **=AddUp(2,5)**. The cell produces the result 7. Programmers would say: you **called** the AddUp function, **passed** it the values 2 and 5 and then it **returned** the value 7. (Thanks to the remarkable powers of late twentieth-century computing, you are now relieved of the job of calculating this difficult result.)

 Q&A *Why should I bother with a function like this when I could just use SUM instead?*

> This was just an easy example to show you how these functions are created. Once you get the idea of how functions work, read the section, "Now how do I make some really useful functions?".

Another use of the function is shown in figure 4.1 where the values are in other spreadsheet cells. The values in cells D5 and D6 are passed to AddUp.

Fig. 4.1
AddUp is being used just like one of Excel's built-in worksheet functions.

	A	B	C	D	E	F	G	H
				=AddUp(D5,D6)				
1								
2								
3								
4			January	February				
5		Joe	$23,468	$14,370				
6		Nancy	$19,633	$66,670				
7								
8								
9			Jan Sales	Feb Sales				
10			$43,101	=AddUp(D5,D6)				
11								
12								
13								
14								
15								
16								
17								
18								

Sheet1 / Sheet2 / Sheet3 / Sheet4 / Sheet5 / Sheet6

Different ways to access functions

Just like macros, your function is saved in a module which is a part of an Excel workbook. You can access your function from anywhere else in the workbook. Within that workbook, you can use your function by typing its name into a formula, as described in the previous section.

Catch the bug

This function has two mistakes in the code:

```
TimesTwo(x)
    TimesTwo = 2 * x
End
```

Answer: *All functions must begin with the word* Function. *In this case, the first line should read* Function TimesTwo(x). *The last line of every function is* End Function.

The corrected code reads:

```
Function TimesTwo(x)
    TimesTwo = 2 * x
End Function
```

You can also use the function with the Function Wizard. Choose Insert, Function; select the User Defined category and then select the function as shown in figure 4.2. The Function Wizard also prompts you to enter the values for x and y. Clicking Finish enters the function in the cell, and Excel automatically calculates the result.

Fig. 4.2
User-defined worksheet functions are automatically added to the Function Wizard.

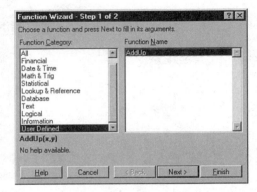

Q&A *Why is there no User Defined category in my Function Wizard?*

The category of User Defined functions only appears when you've created at least one function in that workbook or in another open workbook. First create a function in a module sheet, and then have a look at the dialog box again.

Of course, you won't spend the rest of your Excel career in that same workbook, so you need to be able to access the function from other workbooks. There are a number of ways to do this:

- Copy the function from a module in one workbook and paste it into a module in another workbook.

- Copy the entire module sheet from one workbook to another workbook by choosing Edit, Move or Copy Sheet.

- Put the function into the PERSONAL.XLS workbook to make it accessible to all worksheets.

It's possible to use a function from one workbook in a different workbook if both are open at the same time. This isn't usually a good idea. If you close the one where you created the function, the other one will forget about the function and display #NAME? in the cell. Save this technique for situations where you're sure both workbooks will be used together.

Now, how do I make some really useful functions?

Somehow, I suspect that the AddUp function isn't quite what you had in mind as a way to enhance your productivity in Excel. It's just a pale imitation of Excel's SUM function, after all. It can't even add more than two numbers together.

In order to go further with user-defined worksheet functions, you'll take a slight detour and learn a little background about programming. These topics are discussed in much greater detail in later chapters. For now, here's just enough to give you the ability to write functions that actually help you in your work.

A crash course in variables

To learn more about variables, see Chapter 9, "Variables."

In AddUp, you told the function to expect to receive two values, which it would add together. In order to do this, you created variables called x and y as placeholders for the incoming values. Variables are just that—named placeholders that accept values.

How can I use this in the real world?

You're fast becoming a VBA pro, but that may not be true of everyone who works with you. You can create user-defined worksheet functions for others, and they can access them using the Function Wizard, without ever being aware of the VBA world behind the scenes. This also will assure that they use the right number of values for your function.

One thing that will make the Function Wizard particularly easy to use is to name your variables something descriptive. When a variable is called TaxRate, it's much more obvious what kinds of values it's for than if it's called Moe or x.

You can create variables by naming them when you need them. The first line of AddUp

```
Function AddUp(x,y)
```

created the variables x and y. After the function is completed, x and y lose their values and become placeholders again, just waiting for values to be passed to them.

You can use many variables in a function. Here's a function that adds 2 to a number and then multiplies the result by 3. To achieve this, it uses three variables called Moe, Larry, and Curly:

```
Function Stooges(Moe)
    Larry = Moe + 1
    Curly = Larry + 1
    Stooges = Curly * 3
End Function
```

The first line starts the function Stooges and creates the placeholder/variable Moe. When the function is called, the value passed to it is put in the placeholder reserved by Moe. The second line says, "Take the value of Moe, add one to it, then put this value in the Larry placeholder (which gets created as soon as it is mentioned in this line)." Or, as programmers would say, "Assign Moe plus one to the variable Larry." The third line takes the value just assigned to Larry, adds one to it, and assigns this value to Curly. The fourth line tells the function to return the value of Curly times three.

You *can* use names like this for your variables, but in many cases, it makes sense to use names that are relevant and easy to remember. In a program where you're dealing with finances, you might use variable names like PrimeRate, AccountBalance, and TotalEarnings. Sometimes, though, you just call a variable into existence for a few lines and then forget about it. In these cases, it makes more sense to use something generic and quick to type, like x or i.

There are certain restrictions on what your variables can be named. Here are some of the rules:

- No spaces can be used in variable names. Prime Rate is not a valid name.

- Variables can use both letters and numbers, but the first character must be a letter. So, Stooge3 is a good variable name but 3rdStooge isn't.

- You cannot use these characters in a variable name: **. ! # $ % &** .

 TIP   **Although spaces can't be used in variable names, the underscore** character is often used as a substitute. So, you could call a variable Prime_Rate.

Much, much more can be said about variables. You can:

- Create variables that are used in more than one function

- Create variables that remember their value even after the function is done

- Create variables that only accept certain kinds of values

These uses and others are discussed in Chapter 9, "Variables." You can skip ahead and read those sections or go on using variables with what you've learned so far.

Some operators to work with

As an Excel user, you're probably already familiar with quite a few operators. The most common are the arithmetic operators. An example is the addition operator (+). You can use arithmetic operators in your VBA code to put together complicated mathematical formulas for use as user-defined worksheet functions. The VBA operators are listed in table 4.1.

Table 4.1 VBA's arithmetic operators

Operator	Name	Example
+	Addition	x + y adds x to y
−	Subtraction	x − y subtracts y from x
*	Multiplication	x * y multiplies x and y
/	Division	x / y divides x by y
^	Exponentiation	x ^ y raises x to the y power: x^y

Combining them, you can put together some very complicated mathematical expressions the same way you do in Excel formulas.

Building your programming vocabulary: VBA built-in functions

Just as Excel has built-in functions, VBA has built-in functions.

To learn about using more built-in functions in your VBA programs, see Chapter 8, "VBA Procedures."

 ## Plain English, please!

What? More uses of the word **Function**? In addition to Excel's predefined worksheet functions and functions that you write in VBA, there are also functions that are built into VBA. So far, we have the following meanings for functions:

- A type of VBA procedure that returns a value

- A special word in Excel, like SUM or AVERAGE, that you can put into a formula. (You can define your own functions of this kind, called user-defined worksheet functions, by creating a function of the VBA procedure kind.)

- A special word in VBA that you can put into your code

How can I use this in the real world?

Do you have calculations that take up several cells? One cell might have the number of hours an employee works per week, another cell has the hourly wage, and a third has the total salary earned per week.

Instead, you can write a function that accepts two values—the number of hours and the wage—and returns the total pay for the week. You'll be able to click on the cell and change the wage or hours without changing the function, and keep everything in one cell. Moreover, by naming the variables that the function expects something descriptive like Weekly_Hours and Hourly_Wage, using the Function Wizard to create the formula will make using the function almost completely self-explanatory.

The really confusing part is that VBA built-in functions are different from Excel built-in functions even if they do the same thing. VBA has a built-in function called Sqr that calculates the square root, just like the built-in Excel function SQRT. However, if you try to use SQRT in your VBA programs, it won't work. Sometimes, the VBA and Excel functions will even have the same name, albeit different capitalization. The Abs VBA function works just like the Excel ABS function. If this seems unnecessarily complicated, I agree. But don't worry, the context will generally make the meaning clear.

Table 4.2 lists a few of the simpler built-in VBA functions that you can begin using in your code.

Table 4.2 Some built-in VBA functions

Function	Description	Example
Abs	Absolute Value	Abs(–5) returns 5
Cos	Cosine	Cos(0) returns 1
Int	Integer	Int(3.6) returns 3
Sin	Sine	Sin(0) returns 0
Sqr	Square Root	Sqr(4) returns 2

You use VBA built-in functions in your programming much the same way you use Excel's built-in functions in your formulas.

Speaking of *Sqr( )*

The Sqr( ) function returns the square root of a numeric expression. The general form is as follows:

```
result = Sqr(value)
```

where *value* is any non-negative numeric expression. For example:

```
x = Sqr(16)
```

After running this code, x equals 4.

Below is a function which uses the built-in VBA function Sqr and the exponentiation and addition operators. The function allows you to enter the two legs of a right triangle and calculates the hypotenuse by using the Pythagorean theorem. (That's the formula that you said you'd never use in real life when you learned it in 9th grade.) To obtain the value of the hypotenuse of a right triangle, you need to square each of the other two sides, add the results together, and take the square root. Here's the VBA function that does it:

```
Function Hypotenuse(leg1, leg2)
    Hypotenuse = Sqr(leg1 ^ 2 + leg2 ^ 2)
End Function
```

The first line defines a VBA function called Hypotenuse and sets up two variables, leg1 and leg2.

To understand the second line, start on the right side of the equal sign. This is a computation. leg1 ^ 2 takes the value that was passed to the function for leg1 and squares it. leg2 ^ 2 does the same for the leg2. These values are added together as (leg1 ^ 2 + leg2 ^ 2). Finally, their square root is computed with the built-in VBA function Sqr.

Once the value on the right side is calculated, the result is assigned as the return value of the function. This is accomplished with the code Hypotenuse =.

Not only can you use VBA's built-in functions in your code, you can also use your own VBA functions. So, having written the Hypotenuse function, you can use it in other code in the same workbook. The next section gives an example of functions calling other functions.

Making several functions work together

As a child, the toy I continued to play with the longest was my set of building blocks. I think it was because I could do so many different things with it. I'd line them up like dominoes and topple them, or build skyscrapers, or throw them at my brother. They were very versatile.

You can take small, simple functions and combine them with other functions, macros, and more VBA code to write really extensive programs. Bigger is not necessarily better where programming is concerned, and writing smaller

procedures not only gives you a useful piece of code of its own right, but a building block from which you can create much larger programs. This section presents a longer programming example that creates several functions that call each other.

 Plain English, please!

A **procedure** is a block of programming code. There are two kinds of VBA procedures: subroutines and functions. All macros are VBA subroutines.

Catch the bug

You can enter this code into a module and it will seem to find no problem:

```
Function BadHypotenuse(leg1, leg2)
    BadHypotenuse = SQRT(leg1 ^ 2 + leg2 ^ 2)
End Function
```

But when you try to use it in a formula, a problem occurs. Excel brings up a dialog box and highlights the word SQRT, as shown in the following figure. What's wrong?

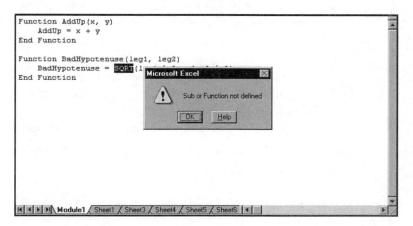

Answer: SQRT is an Excel built-in function, not a VBA function. You need to use the equivalent built-in VBA function Sqr instead.

Suppose you're standing on the ground and your friend Bob is on top of a building. You know how tall the building is in feet, and you have counted how many paces you are from the building. You also know that every pace you take is about 3.2 feet long. Now you want to know how far you are from Bob. (Evidently, it was a slow day at work.)

Since you regularly do this sort of calculation, you want to have a user-defined VBA function called HowFar that allows you to input the height of the building and the number of paces and give you the distance. Here's a way to program it into VBA.

```
Function HowFar(steps, height)
    length = ConvertPaces(steps)
    HowFar = Hypotenuse(length, height)
End Function

Function ConvertPaces(steps)
    ConvertPaces = steps * 3.2
End Function

Function Hypotenuse(leg1, leg2)
    Hypotenuse = Sqr(leg1 ^ 2 + leg2 ^ 2)
End Function
```

 This code defines three functions, HowFar, ConvertPaces, and Hypotenuse. Let's look at the functions separately, starting at the end. The Hypotenuse function is the same as the one described earlier in this chapter; give it two sides of a right triangle and it computes the hypotenuse. ConvertPaces takes the number of steps and then converts it into feet. It supposes that you measured your average pace to be 3.2 feet long. The value that you pass to ConvertPaces (steps) is multiplied by 3.2 to convert it to feet, and then ConvertPaces returns the number of feet you are from the building. The function HowFar is the one that ties it all together. It is HowFar that you enter as a user-defined worksheet function into a spreadsheet formula. Let's look at it line by line.

The first line of HowFar is

```
Function HowFar(steps, height)
```

It defines the function HowFar and creates two variables, steps and height. So, to use HowFar in a formula, you might type =**HowFar(10,50)** when you are 10 steps away from a 50-foot tall building. The second line of `HowFar` reads:

```
length = ConvertPaces(steps)
```

This takes care of several things at once. First, it creates a variable called `length`. Next, it takes the value of steps and passes it to the `ConvertPaces` function to figure out the length in feet. `ConvertPaces` returns the converted value, and it is assigned to the variable `length`. Notice that the function `ConvertPaces` is defined *below* the function `HowFar`, and yet `HowFar` calls `ConvertPaces`. Remember, you can call a function that is anywhere in your workbook, even in another module sheet.

The next line is:

```
HowFar = Hypotenuse(length, height)
```

This line assigns a value to `HowFar`, which will be the final answer that the function produces. (Remember that this is the entire purpose of a function—to return a value!) This line calls the function `Hypotenuse` and sends it the value `length` and `height` to work with.

Hypotenuse goes to work and returns its answer. That's done on the right-hand side of the line: `Hypotenuse(length, height)`. The first part of the line `HowFar =` takes the value that `Hypotenuse` returned and makes it the return value of `HowFar`.

Q&A

Wasn't Hypotenuse supposed to get values for leg1 and leg2, not length and height?

Actually, the names of variables in these functions are only relevant within that function. So, the `HowFar` function sends two values to `Hypotenuse`; it doesn't send their names. `Hypotenuse` receives two values and then calls the first one `leg1` and the second one `leg2`.

When `HowFar` sent the value of steps to `ConvertPaces`, it was only by coincidence that `ConvertPaces` used the same variable name for `steps`. They are actually different variables, which have nothing to do with each other except that the variable steps in `HowFar` was a placeholder that sent its values to a placeholder in `ConvertPaces` that had the same name. It's as if you had two boxes, each one with the label "steps" on it. You then took the contents of one box and transferred it to the other. The same results would have been obtained by having different labels on the boxes.

Summary

This chapter introduced functions, a type of VBA procedure that returns a value. You can write your own VBA functions and then use them in your formulas as user-defined worksheet functions. You learned a little bit about variables and operators, giving you enough knowledge of each to start programming user-defined worksheet functions that are really useful.

Review questions

1 What are the two types of VBA procedures?

2 What is a variable?

3 What is the purpose of a function? (What does a function always accomplish?)

4 What are the two kinds of built-in functions and where are they used?

5 Why is it good to break your code down into small, self-contained procedures?

6 How do you tell a function how many values it will receive when called upon?

Exercises

1 Rewrite the AddUp function so that it can add three values together instead of two.

2 Modify the `Stooges` function so that it only takes three lines instead of five. (Hint: eliminate the `Larry` and `Curly` variables and put all the calculations on one line.)

3 Right now, the `ConvertPaces` function assumes you have a stride length of 3.2 feet. Modify it so that you can enter in the length of your stride. The function will need to receive two values, the number of strides and the length of a stride.

4 Suppose you regularly drive for your work. You are paid $15 an hour for your time on the road and reimbursed $0.20 per mile for the distance you drive. Write a function that will accept values for time spent on the road and number of miles driven and that will return the amount of money the company owes you.

5 You recently went on a sales trip from the U.S. to Canada, and you know how far you drove in kilometers. Write a function that converts kilometers to miles (1 km = 0.6 miles), and then rewrite the function that figured out your expenses so that it calls this new function to convert kilometers to miles.

5

A Little Bit of Programming Goes a Long Way

● **In this chapter:**

● How much programming do I really need to know?

● Can I write code that only runs under certain circumstances?

● Programs can do something over and over again

● What does *With* mean in a program?

Getting just a few key pieces of programming under your belt will give you a huge increase in your VBA capabilities . . . . ▶

Have you ever considered how many different ways there are to ask something in English? In a restaurant, you could ask the waiter for a fork in dozens of ways including: "Could you get me a fork, please?" "I'd like a fork," "I need a fork, if you don't mind," and even "Get me a fork right now!" The particular phrase you'd use would depend on the particulars of the situation, but really you could probably limit yourself to one or two standard types of requests and get along just fine. In fact, if your English skills were limited, you'd probably do just that: pick out a fairly innocuous phrase that gets the job done and use it exclusively until your English skills progressed enough to allow you to add some variety for different situations.

In much the same way, you can get the job done in VBA without knowing a great deal of the language. This chapter shows you several structures of the VBA language that can be used to create many sophisticated and useful programs. Sure, there are other ways to get these jobs done, and some of them are more elegant or more efficient. When you learn them, you'll start to incorporate them into your programming. But why wait to know everything? Get that fork as soon as you know even one way to ask for it.

Performing an action when certain conditions are met

If I'm out for a walk and a dog approaches me, should I pet it? That all depends. Does the dog seem friendly? If so, then my answer is probably yes. If, on the other hand, the dog is snarling with hackles raised and salivating profusely, I might not be so inclined. My decision-making process can be stated as such: If the dog appears friendly, then pet the dog.

VBA provides several different ways to test conditions, but by far the most common and versatile is the If/Then control structure.

The If/Then control structure works just like the thought process about whether to pet the dog. Figure 5.1 shows what the If/Then structure does to control the flow of the program.

66 *Plain English, please!*

A **control structure** is a part of the VBA language that enables you to affect which part of a program runs. Loops and If/Then statements are both control structures.

A procedure without any control structures would simply start at the beginning and run straight to the end without stopping. By adding these structures, you can make your programs sensitive to the context, by affecting the order in which statements are run, how many times they run, or whether they are run at all. Your program can make these decisions by using control structures to look at the existing circumstances. 99

Fig. 5.1
Which path VBA follows depends on whether the condition is true or not.

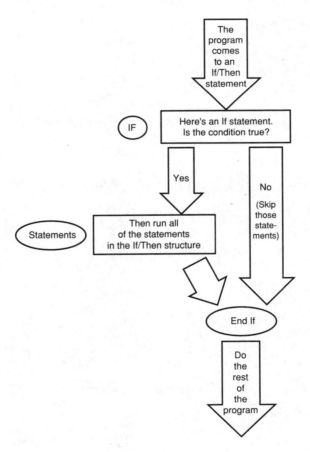

Testing whether a number fulfills a condition

Suppose that a salesman gets a commission bonus of $1,000 if his monthly sales exceed $100,000. The following function looks at the sales and decides whether to add the bonus or not.

```
Function Commission(GrossSales)
    Commission = GrossSales * 0.03
    If GrossSales > 100000 Then Commission = Commission + 1000
End Function
```

This function uses the single line version of If/Then. The first line of the function gives it the name Commission and declares the variable GrossSales. Whatever value is assigned in the function to Commission will be the return value of the function.

The next line computes the commission by multiplying GrossSales by 0.03. A return value has been assigned to Commission, but the program is not finished yet. The next line uses the one-line syntax of the If/Then control structure.

Speaking of *If/Then*

There are two forms of the If/Then statement: a one-line version and a multiple-line version.

The general form of the one line version is

```
If condition Then statement
```

where *condition* is something that VBA can determine to be true or false, and *statement* is the code that runs if *condition* is true.

The general form of the multiple-line version is

```
If condition Then
    statements
End If
```

where *statements* is one or several statements that runs if *condition* is true.

To learn about assignments, see Chapter 7, "Putting Together Lines of VBA Code."

This line starts by testing a condition. Is the value of `GrossSales` greater than `100000`? If this is the case, the rest of the line is executed. If not, VBA ignores the rest of the line. The rest of the line, `Commission = Commission + 1000`, assigns a new value to `Commission`, that of the old value which was computed on the preceding line, plus `1000`. You can read this line as, "Let Commission equal Commission plus `1000`."

You can test this function by entering the formulas **=Commission(50000)** and **=Commission(150000)** into worksheet cells and seeing the results. In the first case, the bonus will not be added, but in the second case it will.

Other ways to compare numbers

The most common conditions that are tested involve numbers. In order to perform a test on two numbers, you need to compare them in some way, such as deciding if they are equal or if one is smaller than another. In VBA, you compare numeric values by putting a comparison operator between them. In the preceding example, the greater than (>) operator was used to compare the value of GrossSales to 100,000.

 Plain English, please!

A comparison operator is a symbol that is used to compare two numbers. The equal sign is perhaps the most familiar comparison operator.

The VBA comparison operators are listed in table 5.1. Two examples are given for each operator—one that would evaluate to be True, and one that would evaluate to be False if used as the condition in an If/Then statement.

Table 5.1 Comparison Operators

Operator	Meaning	True Example	False Example
=	Equals	5 = 10/2	3 = 0
>	Greater than	10 > 6.7	10 > 10
<	Less than	–2 < 0	9 < 8
>=	Greater than or equal to	4 >= 4	4 >= 5
<=	Less than or equal to	3 <= 5	3 <= –5
<>	Not equal to	6 <> 7/2	6 <> 6

To learn more about VBA expressions, see Chapter 7, "Putting Together Lines of VBA Code."

Putting two values together with a comparison operator gives you a conditional expression that VBA can test as True or False. Thus, comparison operators are very commonly used with If/Then structures.

Comparing text

If/Then statements are not restricted to testing conditions on numbers. Text strings are fair game, too. The equal and not equal comparison operators are useful for comparing text strings.

 *Plain English, please!*

A **string** is bunch of characters, usually text. Just like numbers, words and letters can be assigned to variables in VBA, and compared to each other. Examples of strings are: "Nancy," "The Houston Rockets," or "123 Main Street." All of these are text strings and can be assigned to variables as values.

The following subroutine asks the user's name, and if the user is named Sam, it brings up a message box. It uses the second syntax of the If/Then structure.

```
Sub Greeting()
    user = InputBox("Who are you?")
    If user = "Sam" Then
        Beep
        MsgBox "Hi Sam"
    End If
End Sub
```

How can I use this in the real world?

A few possible ways that If/Then tests could be used include the following programming scenarios:

- If the text entered in a cell is "Taxes," then run the subroutine that fills in tax information below that cell.

- Present a dialog box to the user which asks, "Do you want to save your changes?" If the user selects "Yes," then save the changes.

- Check the system time to see if a certain hour has been reached. If so, run a program that reminds the user to make a backup copy of recent work.

InputBox is a built-in VBA function that returns the value of whatever the user types in. This procedure creates a variable called `user` and assigns the return value of InputBox to it. The third line checks to see if this text is Sam. Notice that for a text comparison, quotation marks are used around the word Sam, otherwise VBA thinks it's a variable rather than a string.

To learn about using string variables, see Chapter 9, "Variables."

If the text entered was `Sam`, the two lines in the If/Then block are executed; the computer beeps and a message box appears.

Testing multiple conditions together: And, Or

Sometimes, you'll want to require that several conditions be true before performing a certain action. Or, you may wish to perform an action if any one of several conditions is true.

And allows you to require multiple conditions to be true. For instance, to be very cautious about strange dogs, you might want to avoid large ones even if they're friendly. Then, your conditional statement would be, "If a dog looks friendly and he is small, then pet him." Here you're requiring that two conditions be true.

Or lets you choose among conditions. Maybe having only one of two conditions is enough for you. For example, if the dog looks friendly or is wearing a muzzle, then pet him.

Speaking of *And*

The And operator is used to join two expressions into a new one which is true if and only if *both* of the individual expressions are true. The general form of And is

    condition1 And condition2

where *condition1* and *condition2* can each be evaluated to true or false individually.

In this example, the Beep statement will be executed because both conditions are true.

```
Sub UsesAnd()
    x = 4
    If x > 3 And x < 10 Then Beep
End Sub
```

TIP **Or will work if one or both of the conditions are true. If you want** to run code only when one condition is true, not both, then use Xor instead of Or.

Making things happen when the condition isn't true: Else

Sometimes, you not only want to do something when a condition is true, you want to do something else if it is false. In the dog scenario, this might work out as, "If the dog is friendly, then pet him. Otherwise, run away as fast as you can." The VBA word for otherwise is Else.

Here's a procedure of code that checks to see if a user enters the correct password when prompted.

```
Sub PasswordCheck()
    password = InputBox("Please enter the password.")
    If password = "pzx054" Then
        MsgBox "Thank You"
        RestrictedAccess
    Else
        MsgBox "Sorry, that is the wrong password."
    End If
End Sub
```

Speaking of *Or*

The Or operator is used to join two conditions into a new one which is true if one or both of the individual conditions are true. The general form of Or is

condition1 Or *condition2*

where *condition1* and *condition2* can each be evaluated as true or false individually.

In this example, the Beep statement will be executed because the first condition is true. Notice that the second condition is false, but only one of them needs to be true.

```
Sub UsesOr()
    x = 4
    If x > 3 Or x = 10 Then Beep
End Sub
```

This procedure starts by prompting the user to enter a password. The text entered in the inputbox by the user is assigned to the variable `password`. The next line begins the If/Then/Else structure and checks to see whether the password the user entered is the correct one.

The condition being tested is

```
password = "pzx054"
```

This will be evaluated as true if the text entered by the user is `pzx054`. If so, then two statements are run as a result. The first is a message box that says `Thank You`. The second runs another program written elsewhere called `RestrictedAccess`.

If the text entered into the input box was not `pzx054`, these two statements are not run. Instead, the program skips down to the `Else` line and displays a message box explaining that was the wrong password. Notice that the RestrictedAccess program does *not* get run in this case.

This code contains an example of calling one procedure from within another. If you don't have a procedure called `RestrictedAccess` somewhere in the workbook, this procedure will not be able to run.

To learn about ElseIf and Select Case, see Chapter 10, "Ways to Control the Flow of Your Programs."

If/Then/Else is a good structure to use when there are two different courses of action you want your program to decide between. When you have three or more courses of action, you'll want to use a different control structure such as ElseIf or Select Case.

Speaking of *If/Then/Else*

The general form of If/Then/Else is

```
If condition Then
    statements
Else
    otherstatements
End If
```

There are two different sets of statements. One set, *statements*, will be run if *condition* is true. The other set, *otherstatements*, will be run if *condition* is false.

Catch the bug

When you run this code, it tells you that the value of x is greater than 0, but x is defined to be –5 which is less than 0. What's the problem?

```
Sub PrettyWeird()
    x = -5
    If x Then
        MsgBox "The value of x is greater than 0."
    Else
        MsgBox "The value of x is less than 0."
    End If
End Sub
```

Answer: *The problem was a simple typo on the If/Then line. The line should read*

```
If x > 0 Then
```

What is pretty weird is that the code ran at all. Somehow the condition that was incorrectly entered was evaluated to be true.

This is actually an interesting and subtle feature of VBA. The expression being evaluated was merely x, a numeric value. When VBA looks at a numeric value by itself, if it is 0 it makes it false and if it is anything other than 0 it makes it true.

So, even though it is hard to see any condition that VBA could evaluate as either true or false in the PrettyWeird procedure, VBA finds one. It looks at the value of the variable and because it is not 0, it evaluates it as true.

The point to keep in mind is that if VBA is not evaluating conditions the way you think it should, remember that VBA has pretty weird ideas about numbers being true and false.

Writing programs that repeat steps

Suppose there's a long line of friendly dogs and you want to tell your friend to pat each one on the head. You could give really wordy instructions like "Pat the first dog, then pat the second dog, then pat the third dog..." and keep going until you got to the end of the line or ran out of breath. Or, you could say, "Start at the beginning of the line and pat each dog until you get to the end." Clearly, the second way will require much less effort when there's a long line of dogs.

Often, you'll want to automate a task that performs an action many times in your programs. By creating a **loop**, VBA can repeat a step over and over until you want it to stop.

Repeating a step doesn't mean you need to do exactly the same thing on each go-around, though. For example, if you were doing a dog-patting loop, you would pat higher or lower for each dog, depending on the height of the dog's head. A **loop** means that you're doing *something* similar on each go-around, but it often varies from iteration to iteration.

To learn about other kinds of loops, see Chapter 10, "Ways to Control the Flow of Your Programs."

There are many different kinds of loops. Some let you repeat an action a certain number of times, some repeat an action until a condition is met, and some go on forever. For now, let's take a look at the For/Next loop which will repeat a loop a certain number of times, and the Do While loop which will allow you to repeat an action while a condition is true.

A loop works by having a line of code that marks its beginning. This line is where you specify what conditions or numbers will control how many times the loop is run. This line is followed by one or many more lines of code that are executed during one round of the loop. At the bottom of the loop is a line marking the end. When this line is reached, the program determines whether the loop should be run again or whether it's time to move on. This is determined by the conditions or values set forth in the top line of the loop. Figure 5.2 shows the path VBA takes through a loop.

Fig. 5.2
There are different kinds of loops but they all have a starting line, a body where their instructions are ended, or an ending line.

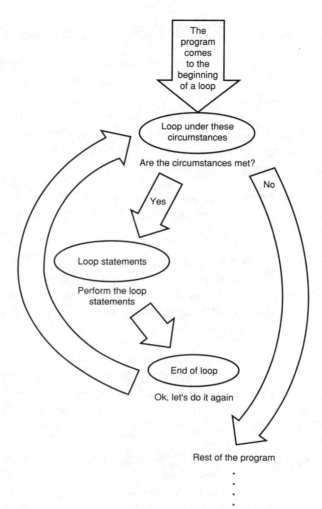

The program comes to the beginning of a loop

Loop under these circumstances

Are the circumstances met?

No

Yes

Loop statements

Perform the loop statements

End of loop

Ok, let's do it again

Rest of the program

Repeating some code a certain number of times

There are many situations where you might want to repeat code a certain number of times. You can fill values into a row of spreadsheet cells this way, each time around on the loop putting a value into a new cell. Or, you could prompt a user to supply values to go in a number of different categories. (Each category would be supplied during a round of the loop.) To create such a loop, use For/Next.

Here's an example of a For/Next loop in action.

```
Sub MyFirstLoop()
    Limit = 5

    'about to enter the loop the loop
    For n = 1 To Limit
        MsgBox "The current number is " & n
    Next n
    'out of the loop

    MsgBox "Now you've left the loop!"
End Sub
```

The variable `Limit` is given the value 5. The line beginning with `For` sets up a loop that will repeat until *n* equals the value of `Limit`—five times. This line also assigns an initial value of 1 to *n*.

The code to be repeated is a message box statement. On each round of the loop, it will display some text and the value of *n*. While *n* is 1, for example, the message box will look like figure 5.3.

Speaking of *For/Next*

Use For/Next with the following syntax:

```
For counter = start To end
    statements
Next counter
```

The first line establishes the number of times you want to repeat the loop by assigning values *start* and *end*, and designates a variable, *counter*, to keep track of how many times the loop has been performed. The initial value of *counter* will be the value of *start*, and the loop will increase by one each time it reaches the next line. As long as the value of *counter* does not exceed end, the Next line will send the program back to the beginning of the loop.

After the first line, whatever statements are to be executed during the loop are inserted. The last line changes the value of *counter* to the next value.

Fig. 5.3
The number on the
message box changes
with each iteration of
the loop.

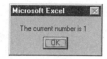

After the message box is displayed, the line `Next n` is reached. On this line, the value of *n* gets incremented by one. If the value of *n* is not greater than `Limit`, the program goes back up to the top of the loop again. When the value becomes greater than `Limit`, the program continues on to the next line, displaying another message box which indicates the loop is done.

TIP Don't change the value of the *counter* variable (the one that is *n* in the previous example) in the body of the loop. Remember, it's trying to keep track of how many times the loop has been run. If you change its value, you'll get unexpected results.

Repeating code while a condition is met

To learn about other kinds of Do loops, see Chapter 10, "Ways to Control the Flow of Your Programs."

It's hard to put a number on some things. You want to repeat a process until an end is reached, but sometimes you don't quite know when that end will be. A Do loop is what you need for this, so let's take a look at Do While.

How can I use this in the real world?

In Chapter 12, you'll learn how to get information in and out of worksheets. Then, you can write a program that loops from 1 to 12 for the months of the year. On each loop iteration, the program could open the monthly report from that month, copy information from a particular cell, and write it in a new workbook. This way you could create a summary report without having to manually open all 12 monthly reports.

Another tool that will add to the usefulness of loops is to create an array, as described in Chapter 13. An **array** is just a numbered list; it could be of names or categories. Then on each round of the loop, you can affect a different element on the list.

This procedure uses a Do While loop. It keeps prompting the user to enter a name as long as the last name entered was not Rosenkranz.

```
Sub NameChecker()
    User = "Guildenstern"
    Do While User <> "Rosenkranz"
        User = InputBox("What is your name?")
    Loop
End Sub
```

The first line of the body of this procedure assigns an initial value, Guildenstern, to the variable user. The expression on the following line, User <> "Rosenkranz", compares User to the text string Rosenkranz. If User *is not* Rosenkranz, it will be evaluated as True. Since the initial value was not Rosenkranz, this expression is true, and so the body of the loop gets run.

The body of the loop is a line that assigns a new value to User by prompting the user for a name. The user enters a name which is assigned to the variable User. The next line sends the program back up to the Do While line. Once again, this line checks the expression to see if it is different from Rosenkranz. If it is, then the loop is run. If it is not different—in other words, if the text entered was Rosenkranz—then the loop is skipped. Because there is nothing left of the procedure after the loop, the procedure ends.

Speaking of *Do While*

```
Do While condition
    statements
Loop
```

The first line starts with Do While and is followed by a condition that VBA can evaluate to be true or false. Whenever this condition is true, the statements in the loop will be run. If this is false, the statements in the loop will be skipped.

The number of statements can be one, many, or even none. After the statements have been run, the Loop line sends the program back up to the Do While line to see if the condition is still true.

What's the *With* that the macro recorder keeps using?

You don't want to know everything there is to know about VBA, but it would be nice to get an idea of the things you see every day, right?

The macro recorder often uses a statement called With. You may not choose to implement this into your own programming, but you should know what the recorder is up to.

For example, here's an excerpt from a macro recorded by the macro recorder:

```
With Selection.Font
    .Name = "Arial"
    .FontStyle = "Regular"
    .Size = 8
End With
```

Catch the bug

If you run this procedure, nothing seems to happen except that the computer gets tied up. You need to press the Esc key, which brings up an error message. Click on End to get your cursor back. What's wrong?

```
Sub InfiniteLoop()
    x = 5
    Do While x < 10
        x = x - 1
    Loop
End Sub
```

Answer: x is given an initial value of 5. The loop will run as long as x is less than 10. Look at the statement inside the loop. All it does is decrease the value of x. Since x started out being less than 10 and only gets decreased, the condition that x be less than 10 will always be true.

One way to fix this is by changing the line that decreased x to

```
x = x + 1
```

Even without knowing all of the VBA rules that go into this piece of code, it's pretty easy to figure out what it's doing: it's changing the font of the current selection to 8-point Arial Regular. What is the role of the With and the End With, though?

To learn about working with objects and properties, see Chapter 11, "How VBA Refers to Things in Excel."

The With statement is a way of working with **objects**. In the previous example, Selection.Font is an object. It has many different properties including Name, FontStyle, and Size. If you wanted to change the font size of a selection on a single line of code, you'd type:

Selection.Font.Size = 8

But if you want to change several properties of the Selection.Font object, the With statement would make it faster for you to type, and faster for VBA to run. You first identify the object you want to work with and then list all the properties you want to change. You only need to type the name of the object once, which is a time-saver when there are several things being done to that object. Converting the above line into a With format would give you

```
With Selection.Font
    .Size = 8
End With
```

This code does exactly the same thing as the one-line version above. With Selection.Font identifies the object to which the changes are to be made. The lines that follow up until the End With line describe the properties for the object that should be changed.

Summary

In this chapter, you learned that getting just a few key pieces of programming under your belt will give you a large increase in your VBA capabilities. Very useful structures include If/Then (which allows you to selectively run code) and loops (which allow you to repeat code many times). This chapter also explained the mysterious With statement that the macro recorder is so fond of.

Review questions

1 What is a control structure?

2 What does an If/Then statement do?

3 What does a loop do?

4 How is the For/Next loop different from the Do While loop?

5 Why is the With statement useful?

6 How can you test more than one condition in an If/Then statement?

Exercises

1 Change the GrossSales function so it no longer gives a bonus. Instead, if the sales level is less than $50,000, make it subtract $250 from the commission as a penalty.

2 In the UsesOr program, make the If/Then statement test to see if both conditions are true by changing Or to And. Will it beep now?

3 Change the MyFirstLoop program so that the loop will repeat 10 times instead of five.

4 In the Greeting Program, add an Else clause so that if the name entered is not Sam, the program beeps.

5 Rewrite the following code example using With:

```
Sub Macro3()
    Selection.Font.Bold = True
    Selection.Font.Italic = True
    Selection.Font.Underline = xlSingle
End Sub
```

6 In the Greeting program, it's possible that Sam would enter his name as Sam or sam. Modify the program so that with either capitalization, the greeting message box will appear.

7 Use a For/Next loop to write a program that adds together all of the numbers between 1 and a value that you specify.

VBA Information Online

● **In this chapter:**

● **What kinds of things can you look up in the online help?**

● **How help files are organized**

● **Look alphabetically or by subject**

● **Can I use these examples in my own programs?**

● **Which object is which?**

For definitions and examples of virtually everything in the VBA language, check out Excel's online Visual Basic reference. . . . . ●

I have two pet peeves regarding programming documentation. First of all, I hate to sit with two or three manuals and user's guides balanced on my desk (and often on my knees). Second, I don't understand why so many programming books are filled with appendixes that simply rehash reference information that comes with the software product. Why should I pay for that twice? Give me something useful instead.

Excel includes a complete reference guide online. It's a great way to look things up without having to reach for the manual. And since it contains a complete list of all VBA programming terms, you won't find that information duplicated in this book.

The online help is a reference in the best and worst senses of the word. It contains definitions and examples of virtually everything in the VBA language, but the information is quite condensed and doesn't necessarily explain things in non-technical terms. But that's what this book is for.

Are your Visual Basic help files installed?

VBA is a bit of an insider's feature of Excel. Most people don't know (and don't care) that there is a whole programming language embedded in their spreadsheet. Thus, the default installation for Excel doesn't install the Visual Basic help files.

They are a terrific resource, however, so go ahead and install them if you haven't already. You can do this by opening the Windows 95 Control Panel and running Add/Remove Programs. From the list of available programs, choose Microsoft Excel or Microsoft Office and then click on the Add/Remove button. You are prompted as to which components you want to change. You'll need to find the Excel Visual Basic help files component and check it. This will require your original program disks or CD.

Finding the Visual Basic help files can be a little tricky, since you'll need to maneuver through several dialog boxes. If you originally installed Excel as a part of Microsoft Office, then here are the steps for adding the Visual Basic help files to your installation:

1   From the Windows 95 Start menu, choose Settings, Control Panel.

2   Double-click on Add/Remove Programs.

3 Select the Install/Uninstall tab in the Add/Remove Programs Properties sheet.

4 Select Microsoft Office from the list, and click on the Add/Remove button. Follow the directions that appear on-screen for inserting your Office CD or disks.

5 In the Office Setup dialog box that appears, click on the Add/Remove button.

6 Select Microsoft Excel from the Options list and click on the Change Option button.

7 Select Online Help and Samples from the Options list, and click on the Change Option button.

8 Finally—here it is! Put a check mark next to the box by Online Help for Visual Basic, as shown in figure 6.1.

Fig. 6.1
Check the Online Help for Visual Basic option here.

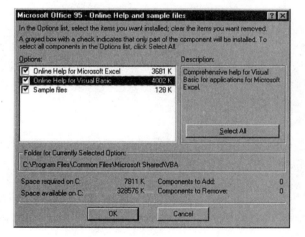

9 Click on the OK button, then in the next dialog box, click OK again. Finally, click Continue. The Excel Visual Basic help files are now added to your computer.

Adding the VBA help files if you originally installed Excel as a solo application (rather than as a part of Office) is done in a way very similar to the steps listed above. You won't have to select Excel from the Office Setup dialog box, however.

Navigating through Excel's online help

Excel has a *lot* of help available online. Once installed, the VBA help is in there with the rest of Excel's help topics. All of the help components, including the VBA reference, can be accessed through the Help Topics dialog box. To display the Help Topics, choose Help, Microsoft Excel Help Topics, and the dialog box shown in figure 6.2 appears.

Fig. 6.2
If you've never used the Help system before, you may get the message to wait while the Help index is compiled. It won't take long; then you'll get this dialog box.

The dialog box is divided into four tabbed pages. The first of these, the Contents page, is shown in figure 6.1. The two categories that are of the most interest to us are "Getting Started with Visual Basic" and "Microsoft Excel Visual Basic Reference." You may have to scroll down to find them. You can see both of these topics near the bottom of the list in figure 6.2.

Q&A *Where are these two topics? I can't find them even though I scrolled through the whole list.*

You may need to install the help files. See the previous section for instructions on how to do this.

Each of the different tabbed pages in the dialog box will lead you to the same places. The difference between them is how you get there. It is just like looking up a page number by using the table of contents versus the index of a book. They both lead you to the same place in the book via different routes.

Here's what the different pages of the dialog box are for:

- **Contents** works like the table of contents in a book, allowing you to browse topics by category.

- **Index** lets you search for the name of a help topic.

- **Find** lets you search for any text within a help topic.

- **Answer Wizard** accepts questions in English and provides "how-to" style answers.

Using the Contents

When do you use the table of contents in a book? If you don't have a particular word or a narrowly defined topic in mind, the table of contents will give you an idea of where to look. It's also useful if you don't have a specific question in mind, but you just want to see what there is available. Use the Excel Help Contents the same way.

There are two sections of Contents that apply to Excel VBA programming. One is geared towards teaching you how to program in VBA; the other contains a comprehensive reference to the VBA language, listing all of its keywords and components. This is the Microsoft Excel Visual Basic Reference. If you are using Excel as a part of Office, you might see a third topic called Microsoft Office Visual Basic Reference. This covers information on some VBA features that apply to Office as a whole. This book doesn't cover these features, but take a look at the help topics available there if you're curious.

For now, let's take a look at the Microsoft Excel Visual Basic Reference. To look at its subtopics, select this line and then click on the Open button. The topics and subcategories of the reference appear as shown in figure 6.3. The open book icon next to the Microsoft Excel Visual Basic Reference means that its components are being displayed. The page icons show a help topic destination. Other book icons lead to more topics.

Two topics and six subcategories of the Visual Basic Reference are shown in this figure. Of the two topics, the Microsoft Excel Object Model is particularly useful and is discussed later in this chapter in the section, "I'm lost in a sea of objects!". The other topic deals with changes that have been made to the VBA language with the latest release of Excel for Windows 95.

Fig. 6.3
Tables of Contents are
a great place to start
when you're looking
for ideas.

Open book:
Contents are
displayed

Page: Help topic

Closed book:
More topics under
this heading

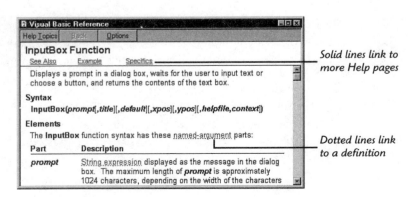

The first five subcategories—Functions, Methods, Objects, Properties, and
Statements—each contain an alphabetical listing of all of these VBA components. Once you locate the function or property or whatever you're looking
for, you'll have a description, syntax, and an example of it being used in code.

For example, if you wanted to get information on the InputBox function:

1 Double-click on the Functions book icon to show its subcategories.

2 Double-click on the book icon for the letter *I* to display all of the VBA
functions that start with the letter *I*.

3 Double-click on the InputBox Function topic to bring up the help
information on that topic. The help screen for this function appears as
shown in figure 6.4.

Fig. 6.4
The underlined words
in a help file let you
connect to related
topics with the click
of a button.

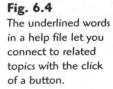

Solid lines link to
more Help pages

Dotted lines link
to a definition

Before you is a great deal of information about the InputBox Function and its syntax. Examples of how to use it, and definitions of technical terms and related topics are only a click away.

TIP **Once you've reached a help topic, clicking the Help Topics button** at the top left of the window will bring you back to the main Help Topics dialog box.

Searching for a particular topic or word

If you already know the name of what you're looking for, going through the Contents can be a roundabout method. You're better off using the Index or Find pages of the Help Topics dialog box:

- The Index looks things up by topic titles. If you're interested in what you can do with the menu editor, type **menu** into the text box, and the list box below will jump to the relevant part of the index. Once you see a suitable entry, click on it in the list box and then click on the Display button. Depending on the entry chosen, this may bring you to a help topic immediately, or it may bring up a dialog box with a list of subtopics to choose from.

- Find will look through *all* the text in all the help topics to get the information you're looking for. You can type one or several words (or symbols) in Find's text box. All topics that contain this word or words anywhere in their text appear below. Select the one you want and click the Display button.

  The first time that you use Find, Excel prompts you to build the Find database. It takes a couple of minutes, but you won't have to do it again.

TIP **Try Index first when looking for help on a particular word or topic.** Index is less likely to find irrelevant information. Try Find if you can't get what you want in Index.

Help topics contain links to more information

One of the great advantages to online reference material is the way you can jump from one piece of information to another. Excel's help provides access to definitions, examples, and related subjects. These are available by clicking on marked text or icons.

Text that is **linked** to other information is green and underlined. Underlines appear as solid or dotted depending on the kind of link:

- A dotted underline indicates that the link is to a **definition**. In figure 6.4, there are links to definitions of named-argument and String expression. Clicking on one of these will bring up a definition of the term in a window that pops up on top of the current window. Clicking the mouse button again makes the definition go away.

- A solid underline indicates a more extensive link that brings up another independent window. These links can be used to code examples, related topics, or other information.

Hey, there's an entire user's guide here!

Looking up words or topics alphabetically works if you know more or less what you're doing. The online help also includes a section called "Getting Started with Visual Basic," which provides step-by-step instructions on how to create programs with Visual Basic. The information provided tends to be condensed and assumes you know a bit about programming, but it's worth a look when you're stuck trying to figure out how to do something.

These topics can be accessed through the Contents page of the Help Topics dialog box. They are listed in a section just above the Microsoft Excel Visual Basic Reference.

Sometimes reading multiple descriptions of how to do something will make it clearer. If something in this book doesn't quite click, have a look at the online help's version as well. Some of it is pretty technical, but it can give you added insight.

Finding help on specific keywords

Plain English, please!

A **keyword** is a word or symbol that is recognized as part of the VBA language. These include function and procedure names, operators, objects, and properties.

Suppose you've decided to write a procedure that will generate a random number for you. You already know all about writing procedures, and all you want to know is how to do the random number part. You imagine that there's got to be a VBA built-in function that generates a random number, and you'd like to find out what it is and how it's used.

The last thing you want to do is to read through a whole lot of irrelevant information. Here's where the online help can really be useful. You can cut right to the chase and find the information you need without having to sort through a bunch of information you don't want to know.

Looking for a keyword when you don't know its name

When you know what something does but don't know the name of it, the Index page of the Help Topics dialog box is a good place to start. By typing **random** into the text box, the topics that have the word *random* in their name appear (see fig. 6.5).

Fig. 6.5
Typing **random** into the text box brings up all help topics with the word random in their title, as well as other help topics with similar spellings.

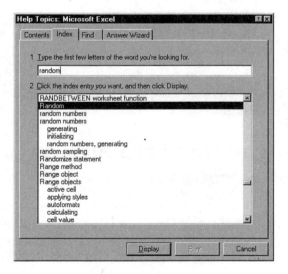

The entry `random numbers, generating` looks promising. Displaying this topic will get you the information you're looking for. You find out that the Rnd function will do the trick.

Getting help on a specific keyword

If you already knew that the Rnd function existed but you wanted to learn how to use it, you could still access the information through the Help Topics dialog box. However, there is a much more efficient way to bring up the information you want.

While in a module sheet, you can type the name of the keyword and when the cursor is anywhere in that word, press F1 on the keyboard. This will bring up the help topic for that word.

TIP **You don't need to select the word to get the help; just position** your cursor anywhere inside it, including at the end. That way, you can just type the word and immediately press F1 to get help.

Q&A *I tried it with a different keyword and got a message saying* Keyword not found. *What did I do wrong?*

If you selected part of a word or more than one word before pressing F1, Excel looks for a help topic that corresponds to the selection. Thus, if you selected the Rn in Rnd, Excel will try and find the Rn topic. You don't need to select any text to bring up the keyword's help file; just position your cursor in or immediately after the word.

It may, however, be Excel's fault. Some keywords, including all of the operators which are a single symbol like & or * are not available for this kind of help access.

Making sense of the built-in language reference

Once you've found the topic you're looking for, you need to be able to figure out what all those things in the dialog box mean. For example, the InputBox Function help page shown in figure 6.6 starts out simply enough. It tells you the name of the function and provides a brief description of what it does. Then it goes on to give the syntax for the function and how it's used, and it starts to look pretty convoluted.

Below the syntax is a description of the different elements, but it's not immediately apparent how to use this syntax:

```
InputBox(prompt[,title][,default][,xpos][,ypos][,helpfile,context])
```

Fig. 6.6
Sometimes Excel's
online help can seem
too complicated to be
truly helpful. What's
that line supposed to
mean, anyway?

The formal syntax
for InputBox

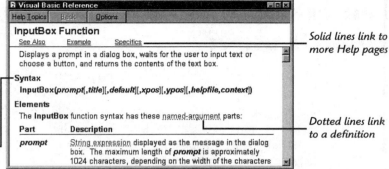

Solid lines link to
more Help pages

Dotted lines link
to a definition

To make sense of this, remember a simple tip—everything that's in rectangular brackets is optional. So, if we get rid of the rectangular brackets and their contents we wind up with

    InputBox(*prompt*)

which is a lot easier to understand. Just like in the Speaking VBA elements throughout the book, an item appearing in italics is one that you're supposed to replace with your own values. So, *prompt* is where you put in a text expression. To create an input box that asks users for their name, type

    InputBox("What is your name?")

When I'm learning a new keyword and figuring out its syntax, I try to start with the minimum. The title option looks like a good thing to add to the basic recipe above. To figure out what the syntax is like when including a title, I just put in the contents of that set of rectangular brackets. For instance, [,title] appears in the syntax line, so adding the contents of those brackets to my simple syntax gives me

    InputBox(*prompt*, *title*)

This seems easy enough and inserting a text expression for *title* will produce an input box with the title that you supplied.

TIP   **Don't be cowed by the complexity of the syntax of new keywords.**
Just take out all extraneous options and add things a little at a time.

Need an example of how something is used?

Imagine trying to describe what a spiral staircase looks like to someone who has never seen one. You can take a vague approach, "It's steps that go up and around," or you could try a very precise technical definition, "A helix whose axis is vertical with horizontal steps joining the…" Both leave something to be desired. Really, the best way to describe it is to point to one and say, "Look!"

After muddling through the syntax and description of a keyword, you may want to see it in action to better understand how it's used. The online reference has many code examples; you cannot only read them to learn how something is used, but you can also copy and paste these examples into your own code and modify them to suit your needs.

Find the code examples

There are a couple of places you'll find code examples. The most obvious is in an example link. In the InputBox help topic shown in figure 6.6, the underlined word `Example` is actually a link to another page of help with examples of InputBox being used in code. Most keyword help pages will have Example links like this.

There are other places you'll find sample code, though. The Getting Started with Visual Basic sections of Excel's online help will often contain longer examples of more general topics, such as creating loops or writing subroutines. There often also are general examples and Excel-specific examples available on a certain subject. It's not a trivial matter to find all of the possible code samples for a given subject, but if you can find one that's close to what you need, you can often drop it right into your program with very minor adjustments.

Let's look at what code examples we can find that involve For/Next loops. Start off in the Index, typing **For** into the text box. An entry called For Next Statements appears. That seems promising, so click on this entry and then on the Display button to display the topics shown in figure 6.7.

Fig. 6.7
Want help on For/Next loops? Take your pick of topics.

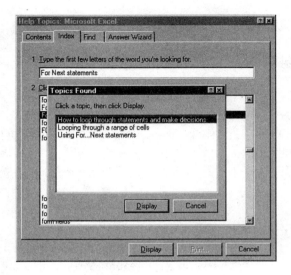

Choose `Using For...Next Statements`. A help topic appears with some general information on the subject. Although it doesn't contain an example link, it contains two examples in the text. This topic does contain two links, a See Also and a For...Next link. Click on the For...Next link.

Now the formal keyword help topic for For...Next appears. This is the one with the cryptic syntax explanations. It also has an Example link. Click on this link, and you'll find that there are two possible example pages for this subject: `For...Next Statement Example`, and `For...Next Statement Example (Microsoft Excel)`. Both of these will bring up a help page with one or more examples of the For...Next statement in action.

TIP Examples that say `(Microsoft Excel)` usually involve sending information to and from worksheet cells or working with other parts of the Excel environment.

Modify the examples for use in your own programs

Code examples can be copied and pasted from anywhere in a help topic to your module sheets. You do this just as you would any other kind of text:

1 Select the text you wish to copy.

2 Choose <u>E</u>dit, <u>C</u>opy or press Ctrl+C.

3 Bring up a module sheet, and position your cursor where you'd like the example to go.

4 Choose Edit, Paste or press Ctrl+V.

Once the code is in a module sheet, you can try running it as-is to see how it works, or change it to suit your own needs. To run it as it is, make sure that it's part of a valid procedure and that everything it refers to is appropriate to your situation. For instance, if a code example tries to open up a particular file that you haven't created on your computer, it won't be able to run.

When modifying code examples, you want to understand what is part of this particular structure or keyword's syntax, and what's optional. That's the point of the red text in the Example links; red words and symbols are essential parts of the syntax, and black words are ones that you can replace with your own. So, if you've copied an example from an Example link, look back at the link to see what was in red. Leave these parts in and replace the others with values and names relevant to your situation. In the following example, I take the Select Case help example and replace all of the black text, leaving the red text intact.

Select Case is an alternative to an If/Then/Else statement. It works particularly well when there are many different conditional expressions. I wanted to create a program that would ask someone about her mood and give an appropriate reply.

To create this, I took the code example for the Select Case Statement shown in figure 6.8. In the help example, it's used to display information about the value of a variable. I modified it for my own uses.

Fig. 6.8
Microsoft employs some pretty good programmers. Why not just adopt their code for use in your programs?

Words that appear in red are required parts of the syntax

```
Visual Basic Example                                          _ □ X
Select Case Statement Example

This example uses the Select Case statement to evaluate the value of a variable.  The second
Case clause contains the value of the variable being evaluated and therefore only the statement
associated with it is executed.

Number = 8                              ' Initialize variable.
Select Case Number                      ' Evaluate Number.
Case 1 To 5                             ' Number between 1 and 5.
    MyString = "Between 1 and 5"
Case 6, 7, 8, 9, 10                     ' Number between 6 and 10.
    ' This is the only Case clause that evaluates to True.
    MyString = "Between 6 and 10"
Case Else                               ' Other values.
    MyString = "Not between 1 and 10"
End Select
```

Here's my modification of the online help example:

```
Sub MoodPhrase()
    Mood = InputBox("What is your mood?")

    Select Case Mood
    Case "good", "Good"
        MyString = "Accentuate the positive!"
    Case "bad", "Bad"
        MyString = "Eliminate the negative!"
    Case Else
        MyString = "Don't mess with Mr. In-between!"
    End Select

    MsgBox MyString
End Sub
```

MoodPhrase is a modified version of the example code for the `Select Case` statement. The Number variable from the example has been renamed Mood. Rather than pre-assign a value like in the example, this program asks the user to supply the value of the mood variable with an input box.

In the `Select Case` block, Number was replaced with Mood and the values that would have applied to Number have been replaced with the values that could apply to mood. The line

```
Case "good","Good"
```

will execute the following line if the value of Mood is one of the two strings: good or Good. This replaced the line in the example which was the case when number was between 1 and 5.

How can I use this in the real world?

You can create a custom dialog box that opens whenever Excel is run, and which allows users to select what kind of document they wish to create. In Chapter 19, you'll learn how to create list boxes. That way you can create a list containing items such as "Sample Data" or "Monthly Report."

When the user selects one of these items, the Select Case statement could then be used in the code to bring up the appropriate template without the users ever having to understand what a template is.

At the end of the modified version, a message box has been added to show the result.

Notice that the entire Select Case structure has been preserved from the example and none of the red words have been changed.

I'm lost in a sea of objects!

Worksheets, menus, cells, charts, toolbars, fonts... there are so many different things in Excel that you can manipulate with VBA. How do you find them all? What are their names? What are the names of the settings that you want to change?

To learn more about objects, properties, and methods, see Chapter 11, "How VBA Refers to Things in Excel."

The **object model** is a great tool for addressing these issues. It includes a schematic chart of all the objects in Excel. Once you've found the right object, there are links to all the different properties and methods for that object.

You can get to the object model through the Help Topics dialog box in one of two ways:

- Type **object model** into the text box on the Index page.

- Look up the object topic in the Contents page. It's listed under Microsoft Excel Visual Basic Reference.

The unexpanded version of the object model is shown in figure 6.9. Because some objects, like worksheets, have so many objects inside them, the whole object model can't fit on one page. The red arrows to the right of the Worksheet, DialogSheet, and Chart entries will expand that part of the object model while hiding other parts.

 TIP   **The Object Model should not be confused with the Object** Browser that's discussed in Chapter 11.

When you click on any rectangle in the object model, it will bring up the help page on that particular object. The help page will include links to the properties and methods of that object.

Fig. 6.9
Like a family tree, the Object Model helps you figure out who is related to whom.

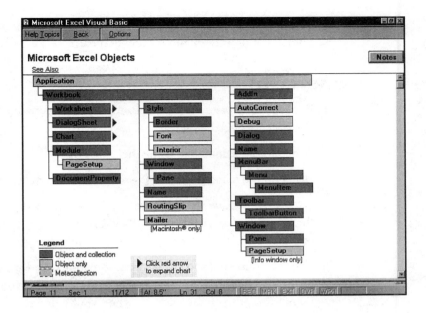

Summary

There is a plethora of information available through Excel's online help. You can learn how to perform a task, get the syntax on a particular keyword, or find an elusive object. There are also code examples showing different components of VBA in action. These code examples can be copied and pasted into your programs and changed to suit your needs.

Review questions

1 Where would you find a list of all of the different statements in VBA?

2 How would you use the Help Topics dialog box to show you what topics exist on the subject of loops?

3 If you're working in a module sheet and can't quite remember the syntax for a keyword you just typed, what is the fastest way to access its help topic?

4 When you're looking at an Example page, how can you identify which parts of the syntax are mandatory and which parts you can replace with your own choices?

5 When learning a new keyword and looking up its syntax in the online help, what do rectangular brackets mean?

Exercises

1 Find the help page on the Caption property, using the Contents page of the Help Topics dialog box.

2 Bring up the same page using the Index instead.

3 Bring up the same page from within a module sheet by pressing F1.

4 Find the InputBox example page. Copy all the code up to and including the first line that uses an InputBox function. Copy this to a module sheet and create a procedure that runs this code.

5 Use the online help to get information about the Date statement and write a procedure that changes the system date in your computer. (Don't forget to change it back when you're done!)

Putting Together Lines of VBA Code

In this chapter:

- **The sentence structure of VBA**

- **So what is an expression anyway?**

- **Calculating values and testing for true and false**

- **How to give a variable its value**

- **Make your code more readable: Group things together**

Without being aware of it, you already know many rules for putting together lines of code. Knowing why this code works will add to your understanding of VBA . . . . **>**

To write a professional business letter, your writing must be acceptable on several levels. Individual words must be spelled correctly, sentences should be constructed properly with no sentence fragments or dangling participles, and paragraphs should unify common themes. The grammar, though, mostly takes place on the sentence level.

VBA code needs to work on similar levels. Putting together usable lines of code is much like writing a grammatically correct sentence in English. This chapter looks at some of the rules for constructing a line of code. As with English, you'll find that much of it is what you already know without being fully aware of all the rules. Knowing *why* it works will add to your understanding of VBA and help you add to your collection of programming tools.

The information in this chapter can get pretty technical, and there's some new terminology being used. Don't let it get you down, though. In English, you use interjections and subordinate clauses all the time without thinking about it. If your programs are running, that's all that really matters.

Issue commands with statements

The **statement** is the fundamental unit of VBA instructions. Programming is all about giving the computer instructions to carry out, and any single instruction that you give is a statement.

What kind of instructions can you give with statements? Here are some examples describing various instructions to VBA followed by the corresponding VBA statement. Each one of these is a self-contained line of VBA programming code:

- Display a message box that says "Good Morning"

    ```
    MsgBox "Good Morning"
    ```

- Assign the value of 5 to the variable called "Tidling"

    ```
    Tidling = 5
    ```

- Set aside the name "Expenses" as a variable

    ```
    Dim Expenses
    ```

- Run the macro called "Scheduler"

```
Scheduler
```

In fact, most single lines of VBA code are actually statements.

Excel's built-in statements

Many statements are predefined in Excel. MsgBox and Beep are two such examples. They differ in an important way: Beep can stand alone on a line as an Excel statement, whereas MsgBox cannot. You must write out the text that goes into the MsgBox, such as **MsgBox "Hello"**. The MsgBox statement needs an argument; in this case, `"Hello"` is the argument.

 Plain English, please!

An **argument** is the term for a value that you provide to a procedure.

To learn about using online Help, see Chapter 6, "VBA Information Online."

Excel's online Help includes a complete list of VBA statements, along with examples of how they can be used.

Your own programs can be statements, too

Often, you will write a procedure that runs another procedure. To do this, you write a VBA statement to call the other procedure.

```
Sub RunThreeMacros ()
    Macro1
    Macro2
    Macro3
End Sub
```

This procedure runs three macros that you've created elsewhere in the workbook. Each of the three lines in the body of this procedure is a statement that runs one of these macros.

To learn about passing values to different procedures, see Chapter 8, "VBA Procedures."

In the example above, the statements did not require arguments. If you are calling procedures that require values, you'll need to provide an argument. For example:

```
Sub BeepingMessage(Message)
    Beep
    MsgBox Message
End Sub
```

```
Sub AnotherSub ()
    BeepingMessage "hello there"
End Sub
```

The first subroutine, `BeepingMessage`, expects to receive a value when it is called. It beeps and then puts the received value as the text in its message box. The second subroutine, `AnotherSub`, calls the `BeepingMessage` procedure. Since `BeepingMessage` requires a value, the argument `"hello there"` is given.

Notice that `AnotherSub` is a macro; it requires no arguments and will show up in the Macro dialog box. Because `BeepingMessage` requires an argument, you can only run it with a line of code in another procedure that calls it and provides the argument.

Work things out with expressions

Throughout the Speaking VBA portions of this book, you'll find the word *expression* used in italics, meaning that you are supposed to put in a relevant expression. In VBA, the term expression has a specific meaning.

 Plain English, please!

An **expression** is any combination of numbers, functions, and symbols that VBA uses to produce a value. The key concept is that when VBA encounters an expression, it produces a value. **99**

An expression is never an entire statement and is never able to stand alone as a line of VBA code. Rather, it is a part of a statement. You can compare it to an incomplete part of a sentence in English. The words "next to the bookshelf" don't comprise a sentence on their own, but can be used as a part of a sentence.

The result yielded by an expression can be a number, text, or a true or false value. Any type of VBA data can be the result of an expression.

When VBA encounters an expression, it **evaluates** it. Some expressions are already pretty much evaluated. The number 5 or the string "Jerome" are both ready to go. But the expression 5+2 is evaluated by VBA as 7. Variables are also expressions, and VBA evaluates them as whatever value is currently assigned.

Expressions that calculate values

As an Excel user, you use expressions all the time. When entering a formula in a worksheet cell, everything except the equal sign is an expression. Similarly in VBA, combinations of numbers, functions, and symbols create expressions that yield numeric results.

Here are some numeric VBA expressions:

`(4 + 7)/2`	Excel will evaluate this to be 5.5
`TaxRate`	This expression will be evaluated as whatever value is assigned to the variable TaxRate
`35`	Yes! A single number is an expression, too
`Expenses * 2`	If Expenses was previously defined to be 350, then this expression will be evaluated as 700

Numeric expressions can be used anywhere that VBA is looking for a value. For example,

```
DoubleExpenses = Expenses * 2
```

is a valid VBA statement that assigns the result of the expression on the right to the variable on the left.

Expressions that test for true or false

A common use of an expression is in If/Then statements or other places where the truth or falsehood of something will affect how the code runs.

Consider the code

```
CurrentValue < 8
```

Assuming that `CurrentValue` is a variable containing some numeric value, VBA can look at this code and decide whether it is true or not. Thus, it is an expression that VBA can evaluate as True or False.

```
Sub MeasureUp()
    CurrentValue = ActiveCell.Value
    If CurrentValue < 8 Then MsgBox "That's too little"
End Sub
```

This procedure is designed to be run while a cell with a numeric value is selected. The value of that cell is assigned to the variable CurrentValue.

On the next line, VBA evaluates the expression CurrentValue < 8. If it is found to be true, VBA goes on to produce a message box.

You can use a function's return value as an expression

To learn more about functions, see Chapter 8, "VBA Procedures."

Expressions and functions seem to have something in common. An expression is anything that VBA can chew on and produce a value. A function is a procedure whose job is to return a value. So, it makes sense to use a function to create an expression.

The following is an example that uses a function as the conditional expression in an If/Then statement.

```
Function AddSalesTax(Price)
    TaxRate = 0.054
    Totaltax = Price * TaxRate
    AddSalesTax = Price + Totaltax
End Function

Sub ComputeTax()
    Amount = ActiveCell.Value
    If AddSalesTax(Amount) > 500 Then
        MsgBox "Wow, that's more than $500 with tax."
    End If
End Sub
```

The first procedure, the AddSalesTax function, takes a number and computes the total price that would be paid with a 5.4 percent sales tax rate. It returns this value.

The second procedure, ComputeTax, takes the value of the active cell and assigns it to Amount. On the next line, the If/Then statement calls the AddSalesTax function, sending it the value of Amount. The return value is compared to 500 and if it is greater than 500, the contents of the If/Then block are run.

Anywhere that an expression is called for, a function can be used. Usually a function requires that an expression be supplied for it to work on. You can use another function to supply this expression. If this seems confusing, read the breakdown of the following example carefully.

```
Sub Compute()
    Result = Sqr(TimesTwo(8))
End Sub

Function TimesTwo(x)
    TimesTwo = x * 2
End Function
```

The subroutine Compute consists of one instruction—to assign a value to the variable Result. The value that it is to assign is going to be the return value of the Sqr function. (Recall that the Sqr function returns the square root of its argument.)

What exactly is the argument of the Sqr function? It is TimesTwo(8), an expression made from a function call. TimesTwo(8) means send the value of 8 to the TimesTwo function and use the return value. This turns out to be 16. So Sqr will do its work on 16 and will come up with 4, the value assigned to Result.

Catch the bug

The following procedure is supposed to multiply x by 2 and display the result. What's wrong?

```
Sub BadTimesTwo()
    x = 4
    x * 2
    MsgBox x
End Sub
```

Answer: The problem is in the middle line. This is an expression, not a statement. This line multiplies x by 2 but then doesn't know what to do with the result. An expression by itself is not a valid line of code.

*To correct the problem, change the middle line to **x = x * 2**.*

Build bigger expressions with operators

In order to make complicated expressions, you need some way of combining or comparing values in interesting ways. The tools required are **operators**.

Operators fall into four different categories:

- Arithmetic operators (such as * and +) create numeric expressions

- Comparison operators (such as < or >=) are used when comparing different values

- Concatenation operators combine text strings

- Logical operators combine multiple true/false expressions into one

To learn how to look up operators online, see Chapter 6, "VBA Information Online."

A listing of all VBA operators with explanations and examples is available in the online Visual Basic Reference by looking up Operators in the index. The following sections describe how these operators can be used.

Combining numeric and text expressions

To learn more about using arithmetic operators, see Chapter 4, "Write Your Own Worksheet Functions."

You are probably quite familiar with arithmetic operators from your work in Excel. You can use them to build complicated numeric expressions out of numbers, variables, and other expressions. Here's an expression that uses the addition and division arithmetic operators with several expressions.

```
(TimesTwo(6) + Sqr(9.4) + TotalValue) / 53
```

Concatenation operators work on text. What can you do with text? Not much except stick bits of it together. Both & and + work the same way—they join two text strings together. This statement will produce a message box with the text Frodo Baggins.

```
MsgBox "Frodo B" & "aggins"
```

TIP **Use & instead of + for concatenation. That way, you can keep** yourself and Excel from confusing it with numeric addition.

Creating True/False expressions

To learn more about using comparison operators, see Chapter 5, "A Little Bit of Programming Goes a Long Way."

Comparison operators are most often used as part of If/Then statements or in other places where Excel needs to figure out where something is true. This expression looks at whether the value of a variable is less than or equal to 10. If x is less than or equal to 10, the expression will evaluate as true. Otherwise, the expression will be false.

```
x <= 10
```

To learn more about And and Or, see Chapter 5, "A Little Bit of Programming Goes a Long Way."

Logical operators provide a way to take two true or false expressions and combine them into one. All of the logical operators produce a single true or false result out of two true or false component expressions. They vary in which true and false component expressions will produce what result. The most common logical operators are And and Or.

The following example uses the Or and Xor operators. Or creates an expression that is true when either one of its two component expressions is true. Xor creates an expression that is true when one of its component expressions is true but not the other. If both are false or both are true, the end result of Xor will be false.

```
Sub IsOneTrue()
    x = 5
    y = 3

    If x = 5 Or y < 0 Then
        MsgBox "At least one expression is true"
    End If

    If x = 5 Xor y < 0 Then
        MsgBox "Exactly one expression is true"
    End If
End Sub
```

Two expressions are combined with logical operators in this example. The expressions are x = 5 and y < 0. The first one is true and the second is false; however, it's not one of these expressions, but a combination of both that is used in each of the If/Then blocks.

The first If/Then block uses the Or operator, which looks to see if either one of the two expressions is true. Since the first one, x = 5, is true, then the expression

```
x = 5 Or y < 0
```

is also true, and the message box appears.

In the second If/Then block, Xor is used. For the expression

```
x = 5 Xor y < 0
```

to be true, it must be the case that one of the expressions is true, but not the other. This is indeed the situation since y < 0 is false, and the second message box appears as well. If the expression used in this second If/Then block were

```
x = 5 Xor y > 0
```

instead, then it would be false and the second message box would not appear.

Use = to assign values and settings

Often values are assigned to variables or properties in a statement. This is called an **assignment statement**. All assignment statements contain an equal sign.

On the left side of the equal sign will be the variable or property to which you are assigning a value. On the right side of the equal sign will be an expression. Thus x = 4 assigns the expression 4 to the variable x.

Each of the following is an assignment statement and could appear alone on a line of VBA code. In all cases, the expression on the right side of the equal sign could *not* appear alone on a line:

`x = 4`	The expression 4 is assigned to the variable x.
`Distance = Hypotenuse(6,10)`	Hypotenuse is another function procedure. The expression on the right sends it the values 6 and 10 and assigns the return value to `Distance`.

`Selection.Font.Style = Bold`	This assigns the value `Bold` to the `Style` property of the font of the currently selected cells.
`UserName = "Nifty Nancy"`	The text `Nifty Nancy` is an expression which is assigned to the variable `UserName`.

Q&A *Isn't = a comparison operator that you use when you want to see if something equals something else?*

The equal sign does double-duty as both a comparison operator and for assigning values. It's the same symbol but has two different meanings depending on when it's used.

Why do some variables appear on both sides of the equal sign?

Consider an assignment statement like the following:

```
x = x + 7
```

What is going on here? Is x a variable awaiting assignment (on the left), or is it part of an expression that VBA can evaluate (on the right)? The answer is both. You could read this sentence as saying, "Assign a new value to x which is the old value of x plus 7."

In an assignment statement, VBA will start on the right-hand side and evaluate the expression before it assigns it to the variable on the right-hand side.

The dreaded type mismatch error!

VBA values come in all shapes and sizes. Text, numbers, True and False, and settings for different properties are some examples. Each of these is a **data type**.

Although VBA is pretty flexible in letting you mix and match different data types, sometimes you'll run into trouble when VBA expects one kind of data and gets another. This often produces the infamous type mismatch error message shown in figure 7.1.

Fig. 7.1
The type mismatch error appears when VBA expects one kind of data and gets another.

To learn how to specify a data type for a variable, see Chapter 9, "Variables."

To learn how to use the online Visual Basic Reference, see Chapter 6, "VBA Information Online."

To avoid these, you can force a variable to only store a certain type of value, or you can keep your options open but risk running into type mismatch problems and other drawbacks.

A complete listing of all data types is found in the online Visual Basic Reference. The fundamental difference between assigning text strings and numbers is worth mentioning here, however.

To assign a numeric value to a variable or setting, you want a numeric expression on the right of the equal sign in the assignment statement. To assign a text value, you want a text expression. Easy enough? Well, it can be fairly easy to mix them up sometimes.

If you run this subroutine, it will display the first two message boxes and then produce an error on the third. It's a good example of VBA's flexibility and limits with handling data types.

```
Sub Confusion()
    'George is a number and Astro is text
    George = 6
    Astro = "hello"

    'show George, Astro and both
    MsgBox George
    MsgBox Astro
    MsgBox George + Astro
End Sub
```

The variables George and Astro are respectively assigned text and numeric values. Now, MsgBox is a statement that displays text. Although George is a number, VBA is smart enough to show the text 6 in the message box. It automatically converted the number 6 to the text string 6.

Since Astro has a text value, the second MsgBox statement is doing nothing that's surprising.

The third MsgBox statement is what produces the error. If George and Astro were both text values, the + operator would just string them together. If they were both numbers, the + operator would add them and display the result in the message box. But VBA finds itself trying to add a word and a number and can't handle it.

Catch the bug

Why does this procedure produce a type mismatch error?

```
Sub Shmoo()
    Amount = 9
    x = "Amount"
    Sqr (x)
End Sub
```

Answer: The first line in the body of Shmoo creates a variable called Amount and assigns it the value 9. The next line is the root of the problem, even though it isn't the one producing the error. This line creates a variable called x and assigns it the text expression that is in quotation marks on the right side of the equal sign. Thus, the value assigned to x is the six letters A-m-o-u-n-t which have nothing to do with the variable called Amount.

When VBA tries to calculate the square root of a bunch of letters, it doesn't know what to do; it was expecting a number.

To fix this code, rewrite the middle line as

```
x = Amount
```

Using functions to assign values

The idea behind functions—both built-in or ones you define—is to return a value. When you call a function, you tell it, "Go work this out for me and return with the answer." It's up to you to do something with the answer. This is often achieved by calling the function as part of an assignment statement.

The following procedure uses two functions this way.

```
Sub FuncAssigner()
    horizontal = Cos(0)
    mpg = Mileage(290, 10)
End Sub
```

Two function calls are made in this procedure. Neither one stands alone as a statement, but instead is used as the expression assigned to a variable.

The first line of the body calls VBA's built-in Cos function which returns the cosine of its argument, giving it the value 0 to work on. VBA runs this function and returns the value 1, which is the cosine of 0, assigning it to the variable horizontal.

The next line calls a user-defined function called Mileage which takes two values and returns another. The return value is assigned to the variable mpg.

Why does code get put into blocks and indented?

VBA doesn't care if you indent your code or not. It has no trouble figuring out what the following code is about. At first glance, what do you think? How many procedures are here? Are there any loops or other structures?

```
Sub AddUp()
x = ActiveCell.Value
If x > 10 Then
Beep
MsgBox "Wow, that's a lot!"
Beep
End If
Total = 0
For Current = 1 To 10
Total = Total + Current
MsgBox Total
Next Current
End Sub
```

Here's the reader-friendly version of the same code. Only the spacing has changed.

```
Sub AddUp()
    x = ActiveCell.Value
    If x > 10 Then
        Beep
        MsgBox "Wow, that's a lot!"
        Beep
    End If
    Total = 0
    For Current = 1 To 10
        Total = Total + Current
        MsgBox Total
    Next Current
End Sub
```

Notice that in the second version, it is easy to pick out which statements are part of the If/Then structure. Only if x > 10 will those three indented lines be executed. Likewise, the two lines of code that are repeated in the loop are immediately apparent. It's easy to see where procedures begin and end and which lines of code are run together.

To learn how to nest one control structure within another, see Chapter 10, "Ways to Control the Flow of Your Programs."

With multiple line structures, like loops and If/Then statements, indent the contents as shown in figure 7.2. Sometimes, you'll wind up with a loop within an If/Then or something equally complicated. By scanning straight down from an If statement, you'll be able to find where it ends when you reach the Then.

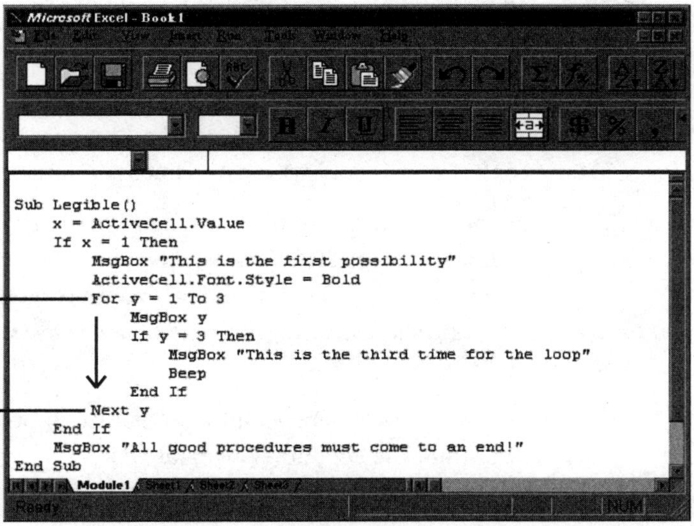

Fig. 7.2
By following an If or For statement vertically down the page, you can see where it ends.

This loop begins here...

...and ends here

Summary

In this chapter, you learned that most lines of VBA are statements: they issue commands to VBA. An expression is a building block of a statement. It can be a simple value or a complicated combination of functions, variables, and operators which is evaluated to give a value. Assignment statements give the result of an expression to a variable. Finally, you learned how much easier it is to read well-organized, indented code.

Review questions

1 What is a statement?

2 Can an expression be a statement?

3 What operator is used to combine text strings?

4 What does a logical operator do?

5 How would you set the value of x to the cosine of the variable Angle?

6 Will this statement produce a beep?

```
If 5 = 0 Or 7 < 9 Then Beep
```

Exercises

1 Fix the Confusion subroutine in this chapter by assigning a numeric value to the variable Astro.

2 Change the MeasureUp example so that the message box will appear if CurrentValue > 8 and will say, "That's too much."

3 Assign your first name to the variable FirstName and your last name to the variable LastName. Now create a message box that uses the & operator to display your first and last names together. (Hint: You won't need quotation marks around FirstName or LastName in the MsgBox statement.)

4 Change the IsOneTrue procedure so that the first message box will appear but not the second. Now change it so that neither one will appear.

5 Indent this code to make it more readable. (Notice that the For/Next loop is contained inside of the If/Then block.)

```
Sub HardToRead()
For x = 1 to 4
Beep
MsgBox "The current number is " & x
If x = 4 Then
MsgBox "This is the last one
EndIf
Next x
End Sub
```

6 Write a procedure that assigns a number to three variables called x, y, and z, and then assigns the average of these variables to a variable called w.

8

VBA Procedures

● In this chapter:

● What's the difference between a subroutine and a function?

● Why can't I use all my programs as macros?

● Stop that procedure!

● Build large programs out of smaller, more manageable pieces

● Give your programs values to work with

Breaking your code down into procedures makes programs more versatile and easy to fix . . . . ⊙

I f statements are the sentences of the VBA language, then procedures are the paragraphs. When writing prose, each paragraph should deal with a single subject, have a beginning line and a concluding line, and be concise. VBA procedures are well-defined blocks of code that run together, and they should adhere to the same rules.

Unlike writing prose, however, programs can hop around from procedure to procedure without regard for where they are located. As a programmer, it's your job to make each one a self-contained unit and to make your programs work with them in an orderly fashion, sending values from one to the other, and putting the results to good use.

Two kinds of VBA procedures are discussed in this chapter: subroutines and functions. You've probably already become somewhat familiar with using these. The real topics of this chapter are the differences between them, their nuances of use, and how to effectively use several of them together.

Subroutines

The first kind of VBA procedure is a **subroutine**. Subroutines fall into two main categories. Some can be used as macros and some cannot. The distinction between these two types is based on whether or not the procedure has values sent to it when it is called. A macro cannot require that any values be sent to it in order to run. A macro can still look up values while it's running, however.

 Plain English, please!

Subroutine, sub procedure, and **sub** all refer to the same thing: a Visual Basic procedure that is created using the Sub statement. **99**

Which subroutines are macros?

Any time you record a macro with the macro recorder, a subroutine is created for you. This subroutine will always have an empty argument list, such as the one in this line of code:

```
Sub Macro1()
```

There is nothing in the parentheses that follow the name of the procedure, and, thus, it doesn't expect to have any values sent to it.

You can also write a subroutine from scratch with an empty argument list. The following example couldn't be created with the macro recorder, because there's no way to get the macro recorder to produce a message box.

```
Sub NoArgs()
    MsgBox "This procedure has no arguments"
End Sub
```

To learn how to assign macros to custom menu items, see Chapter 15, "Change the Menus: No Programming Required!"

Although this procedure was typed into a module sheet, it's still a macro. Why? A macro is any subroutine that has an empty argument list. This procedure will show up in the macro dialog box and can be assigned to a custom menu item. This is only true of macros.

So, what kind of subroutine is *not* a macro? Any sub that has one or several items in its argument list is not a macro. So, you can tell whether a procedure is a macro or not by taking a quick look at the first line. If it starts with the word Sub and has nothing in its parentheses, it's a macro. If there's anything at all in the parentheses, or if it starts with the word Function, it isn't a macro.

Subroutines that accept values

Sometimes, you'll want a subroutine to accept one or more values. To create such a subroutine, you must specify how many values it will receive every time it is run. To do this, put a name for each value in the argument list on the first line of the subroutine.

Speaking of *Sub*

The syntax for the Sub statement is

```
Sub name (arguments)
    statements
End Sub
```

where *name* is the name of the procedure, *arguments* is a list of variables representing values that are passed to the sub (this list can be empty), and *statements* are the lines of code that are run as a part of the sub.

❝ Plain English, please!

What's all the fighting about? An **argument** is a placeholder for a value that is needed for a procedure to run. ❞

This procedure has two arguments: `Income` and `HouseholdSize`.

```
Sub DetermineBenefits(Income, HouseholdSize)
    If Income < 1000 Then
        Qualify = True
    ElseIf Income < 1500 And HouseholdSize > 2 Then
        Qualify = True
    Else
        Qualify = False
    End If
End Sub
```

The first line of this procedure creates the name of the procedure and its two arguments. When the procedure is called, two values will have to be sent or the procedure cannot run. Once it receives these values, it uses them to determine whether a household qualifies for benefits based on their income level and number of members in the household. If they qualify, then a value of `True` is assigned to the variable `Qualify`. If not, then `False` is assigned.

The way to call a procedure such as this one is discussed in greater detail later in this chapter. As an example, however, the following line of code would be an appropriate way to call this procedure:

```
DetermineBenefits 1300, 3
```

Notice that this line doesn't mention anything about the names of the arguments. The arguments are just placeholders, and the values are automatically put into the placeholders. Since `1300` is listed first, it will be sent to the `Income` placeholder, and `3` will go to the `HouseholdSize` placeholder.

Q&A **Why can't I run the DetermineBenefits procedures by clicking on the Play button of the Visual Basic toolbar?**

Only macros can be run this way. You also can't run this procedure by using the Macro dialog box or assign it to a menu item. It can only be called by other lines of VBA code.

Functions

Functions are the second kind of VBA procedure. The whole purpose of a function is to come up with a single value when called. This is called the **return value**. It's this purpose that distinguishes functions from subroutines.

This function takes three arguments. Its return value is the product of the first two plus the third.

```
Function TakeThree(x, y, z)
    TakeThree = x * y + z
End Function
```

Functions go beyond user-defined worksheet functions

To learn how to create user-defined worksheet functions, see Chapter 4, "Write Your Own Excel Functions."

One of the simplest types of functions is a user-defined worksheet function. These are functions that you use in worksheet cell formulas, just like an Excel built-in worksheet function. The TakeThree function above is one of these. You could enter the formula **=TakeThree(5,7,34)** into a spreadsheet cell just as if it were one of Excel's built-in functions.

There is much more that functions can do. Functions can perform all of the kinds of things that subroutines do.

Speaking of *Function*

The syntax for Function is

```
Function name(arguments)
    statements
    name = expression
End Function
```

where *name* is the name of the procedure, *arguments* is a list of variables representing values that are passed to the function, and *statements* are various lines of code, one of which will be of the form *name = expression*. This is the same *name* as on the first line and the value of *expression* is assigned to it. This becomes the return value of the function.

For example, functions can:

- Add or remove sheets in a workbook

- Change the values of spreadsheet cells

- Change the look of the Excel environment

Sometimes, the fact that the function returns a value is only a small part of its purpose. If, however, a function performs any of the things listed above, then it cannot be used as a user-defined worksheet function. User-defined worksheet functions are pretty much limited to making calculations.

The following code won't work as a worksheet function because it tries to set the font style of the cell to bold.

```
Function Oops(x)
    Selection.Font.Bold = True
    Oops = 5 * x
End Function
```

If you try to use a function that does one of the off-limit activities in a spreadsheet formula, then #VALUE! appears in the worksheet cell. Figure 8.1 shows the result of trying to use the Oops function in a worksheet formula.

Fig. 8.1
When you see #VALUE! in a cell, you know that Excel is having trouble with the formula.

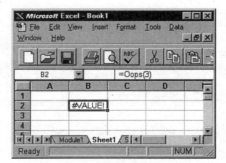

Functions can accept values or not

Functions don't have to have values sent to them. They can return a value based on other criteria. It might seem like a function that doesn't have any arguments passed to it will always return the same value. But this is not the case. Functions can look up information from a variety of places, including checking the contents of cell, prompting the user for information, or looking up current system status. For example:

```
Function WhenIsIt()
    Answer = InputBox("Do you want the date or the time?")
    If Answer = "date" Then
        current = Date
    ElseIf Answer = "time" Then
        current = Time
    Else
        MsgBox "Sorry, that's not a valid response"
        current = "Invalid Response"
    End If
    WhenIsIt = current
End Function
```

This function has an empty argument list. It displays an input box to ask whether the user would like to know the date or time. Based on the response, the function looks up the current time or date using Excel's built-in Time and Date functions and assigns the value it retrieves to the variable current.

If neither "date" nor "time" is entered into the input box, then a message box appears and a string "Invalid Response" is assigned to current. Finally the value of current is set as the return value of the function.

Notice that even though no arguments were passed to WhenIsIt, it still managed to retrieve information that will make its return value unique each time it is called.

Speaking of *Exit*

In a sub procedure, the syntax of Exit is

```
Exit Sub
```

In a function procedure, the syntax of Exit is

```
Exit Function
```

When VBA encounters an Exit Sub or Exit Function statement, it will immediately leave the procedure and return to the place the procedure was called.

Stopping a procedure before it reaches the end

A procedure is a block of code that runs from beginning to end. Sometimes, you might want a procedure to stop at a certain point before running all subsequent lines of code. You can do this by using the Exit statement.

The following procedure is interrupted halfway through with an Exit Sub statement.

```
Sub LeaveEarly()
    MsgBox "This is before the Exit statement"
    Exit Sub
    MsgBox "This is after the Exit statement"
End Sub
```

In this subroutine, the first message is displayed. Then the Exit Sub statement is encountered, and the program leaves the subroutine. The second message is never displayed because that line of code isn't run.

If you were to run the LeaveEarly procedure by calling it from another procedure, then after VBA exited LeaveEarly, it would return to the procedure that called LeaveEarly and go on to the next line of code.

How can I use this in the real world?

You can write a program that checks for a password. If the password given is incorrect, you can exit the procedure. For example, you can use an input box to get a value from the user and assign it to the variable PassEntered. The code that checks whether the password is correct might look like this:

```
If PassEntered <> "pkz054" Then
    Exit Sub
End If
```

If the value of PassEntered is not equal to pkz054, the procedure will exit immediately. Beneath this code, you can put all of the stuff you don't want the user to get to if the password is wrong.

How to call procedures from within other code

You know how to write them, now how do you use them? Once you've created your functions and procedures, you need to be able to access them. You can, of course, call your macros via the Macros dialog box, and call some of your functions in worksheet formulas as user-defined worksheet functions. The rest of your procedures will be called from within other procedures.

Functions and subs are used differently

To learn more about calling one procedure from another, see Chapter 3, "Using the VBA Editor and the Macro Recorder Together."

A subroutine call is a statement. This means that you can create a complete line of VBA code that consists of simply a subroutine call (with arguments as necessary).

 *Plain English, please!*

Calling a procedure means instructing it to run with a line of VBA code.

If you have a subroutine called GreetUser which requires no arguments, then the line

```
GreetUser
```

is in and of itself a complete VBA statement. A call to a procedure named ComputeVolume that requires three arguments might look like this:

```
ComputeVolume 7, 8, Height
```

where Height is the name of a variable that was assigned a value earlier.

Functions are called differently. A function call does not comprise a complete statement; it is an expression that can be used as a part of a statement. A simple way to build a statement out of a function call is to assign the return value to a variable. For example, you might have a function called CalculateTax that takes two arguments. You can use it like this:

```
Tax = CalculateTax(0.053, 10429)
Price = Cost + Tax
```

On the first line above, the `CalculateTax` function is called and its return value is assigned to the variable `Tax`. The following line puts this variable to use in computing a total price. Using a function call to assign a variable to a value is very straightforward, but not always necessary. The above two lines of code could be combined into one and the `Tax` variable eliminated.

```
Price = Cost + CalculateTax(0.053, 10429)
```

TIP **Don't forget that functions have their arguments enclosed in** parentheses!

Organizing programs into many small procedures

Imagine a large business presentation that is to last for four hours. You're assigned to prepare it. You can get up at the beginning of the presentation and step down four hours later having presented your material. Or, you can get up and announce several other speakers who can follow one after another, presenting their specialties. You can even incorporate a video.

It's this second model that approximates the approach most seasoned programmers take when writing an extensive program. Rather than putting everything into one giant procedure, they break it down as much as possible into smaller procedures. The main program itself might consist entirely of procedure calls such as the following procedure which determines what kind of document a user wishes to create and opens the right template for the job.

```
Sub OpenRightTemplate()
    UserName = InputBox("Please enter your name.")
    If CheckPassword(UserName) = False Then Exit Sub
    GreetUser UserName
    JobType = SpecifyJobType
    GetTemplate JobType
End Sub
```

Most of the names in this procedure refer to other procedures that don't appear in this code listing, so you'll have to stretch your imagination a bit.

Every line in this procedure sends the program to another function or procedure. The first line in the body of the procedure creates the variable `UserName` and calls the `InputBox` function to solicit a value from the user.

Next, the `CheckPassword` function is called with the argument `UserName`. It will return a True or False value. If the value returned is False, the program will exit (presumably, the user entered the wrong password). If the value returned is True, the program goes on to the next line. This runs a subroutine called `GreetUser`, which also takes the argument `UserName`.

Catch the bug

The following figure shows two procedures and a resulting error message that occurs when you try to run the second one. What's the problem?

Answer: *The way you call a function is to use it as a part of a statement. The way that* Adder *was used on the line above the one that caused the error is incorrect. VBA missed it because it assumed that you were trying to use* Adder *like a procedure. The line that caused the error makes mention of* Adder *without supplying an argument, which is required. What needs to be done is to combine these two offending lines into the following:*

```
MsgBox Adder(3)
```

Alternatively, you could keep it as two lines, but then you'd need to come up with a new variable to store the value from one line to the next, like the following:

```
ReturnValue = Adder(3)
MsgBox ReturnValue
```

The next line assigns the return value of a function called `SpecifyJobType` to a variable called `JobType`. Notice that even though `SpecifyJobType` doesn't have any arguments, it's identifiable as a function because it is being used as only half of a statement. It's on the right side of an equal sign—a sure giveaway.

Finally, the `GetTemplate` subroutine is called with the argument `JobType`. It will open the desired template.

Why would you want to write a program this way? You could have put it all into one long procedure. Here are some of the advantages to this technique:

- Programs written in this style are easier to read. It would be hard to tell what this program does if all of the intricacies of checking a password and opening a template were visible together.

- If there's a problem with one part of your program, it's much easier to fix when the program is broken up this way. You can easily isolate the function or subroutine that is causing the problem.

- Code written in small blocks is reusable. You might want to check passwords in a variety of situations. You can use the CheckPassword function for all of them without having to copy it into new procedures.

How can I use this in the real world?

A manufacturer might have a complex formula for calculating the production cost of a product. This formula is based on the current price of raw materials, employee wage rates, and which manufacturing plant is used to produce it.

A procedure can be written to accept these values by reading them off of spreadsheet cells. Then you can play "What if?" on a spreadsheet—"What if we make it with materials from this supplier in the Oakland plant? How about the Teaneck plant where wages are higher?"

Catch the bug

The Multiplier procedure accepts arguments so it can't be run as a macro. The RunMultiplier program is a macro that calls the Multiplier procedure, providing it with values. Things won't work the way they are, though. What's wrong?

```
Sub Multiplier(x, y, z)
    Product = x * y * z
    MsgBox Product
End Sub

Sub RunMultiplier()
    Multiplier 3, 4
End Sub
```

Answer: *Multiplier requires that three values be sent to it. The line in* *RunMultiplier* *that calls* *Multiplier* *only provides two values and thus causes an error.*

Values that get sent to procedures

There are several different ways to pass arguments to a procedure. You can:

- Give a value specifically, like a number or a text string.

- Use a variable name. The procedure will figure out what the value assigned to that variable was.

- Use a reference to a cell or a range in a spreadsheet. Chapter 12 explains how this is done.

- Provide any kind of expression that VBA can evaluate.

If all you could do was to pass a specific value, you would really be limited. Your code would already have the values you're going to send and thus would produce the same results each time it was run. Instead, the ways to pass an argument listed above let you write programs that won't know what exact values they're going to get until the program is running.

Using Excel's built-in functions in your code

When creating worksheet formulas, there are many, many built-in Excel functions to work with. To see what's available, select Insert, Function. The Function Wizard appears as shown in figure 8.2.

Fig. 8.2
Just look at all those functions! Now, if only you could use them in your VBA code too...

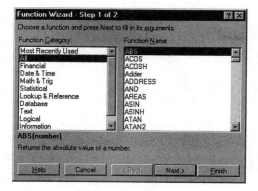

Normally, you'd use these functions in worksheet formulas, but you can incorporate them right into your programming code as well.

Excel built-in functions are called in a way similar to your own functions. However, it is necessary to precede the name of the function with `Application.` so that VBA knows that the function is part of the Excel application, and not a part of VBA.

For example, you can use Excel's Average function in a line of code like the following:

```
MyAverage = Application.Average(18, 24, 29)
```

Specifying data types

There are many values being sent around in this chapter. Arguments of all types are sent to procedures, and functions are generating return values. You can specify ahead of time what kinds of values these should be. For example, you might want to limit a procedure to receiving an integer value rather than a text string.

To learn about specifying data types for variables, see Chapter 9, "Variables."

The reasons you would want to impose these limitations are for efficiency and clarity of code, and to improve VBA's ability to catch your errors for you. They are the same reasons that you would want to specify what kinds of data a variable can accept.

You specify the data type for a procedure argument and for a function's return value in a way similar to that of variables. However, you do not accomplish this by using a Dim statement on a separate line, the way you would for a variable. The first line of the procedure is where the argument is created. A Dim statement would be redundant. If you use a Dim statement to declare a variable that you used elsewhere as an argument, one of two things will happen. If the Dim statement is inside the procedure, it will cause an error. If the Dim statement is outside the procedure, VBA ignores it.

Just remember: if you're using a name for a procedure or an argument, don't declare it as a variable somewhere else.

TIP **Most of the benefits of specifying data types have to do with** making your code more efficient. If you're writing short, simple programs, don't worry about this section.

Which kinds of values do you want your subroutine to accept?

In the DetermineBenefits procedure, both of the arguments require that numeric values be passed when the procedure is called. If a text value is sent, the procedure won't know what to do and will produce a type mismatch error.

 Plain English, please!

Passing values means that you are sending values to be used as the arguments for the procedure.

To learn about writing error-handling code, see Chapter 23, "Making Your Programming User-Friendly."

You might want to require that the procedure will only accept integer values as arguments. If you send it a text value, it will still produce a type mismatch error, but it will catch it at an earlier stage and set aside less memory for the argument. It's also easier to write error-handling code if you have a specific line that checks for the type mismatch.

To specify the data type of an argument, you use the As keyword and the data type immediately following the argument name in the first line of the procedure. The following line defines a function that takes one argument, x, which must be an integer:

```
Function NumberOnly(x As Integer)
```

In a procedure that takes more than one argument, you can mix and match your data types and also which arguments are specified. The following line defines a subroutine that takes three arguments: one must be an integer, one a string, and one can take any type of value.

```
Sub ThreeArgs(IncomeLevel As Integer, _
UserName As String, AnyValue)
```

Specify which kind of value a function returns

You can also specify the data type of the value a function returns. This is done with the As keyword, too. However, you must put the As part *outside* of the argument list so that VBA knows it applies to the function and not to one of the arguments. This line of code specifies that the return value of the function will be a Single data type:

```
Function ComputeTax(Tax, Rate) As Single
```

Notice that the As Single part is outside of the parentheses surrounding the argument list. If we change this line very slightly to

```
Function ComputeTax(Tax, Rate As Single)
```

then it is the argument Rate that is affected by the As Single, instead of the ComputeTax return value.

Summary

This chapter gave an overview of two kinds of VBA procedures: functions and subroutines. Special attention was given to creating procedures with arguments and how to call procedures with and without arguments. You also learned how to exit a procedure in the middle, rather than running all the code from beginning to end, and how to incorporate Excel's built-in worksheet functions into your code.

Review questions

1 What is an argument?

2 What does it mean to call a procedure?

3 How are functions different from subroutines?

4 What prevents you from using some functions in worksheet formulas?

5 How could you use Excel's built-in MAX function in VBA code?

6 If you wanted a subroutine to stop running and exit the procedure at a certain point in the middle of the code, how could you make that happen?

7 If you have a function that takes two values, how could you specify that one should be an integer and one a text string?

Exercises

1 Change the TakeThree function so that it only takes two arguments, x and y, and multiplies them together.

2 Try to use the Oops function in a formula in a worksheet cell. Take out the offending line of code and try it again.

3 Suppose that veterans automatically qualify for the benefits of your program. Add a third argument to the DetermineBenefits procedure. Call this argument **Veteran**. Write an additional ElseIf statement that checks whether Veteran is True or False. If it is True, set the value of Qualify to True as well.

4 Write a procedure that takes one argument and produces a message box that says `"The argument sent to me was: "` and then displays the value of the argument. Now write a macro that calls this procedure.

5 Create a function that uses several arguments and returns a value based on that calculation. (If you can, make it a calculation that you actually use on a regular basis.) Write a procedure that calls this function.

6 Write a macro that consists entirely of calls to other procedures (like the OpenRightTemplate procedure). Use at least three procedure calls, one function, one sub, and one requiring arguments. Now write the procedures that it calls. Congratulations. This is how professional programmers put together complicated programs!

Variables

● **In this chapter:**

● Why you should tell Excel about your variables before you use them

● Different kinds of variables

● Can different procedures share the same variables?

● Making variables remember their values

Just like spreadsheet cells, VBA variables can store values, text, dates, and other types of data. . . . . ▶

U sing Excel is all about storing and manipulating values. When you're using a worksheet, you keep each value in a cell. Some cells contain numbers, some contain words, and some are empty, waiting to receive values.

In module sheets, when you're writing code, there are no cells in which to store your values. Instead, you use variables to hold values. Just like spreadsheet cells, VBA variables can store values, text, dates, and other types of data.

In Excel, you can create a formula to add two cells together without specifying what numbers will be in the cells. This lets you experiment with various values. Variables fulfill the same function in VBA programs; you can use different values in your programs, and VBA operates on the variables.

When variables are created

As the examples in the first chapters of this book show you, variables are created by just mentioning them. As soon as a new name is introduced, VBA sets up a variable with this name. While this is a very easy way to work with variables, there are a number of disadvantages associated with it as well. You may decide to name some or all of your variables in advance, and also to limit the kinds of data that can be stored in that variable. Or you may decide to keep on declaring variables on-the-fly since it seems to work fine for you. Like so many things in Excel, there's no one right way to do it—just the way that works best for you.

Variables can be created on-the-fly

Variables can be created by just mentioning them in the code.

```
Sub CalculatePay ()
    PayPeriods = 24
    TotalPay = PayPeriods * 1500
end sub
```

This procedure creates two variables on-the-fly as they are needed. On line 2, the variable `PayPeriods` is created and immediately assigned the value 24. On the following line, the variable `TotalPay` is created and assigned the value `PayPeriods * 1500`.

There are two advantages to this kind of variable. First, you don't have to plan your variables in advance; when you need one, just think up a name. Second, you don't have to worry about what kind of value you're going to use for the variable. You could just have easily written

```
PayPeriods = "Bi-Monthly"
```

on the line and then `PayPeriods` would have a text value instead of a numeric one.

It turns out, however, that there are some disadvantages to this type of variable as well. The fact that you don't name it in advance means that there's no safeguard against typos. Consider the following procedure.

```
Sub BadCalculatePay()
    PayPeriods = 24
    PayCheck = 1500
    Pay = PayCheck * PayPerods
    MsgBox Pay
End Sub
```

Running this procedure will produce the message box shown in figure 9.1.

Fig. 9.1
A small typo in the BadCalculatePay procedure produces a message box with the wrong value

What's the trouble? The entire problem is the typo in the fourth line of code, `PayPeriods` is misspelled as `PayPerods`. VBA thinks that this is a new variable being called into existence, and since no value is given to it, it assigns it the value 0 by default.

Another disadvantage to this type of variable is that because VBA doesn't know what kinds of values you're going to assign to this variable, it's not limiting the amount of memory that it will set aside for whatever value you do assign. For small programs, you might never notice the difference. For larger programs or ones that repeat a step many times, the difference in speed and size of your program can be substantial.

TIP   **If you're getting to the point where you've got several procedures** that call each other or more than a screen's worth of code, it's probably time to start declaring variables.

Imagine that you're scheduling a business lunch at a local restaurant. The maitre d' asks how many will be in your party, but you're not sure. She tells you she can guarantee you seating for however many guests you bring, but you'll have to pay a $100 surcharge for her to do this. If the lunch is really important and you truly have no way of estimating the number of guests, you might agree to this. However, you might instead say, "Well, let's just reserve a table for four, then." Not telling VBA what kind of values a variable will receive is like making the $100 open reservation: convenient and flexible, but costly.

Announce your variables in advance

The process of announcing a variable to VBA is called **declaring a variable**. When you create them on-the-fly, you are declaring them as you put them into use. When you give the variable a value, this is called **assigning a value to a variable**. Sometimes, the term "declaring a variable" is used to mean declaring it in advance. To avoid confusion, I'll refer to this process as **explicit declaration** or **declaring in advance**.

Declaring variables in advance opens up a whole new realm of possibilities. By declaring variables in advance, you can achieve one or more of the following:

- Get VBA to check your typing for possible misspellings

- Use the smallest amount of memory for a variable that will get the job done

- Get VBA to make sure that you're assigning the right kinds of values to your variables

- Create variables that can be used by different procedures

- Create variables that will "remember" their values

One of the most important reasons to declare variables in advance is not that it makes things easier or faster for the computer. It's to make your code more readable for yourself and others who will be working with your code.

In many programming languages, declaring variables is a necessity, and if you're doing extensive VBA programming or writing code that others will also be looking at, you should declare your variables in advance.

TIP **You can write a comment after the variable declaration as a** reminder of what it's used for, for example:

```
Dim ShoeCount  'keeps track of how many shoes I have
```

To make an explicit variable declaration, you add a line of code whose entire purpose is to announce the presence of the variable to VBA. There are a number of different ways to explicitly declare a variable, depending on how you want to use the variable. The simplest form of declaration is to use the Dim keyword.

The CalculatePay procedure, complete with explicit variable declarations, might look like this:

```
Sub CalculatePay()
    Dim PayPeriods
    Dim PayCheck
    PayPeriods = 24
    PayCheck = 1500
End Sub
```

The first two lines are the explicit variable declarations that were added to the procedure, letting VBA know about them in advance.

Once you start using explicit variable definitions, you can let VBA do some proofreading for you. Try typing the following code exactly as it is written, including the capitalization:

Speaking of *Dim*

The Dim statement (Dim stands for Dimension) is used to declare a variable and can also tell Excel how much storage space to set aside for it.

```
Dim VariableName [As DataType]
```

In this line of code, *VariableName* is a valid variable name, and *DataType* specifies the kinds of values that can be assigned to this variable. *As DataType* is optional.

```
Sub Checker()
    Dim MyValue
    myvalue = 4
```

As soon as you press Enter after typing the last line, VBA changes the last line from `myvalue=4` to `MyValue = 4` to reflect the capitalization that you gave in the variable declaration. It recognizes the name and then changes the capitalization to match the way it's written in the variable declaration.

 TIP **When you declare your variables, begin them with a capital letter.** When typing them later in the code, don't capitalize them—let VBA do it for you automatically to help you check your spelling and save your pinkie from that long Shift key stretch.

Forcing yourself to announce your variables in advance

Once you've decided that you will always explicitly declare your variables, it makes sense to have VBA keep an eye on you by *requiring* that you declare all variables explicitly. Otherwise, you might accidentally misspell a variable name, thus causing VBA to create a new variable for you.

VBA will force you to declare all of your variables if you type the words **Option Explicit** at the top of your module sheets. You can do this by typing the words yourself, or you can get VBA to put it on the top of all module sheets automatically. To do this, choose <u>T</u>ools, <u>O</u>ptions to open the Options dialog box, select the Module General tab, and check the box for <u>R</u>equire Variable Declaration as shown in figure 9.2. This adds the line `Option Explicit` to all new modules you create. It doesn't add this line to existing modules, though. If you want to require explicit variable declarations in these modules as well, you have to type the line in yourself.

 TIP **If you write programs that get longer than a few lines, it's a good** idea to require variable declaration.

Fig. 9.2
Excel will keep you
honest on each and
every module sheet if
you check <u>R</u>equire
Variable Declaration.

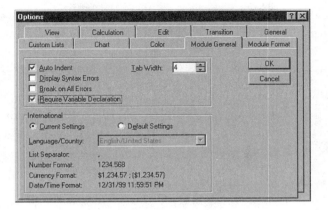

How to specify a type of value for a variable

Imagine that you're on vacation and find the perfect carpeting for your living room, but don't know the exact dimensions of the room. How much should you buy? On the one hand, you want to err on the side of caution and buy too much rather than too little. On the other, you don't want to get ridiculous and

Catch the bug

You can type this code into the editor without encountering any syntax errors. If you try to run it, however, you'll get an error message. What's the problem?

```
Option Explicit

Sub AddUp()
    Dim Total
    Total = 0
    For x = 1 To 10
        Total = Total + x
    Next x
    MsgBox Total
End Sub
```

Answer: *By including* `Option Explicit`, *you are required to declare all variables. The variable x (yes, that's a variable, too) was never declared. You need to add the line* **Dim x** *after the line* `Dim Total`.

buy three times as much as you need. Declaring the type of data that a variable can accept is a similar art. You want to make sure that enough space is set aside for the values you assign to it, but you don't want to make every variable enormous unless you like really slow, memory-hogging programs.

To specify the type of value you want for a variable, you use the As keyword in the line where you declare the variable. Suppose I write a program that counts the number of days left until Christmas. For this purpose, the integer data type does the trick.

 Plain English, please!

> In math, an **integer** is a whole number: one with no decimal points, like 5 or −3. In VBA the integer data type is an integer as in the math definition, but with a restriction on how large it can be.

The following line declares the variable CountDown as an integer, one of the numeric data types.

```
Dim CountDown As Integer
```

If I later try to assign a non-numeric value to CountDown such as the following:

```
CountDown = "hello"
```

VBA produces the error message shown in figure 9.3. VBA expects a whole number for CountDown; when you try to give it a word, it refuses. (Integer and the other data types are discussed below.) This is the Type mismatch error message, and it appears whenever VBA tries to use two different data types together.

Fig. 9.3
Type mismatch—one of VBA's more common error messages—is also one of the few that's easy to understand.

Variables that store numbers or dates

By far the most common type of variable is one that stores a number of some sort. VBA has six different variable types for numbers. Like carpeting, you should choose the smallest one that will be enough for your needs. In many cases, the Integer type, which is the smallest, will do just fine. A variable of the Integer type in VBA can be any whole number between –32,768 and 32,767.

If you have a whole number that might go out of this range, you can use the **long** data type, which will take an integer between –2,147,483,648 and 2,147,483,647.

To learn how to use Excel's online help, see Chapter 6, "VBA Information Online."

When you want to use a decimal point with your numbers, you can choose from **Single**, **Double**, and **Currency types**. A complete list of data types and the values you can assign to them can be found in Excel's online help by looking up the Data Type Summary topic. Pick the one with the smallest number of bytes used that will definitely be big enough to store the values that you will assign to that variable.

Variables declared for such a purpose are called **string variables**. The declaration for a string variable called MyName would be

```
Dim MyName as String
```

The amount of memory a string variable takes up depends on the length of the string assigned to it. The longer the string, the more memory it takes.

Variables to store true or false values

Sometimes you'll want your programs to keep track of a true or false value. The **Boolean** variable type is made just for this purpose. It can accept one of two values—true or false.

How can I use this in the real world?

Boolean data types are useful for keeping track of whether users have selected a certain option. For instance, you might create a program that runs whenever Excel is opened and asks whether the user wishes to automatically save changes before printing. (That way, if the computer hangs during the print job, the work will be saved.)

The user's answer to this query can be stored as a Boolean variable. If she answered yes, it can be stored as True, if no then as False. When the user prints, a program runs that checks the value of this variable. If it is True, it saves the workbook before printing.

Keeping it flexible: The variant variable stores anything

Earlier in this book, no variables were explicitly declared. When you create a variable this way, VBA uses the name to set aside an area in memory for the variable. Since VBA isn't sure whether or not this variable is going to be a number or text, VBA keeps your options open and allows you to assign any value to it. This is called a **variant type variable**, and it accepts any value—numeric, text, or whatever.

TIP   **You can create these variables explicitly, too. In fact, if you have** the statement Option Explicit at the top of your module sheet and you want to use one of these variables, you have no choice but to declare them explicitly.

Syntax Error

Catch the bug

Here's a simple program that tries to multiply a number by two. Why does it produce a type mismatch error?

```
Sub TimesTwo()
    Dim Surbaugh As String
    Dim Doubled As Integer
    Dim Value As Integer

    Surbaugh = "8"
    Doubled = Value * 2
End Sub
```

Answer: When you assign the value 8 to the variable Surbaugh, you are assigning a character to that variable, not a numeric value. Sure, it's the character that happens to be the number 8, but VBA is treating it like any other string: as if it were a letter or symbol. VBA doesn't know how to multiply strings. It makes more sense if you think of assigning a more traditional string, like I am the Lorax to the variable Surbaugh. You wouldn't expect VBA to multiply that by 2. Well, VBA is treating 8 just the same. Surbaugh needs to be an integer or other numeric type for VBA to be able to perform math operations on it.

The advantage to this type of variable is that you won't run into problems by assigning different kinds of values to it. If you set a variable up as a variant, you can freely assign strings, integers, or Boolean values to it. However, variant type variables are the most resource-hungry of variables: they require more time and memory than any other type. One of the main purposes of declaring variable types is to make your programs more efficient. Also, when VBA knows what kind of value to expect for a variable, it can help catch your mistakes by pointing out when you assign the wrong data type. For example, setting the value of an integer variable to `"hello"` produces an error. With variant variables, VBA can't help out with this because it doesn't know what to expect.

 TIP **To create efficient programs, only use variant variables when you** really need a variable to accept different data types for values.

You can explicitly declare a variant variable in one of two ways—with or without writing As Variant. If no data type is given, VBA assumes that you want a variant type variable. So, the declarations `Dim MyVar As Variant` and `Dim MyVar` do exactly the same thing.

Different procedures and modules can use the same variables

To learn how to pass values from one procedure to another, read Chapter 8, "VBA Procedures."

Sometimes you'll want to use a certain value in more than one procedure. One way to do this is by passing values from one procedure to another. This method works when procedures are calling one another, but what about when procedures are completely independent of one another but both need to know the value of a certain variable?

- **Local variables** are variables that are declared in one particular procedure. When VBA is executing code outside that procedure, it forgets that the variable even exists.

- **Module-level variables** are ones that any procedure on a particular module sheet can use.

- **Public variables** are ones that can be shared from module sheet to module sheet.

Whether a variable is Local, Module-level, or Public depends on where and how you declare it.

Declaring variables for use in one procedure only

Most commonly, a variable will only be used in one particular procedure. In this case, you'll want to declare the variable locally. While you could declare these variables in such a way that they could be used by any procedure, it's better to declare them locally. This puts the declaration of the variable near the code where it's used, making it easier to read. It also allows you to use that name in other procedures for different variables.

To declare a local variable, put the declaration statement *inside* a procedure. Declarations go at the beginning of a procedure, before the executable code.

Here's a program that adds the whole numbers from 1 to 100.

```
Sub Gauss()
    Dim Counter As Integer
    Dim X As Integer

    X = 0
    For Counter = 1 To 100
        X = X + Counter
    Next Counter
    MsgBox X
End Sub
```

How can I use this in the real world?

At some point in your program, you might prompt the user to enter his or her name. You could store this value in a variable called UserName that can be used by different procedures.

One procedure that might use this value could be a subroutine that creates a header including the user name. Another one might store a password list by users. The UserName variable becomes a shared reference that different procedures can access.

The two declaration lines create local variables, `Counter` and `X`, since they are declared within the subroutine `Gauss`. After VBA exits this subroutine, `Counter` and `X` are forgotten by VBA.

`X` is initially set to `0`. The For/Next loop executes 100 times, each time increasing the value of `Counter` by 1 and adding this new value to `X`, and then running a total.

A message box displays the final result of the sum of all integers between 1 and 100.

Variables for use anywhere in a module

When a variable needs to be shared by different procedures, you can declare it *before* all the procedures in a module. Here's a code listing for three procedures that work together to calculate expenses based on different categories.

```
Option Explicit

Dim TotalExpenses As Single

Sub CalculateExpenses()
    TotalExpenses = 0
    Travel
    Entertainment
    MsgBox TotalExpenses
End Sub

'add mileage expenses to total
Sub Travel()
    Dim Mileage As Single
    Mileage = 1563 * 0.3
    TotalExpenses = TotalExpenses + Mileage
End Sub

'add entertainment to total
Sub Entertainment()
    Dim Food As Single
    Food = 127.59
    TotalExpenses = TotalExpenses + Food
End Sub
```

code This program declares the following three variables: TotalExpenses, Mileage, and Food. TotalExpenses is declared outside of the procedures, at the top. This makes it a module-wide variable which can be used in any of the procedures. The other two variables are local.

TotalExpenses keeps track of the reimbursable expenses for a business trip. As the program enters and exits the Travel and Entertainment subroutines, values are added to the TotalExpenses variable. Since TotalExpenses is a module-wide variable, VBA doesn't ever "forget" its value.

To put this program to work, you'd run the CalculateExpenses subroutine. Here, the TotalExpenses variable is set to 0 to get ready to start (like clearing your calculator). The next line calls the Travel procedure. VBA now switches procedures and jumps down to the line Sub Travel(). In this procedure, a local variable Mileage is declared, the travel expenses are calculated using the Mileage variable, and then the result is added to TotalExpenses. Then VBA exits the procedure and returns to the CalculateExpenses procedure. When this happens, VBA forgets all about Mileage. For VBA, Mileage only exists when it's executing code in the Travel procedure. However, since TotalExpenses is a module-wide variable, VBA is still keeping its value intact in memory.

Next, the Entertainment procedure is called. This procedure is very similar to the Travel procedure. It takes a local variable, Food, and adds its value to the module-wide variable, TotalExpenses. Now, TotalExpenses has been affected in three different subroutines: CalculateExpenses started by setting it to 0, Travel added its Mileage value, and Entertainment added its Food value. Finally, the result of TotalExpenses, 596.49, is displayed in a message box.

TIP **Use meaningful names for variables that are used by more than** one procedure. You'll remember what TotalExpenses means but might forget what X stands for.

Variables shared by many modules

It's also possible to create variables that are shared by more than one module. (Of course, if you do all of your programming in one module, this isn't an issue.) To create such a variable, you use the keyword Public instead of Dim.

These declarations must take place on the module-level, rather than in a procedure. In the previous code example, `TotalExpenses` could have been declared as a Public variable with the line

```
Public TotalExpenses As Single
```

Then, if the flow of the program moved not only from procedure to procedure within the module, but also to other module sheets, the value of `TotalExpenses` would be available to all procedures in all module sheets.

How can I make a local variable remember its value?

A module-wide or public variable remembers its value for as long as Excel is running. So, if you run one macro that affects a module-wide variable, then do some data entry on a worksheet, then run another macro that affects the same variable, the value is preserved while you do the data entry.

Sometimes, though, you might have a local variable, only used in one procedure, which needs to have a "memory." For example, if you want to track how often you save files, you could write a procedure that is run whenever you save your file. It could keep track of the number of times you save a file, by adding one to its running total each time you call it. The problem is that local variables are "forgotten" whenever VBA exits a subroutine. Each time you run the program, the variable resets itself to 0.

Although you could solve this problem by declaring a module-wide variable, a better solution is generally to use a **static variable**.

```
Sub CountSaves()
    Static TimesSaved As Integer
    TimesSaved = TimesSaved + 1
End Sub
```

❝❝ Plain English, please!

It's just like static cling: A **static variable** is one whose value clings to it even after you leave its procedure. When you come back, the value is still stuck there. **❞❞**

The variable declaration uses the `Static` keyword which sets up a local variable with a memory. Each time this procedure is run, it adds 1 to the `TimesSaved` variable. When VBA exits the procedure, it temporarily forgets that the `TimesSaved` variable exists, but upon running the procedure again, VBA remembers not only the existence of the variable, but also the last value that it had.

Summary

VBA doesn't require you to declare variables, but there are advantages to doing so. By declaring your variables, you make your programs more compact and efficient, allow VBA to check up on whether you're using the right kind of values with the right variables, and get additional proofreading capability out of VBA. You can also create variables that are shared by different procedures and modules, as well as ones that remember their value even after their procedures have stopped running.

Review questions

1 What does it mean to explicitly declare a variable?

2 What is a local variable?

3 How do you declare a variable that expects a whole number to be assigned to it?

4 How can you tell VBA to force you to declare your variables?

5 What data type is used for text?

6 How can you run a procedure that uses a local variable and run the procedure later and find the value of the variable still intact?

7 Why would you use module-wide or public variables?

Exercises

1 Modify the CalculatePay procedure from earlier in this chapter with both variables declared as integers.

2 Add a message box to the CountSaves procedure that displays the value of TimesSaved. Run the procedure a few times to see what happens.

3 Rewrite CountSaves with TimesSaved declared with Dim instead of Static. Include the message box as in Exercise 2 and run the procedure a few times to see what happens.

4 Declare a Public variable in a module sheet. Write a procedure in that sheet that assigns it a value. Create a new module sheet and without redeclaring the variable, write a procedure that displays its value in a message box.

10

Ways to Control the Flow of Your Programs

● In this chapter:

- **The finer points of using If/Then statements**

- **Alternatives to If/Then—when you've got a lot of different cases**

- **What are all the different kinds of loops for?**

- **I want to write code that does something to every sheet in my workbook**

- **Stopping a loop in the middle**

Writing procedures without control structures is like listening to cassette tapes instead of CDs; you have to go straight through from beginning to end . . . . ➤

I hate cassette tapes. You have to listen to them from beginning to end. You can't jump right to the songs you like and play them multiple times. Yes, I know you can fast-forward and rewind, but it's so much work that it interferes with the music. I'm a CD lover, and I program my stereo to play the songs I want, skip the ones I don't, and to play the disk over and over until I stop it.

Using control structures in your procedures gets you out of having to run them from beginning to end. Conditional statements, like If/Then, let you skip the parts you don't want to run. Loops let you repeat other parts. Without control structures, procedures would have to run straight through from beginning to end and would be as cumbersome and frustrating as cassette tapes.

Deciding whether a piece of code should be run

One use for control structures is to decide whether or not a certain section of code should be run. This decision might be based on a value, or on the current state of Excel. For example, if you track your checkbook in Excel, you might want a message box to appear if your balance is particularly low. Or, if you try to run a macro that only works in a worksheet, you could keep it from causing an error if you're in a module sheet by making it check to see what kind of sheet is active.

The control structures that decide whether or not code should be run or which code to run in a situation are called **conditional statements**. These include If/Then and Select Case.

The If/Then structure

In Chapter 5, a simplified syntax of If/Then was given. Here's the full version.

The only required parts of the If/Then/Else syntax are the first and last lines. So, in its simplest form, you could have an If/Then block looking like this:

```
If condition Then
    statements
End If
```

even the statements are optional. You can leave out the middle part and just have a beginning and an end, with no instructions on what to do if the statement evaluates to be true.

 TIP **You might want to use an empty If/Then statement when you plan** to add statements at a later time that are to be run if the condition is true.

Read the next few sections to learn how to add ElseIf and Else clauses.

ElseIf

If the first condition turns out to be false, you might want to explore other alternatives. The ElseIf clause allows you to add as many alternatives as you like.

When VBA gets to an If block, it checks the condition on the top line to see if it is true. If that turns out to be false, it proceeds to check the first ElseIf (assuming there is one). If that one is true, it will run its statements; if not, it will go on to the next ElseIf. When any condition is found to be true, its statements are run and the If loop is exited.

Speaking of If/Then/Else

The general syntax for If/Then/Else is:

```
If condition1 Then
    statements1
[ElseIf condition2 Then
    statements2...
ElseIf conditionN Then
    statementsN]
[Else
    elsestatements]
End If
```

After the If and each ElseIf, a different condition and set of statements can be supplied. Many ElseIf clauses can be used, or none at all. You may have one Else clause, or none.

This example uses two ElseIf clauses.

```
Sub Goldilocks()
    Bear = InputBox("Which bear: Papa, Mama, or Baby?")
    If Bear = "Papa" Then
        MsgBox "Too hard"
    ElseIf Bear = "Mama" Then
        MsgBox "Too soft"
    ElseIf Bear = "Baby" Then
        MsgBox "Just right!"
    End If
End Sub
```

This procedure starts by displaying an input box and assigning whatever text is entered there to the variable Bear. The If block starts and checks to see if the value of Bear is the text string "Papa." If it is, then the appropriate message box is displayed. If not, then VBA proceeds to the first ElseIf statement and checks to see if the value of Bear is "Mama." Again, if it is, then the message box on the next line is displayed. If not, then it goes on to the next ElseIf clause.

So, if "Papa," "Mama," or "Baby" is entered in the input box, a message box associated with that value is displayed. If something different from that is entered, then nothing happens.

Q&A ***Why do I get a syntax error message that says* Must be first statement on the line *every time I try to enter an ElseIf line of code?***

ElseIf needs to be written as one word. You're probably leaving a space between Else and If. Notice that ElseIf turns blue when it is entered as one word, but not when it is entered as two words.

None of the above? Use Else

Sometimes, you'll want to do one thing if a condition is true and something else if it's false. Else will let you define statements that are run when the conditions tested in your If and ElseIf clauses all turn out to be false.

```
Sub CheckForAnnual()
    If ActiveSheet.Name = "Annual Report" Then
        FormatAnnual
    Else
        MsgBox "Can't run macro from this sheet."
    End If
End Sub
```

Catch the bug

The following procedure is supposed to check to see if a profit margin is high enough. A margin of 0.05 is considered to be the minimum acceptable value. If the profit margin is below 0.05, then a message box should appear saying the profit margin is too low. If it is 0.00 or lower, a different message box is supposed to appear. However, this second message box won't appear no matter what value you pass to the procedure. Why?

```
Sub CheckMargin(Margin)
    If Margin < 0.05 Then
        MsgBox "Profit margin is too low."
    ElseIf Margin <= 0 Then
        MsgBox "This price produces no profit!"
    End If
End Sub
```

Answer: *If you pass a value of 0 or lower to this procedure, it first checks to see if it is less than 0.05. Since it is, it doesn't go on to run any ElseIf lines. ElseIf and Else lines are only run if the If and ElseIf lines above them evaluated their condition as false. Once one turns out to be true, none of the ones below it are even looked at.*

To correct the problem, you can change the second line of this program to read as follows:

```
If Margin < 0.05 and Margin > 0 Then
```

Then the first message box will be displayed only when Margin *is between 0 and 0.05, which is when you want it.*

 This macro is designed to prevent a user from running a procedure in a situation where it doesn't apply. Somewhere else in the workbook is a procedure called FormatAnnual which only works properly on the Annual Report worksheet.

When this procedure is run, it checks whether the active sheet is the correct one, Annual Report. If it is, it runs the procedure that formats this sheet. If not, it displays a message box explaining to the user why this macro will not be run.

You can use ElseIf clauses together with an Else. In order, you'd start with an If line, follow with one or several ElseIf lines, then use one Else line, and then an End If.

Select Case lets you choose from many options

Among other things, ElseIf statements allow you to test an expression for many different possible cases. However, using more than one or two ElseIf statements can become unwieldy and make your code difficult to read.

If what you're doing is making decisions based on the value of a particular expression, consider the Select Case statement as an alternative.

The expression that you use in a Select Case statement is usually quite different than one you'd test in an If/Then statement. In a Select Case statement, you don't make it into a true or false statement—you just insert the variable or other expression that you want to evaluate. For example,

Speaking of *Select Case*

The syntax of Select Case is

```
Select Case expression
    Case outcome1
        statements1...
    Case outcomeN
        statementsN
    [Case Else
        elsestatements]
End Select
```

One *expression* is tested for the entire Select Case statement. Each possible outcome you wish to address is listed as *outcome1*, *outcome2* up through *outcomeN*. The *statements* listed below each outcome will be run if that is the correct outcome.

Optionally, you can include the Case Else line with *elsestatements* that will be run if none of the outcomes listed in the Case lines were true.

```
Sub WhichNumber()
    MyNumber = ActiveCell.Value
    Select Case MyNumber
        Case 2
            MsgBox "The number is 2"
        Case 1.75
            Beep
        Case 3 To 10
            MsgBox "The number is between 3 and 10"
    End Select
End Sub
```

This procedure is designed to be run as a macro after entering a number in the current cell of a worksheet. The second line of the procedure creates a variable called `MyNumber` and assigns it the value of the active cell. It is this variable that will provide the following possible outcomes:

- The first line of the Select Case block makes `MyNumber` the expression that will be looked at for possible outcomes. Three possible values for `MyValue` are considered in the Select Case block. The first:

  ```
  Case 2
  ```

  is associated with a message box on the following line. If the value of `MyNumber` is 2, the `Case 2` section of the Select Case block runs, and a message box saying `The number is 2` appears.

- Similarly, if the number is 1.75, the second case is in effect. In this case, the computer beeps.

- The third case deals with the values between 3 and 10. If `MyNumber` is 4 or 8 or 7.999, then the third case is in effect, and a message box saying `The number is between 3 and 10` appears.

Notice that when using a Select Case statement, the name of the variable or expression that you're evaluating is only used on the Select Case line itself. On the individual lines, it isn't mentioned—just the possible values that it could have.

If you want to look at whether your expression is greater than a certain value, it's a bit tricky. Suppose your Select Case block starts out with the line

```
Select Case x
```

This is perfectly acceptable. You're telling VBA that the variable x is the one whose different values will determine which case is in effect. Suppose you want a case to deal with when x is less than 5. This line of code will *not* work:

```
Case x < 5
```

In this Select Case statement, your first line identifies x as the expression you want to look at, and the Case lines have to talk about the outcomes without specifically mentioning x. So, to look at the outcome where x is less than 5, you'd use code like the following:

```
Case Is < 5
```

There's more than one way to repeat code

Loops are used to run a section of code multiple times. VBA provides many different ways to do this, depending on the situation and the reasons for looping.

You don't really need to know each and every kind of loop to make them work for you. It's possible to use a For/Next loop for almost anything that a Do loop can accomplish. However, the different loops make your code more readable and spare you the effort of trying to figure out how you're going to trick a loop that works on counting into testing a condition.

Speaking of *For/Next*

```
For counter = start To end [Step stepvalue]
    statements
Next counter
```

where *counter* is a variable used to keep track of loop iterations, *start* is the initial value of *counter*, and *end* is the final value of *counter*. The *stepvalue* is an optional numerical value you can supply to cause the loop to count by a different increment than by ones. If *stepvalue* is not given, the default value of one is used.

For/Next repeats a certain number of times

In Chapter 5, a simplified syntax of For/Next was given. Here's the full version.

The For/Next loop is a good loop to use when you know how many times you need to loop, or have beginning and ending values for your loop. This procedure calls another procedure, Census, and sends it the value of each decade. Census returns the population for that year.

```
Sub DisplayPop()
    For Decade = 1900 To 1990 Step 10
        Population = Census(Decade)
        MsgBox "In " & Decade & " the population was: " _
        & Population
    Next Decade
End Sub
```

The For/Next loop uses the variable Decade as a counter. Decade starts at the value 1900 and continues until it reaches 1990. The Step value is 10, which means that Decade increases by 10 on each iteration of the loop (1900, 1910, 1920, and so on).

On each round of the loop, the Census procedure is called with the Decade as the argument. Its return value is displayed in a message box.

Do repeats based on conditions

In some circumstances, you don't really know how many times you want a loop to repeat. For example, you might want the user to keep entering data until there is no more. Or, you may want to keep looking at items in a list until you find the one you're looking for, then you can stop. In either of these cases, you can't really predict how many iterations of the loop will be necessary until the end is reached.

Do loops allow a loop to continue an indefinite number of times until a condition is met or as long as a condition is true. There are two kinds of Do loops: Do While and Do Until.

Do something as long as a condition is true

To learn more about the Do While loop, see Chapter 5, "A Little Bit of Programming Goes a Long Way."

The Do While loop lets you repeat an action as long as a condition is true. The following example lets you add party guests to a list until you exceed 100 guests. Since some guests are invited as family groups of two or more, you don't know how many times the loop needs to run before the maximum of 100 guests is reached.

```
Sub InviteGuests()
    TotalInvited = 0
    Do While TotalInvited < 100
        GuestParty = InputBox("Guest party name:")
        NumInParty = InputBox("How many in party?")
        TotalInvited = TotalInvited + NumInParty
        StoreGuestList GuestParty, NumInParty
    Loop
    MsgBox "There's no more room for more guests"
End Sub
```

The InviteGuests subroutine uses a variable called `TotalInvited` keep track of how many people have been invited. The Do loop starts with the line

```
Do While TotalInvited < 100
```

As long as the value of `TotalInvited` is less than 100, the loop will run. The procedure prompts the user for the name of the guest party and how many people will be in that party. These values are stored in the variables `GuestParty` and `NumInParty`. The next line

```
TotalInvited = TotalInvited + NumInParty
```

increases the value of `TotalInvited` by the number of guests just added. The following line calls another procedure that will store the name of the party and the number of guests in that party.

When the Loop line is reached, the program goes back up to the Do While line. `TotalInvited` is evaluated. If it is still less than 100, then the loop is run again. If not, then the program jumps back down to the end of the loop and displays a message box explaining that the limit has been reached.

For the InviteGuests procedure, you didn't know how many times you'd need to run the loop to reach a total of 100. You could have invited 50 couples, or your rather prolific cousins with 12 kids might have used up quite a lot of the available space. The Do While loop let you test a condition before each iteration of the loop.

Do something until a condition becomes true

Do Until is very similar to Do While. The difference is that Do While repeats a block of code as long as something is true. Do Until repeats a block of code as long as something is false: in other words *until* it is true.

The InviteGuests procedure could be rewritten using Do Until by changing one line. The line that starts Do With can be replaced by

```
Do Until TotalInvited >= 100
```

This tells the loop to keep running until the value of `TotalInvited` is greater than or equal to 100. Notice that this will happen exactly when `TotalInvited` is no longer less than 100, which is what the original version looked for.

Q&A **If Do Until and Do While are so similar, why are there two of them?**

It's true that you could get by with just one, but sometimes one will make things easier to read than the other. You can choose the one that makes your program easier to understand.

I want the loop to run at least one time, no matter what

Both Do Until and Do While have another form that puts the While or Until at the bottom. This makes the loop start at the top, go through the entire loop once, and then check to see if the loop should be repeated.

This example makes a message box appear like the one in figure 10.1. If the user selects <u>Y</u>es, it repeats and shows the message box again. If the user selects <u>N</u>o, then the procedure ends.

Fig. 10.1
By pressing a button, the user instructs VBA to keep looping or to stop.

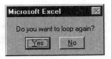

```
Sub DifferentLoop()
    Do
        Beep
        Answer = MsgBox("Loop again?", vbYesNo)
    Loop Until Answer = vbNo
End Sub
```

You would expect to see the Until part up next to the Do, but it's been moved down to the Loop statement. When this procedure begins, it goes right into the loop without checking any conditions. It beeps and displays a message box with Yes and No buttons. The value of the button that is clicked is stored in the variable Answer.

To learn how to use Yes and No buttons in a message box, see Chapter 18, "Ready-Made Dialog Boxes."

On the Loop line, VBA checks to see if the value of Answer is vbNo. This is the value that Answer would have been assigned if the user pressed the No button. If it isn't vbNo, the code will repeat. If it is vbNo, then the loop doesn't run again and the procedure ends.

Catch the bug

In the above example, you could replace

```
Loop Until Answer = vbNo
```

with the line

```
While Answer = vbYes
```

and get identical results. If that's the case, then why doesn't the following procedure ever display a message box?

```
Sub NeverLoops()
    Do While Answer = vbYes
        Beep
        Answer = MsgBox("Do you want to loop again?", vbYesNo)
    Loop
End Sub
```

Answer: When this procedure starts, it checks the value of the variable Answer before it ever displays the dialog box. You haven't assigned the value vbYes to it yet. That's only done when a button is pressed. Thus it looks to see if the value of Answer is vbYes. It isn't, so the loop isn't run even once.

Making loops work for objects and arrays

To learn about objects and collections see Chapter 11, "How VBA Refers to Things in Excel."

To learn about arrays, see Chapter 13, "Working With Lists of Things."

If you had a line of people and you needed to give something to each one, it would be easy. Just start at the front of the line and work your way back. You'd know you were done when you reached the end of the line.

What if that same group of people were milling around in a room, occasionally getting up and moving to new spots? It would be quite difficult to make sure that you got to each one, and that you didn't do someone twice.

If you're trying to write a loop that will affect every object in a collection, or every element in an array, you'll encounter a similar difficulty. Just like the room example, you could come up with some ingenious way to get everyone in order. You needn't do this for collections and arrays, however. VBA provides a way to achieve this automatically with the For Each statement.

This example activates each of the worksheets of the current workbook in turn and prompts you to rename them.

```
Sub RenameWorksheets()
    For Each x In Worksheets
        x.Activate
        x.Name = InputBox("Rename this sheet")
    Next
End Sub
```

The For Each statement uses the variable x as a placeholder for the members of the Worksheets collections. The Activate method brings it to the front so that you can see which sheet is currently assigned to x. Then an input box appears. Whatever text is entered is assigned to the name property of the active sheet, thus changing its name.

Speaking of *For Each*

```
For Each item In group
    statements
Next
```

If you use this type of loop for an array, then *item* is a variable name used as a placeholder for the elements of the array and *group* is the array itself. When working with objects in a collection, then *item* is a variable name as a placeholder for the objects in the collection, and *group* is a collection of objects.

Fig. 10.2
An input box that
lets you rename a
worksheet might be
a useful part of a
custom interface for
a workbook.

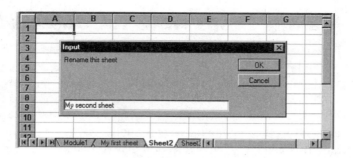

Exit a loop before the end is reached

Just because you've set limits for the maximum number of times a loop
should repeat, doesn't mean that you want it to keep going under all circumstances. This is true both when a loop is set to run a certain number of times
or until a condition is reached.

VBA will immediately exit a loop when it encounters the appropriate exit
statement. To exit a Do While or Do Until loop, use

```
Exit Do
```

To exit a For Next or For Each loop, use

```
Exit For
```

This loop runs once and exits before it can be repeated.

```
Sub LeaveEarly()
    For x = 1 To 5
        MsgBox x
        Exit For
    Next x
End Sub
```

How can I use this in the real world?

You can create a For Each loop that looks at all the cells in a worksheet trying to
find a certain name. Once it's found, there's no reason to check the rest of the
cells.

This is like the old joke: Why do you always find something in the last place you
look? It's because once you find it, you stop looking.

When VBA first starts the loop, it assigns 1 to the variable x and then displays this value. On the next line, an instruction is given to exit the loop. No further iterations of the loop occur.

A very common use of an Exit statement is within an If/Then statement that itself is within a loop. The following section describes this situation.

You can use one control structure within another

Control structures can be **nested**, or placed one inside of another. You can use an If/Then statement inside of a loop, for example.

```
Sub LeaveOnThree()
    For x = 1 To 5
        MsgBox x
        If x = 3 Then
            Exit For
        End If
    Next x
End Sub
```

This procedure uses an If/Then statement within a For/Next. The If/Then tests to see if it is the third iteration of the loop. If it is, then the instruction is given to exit the loop. Otherwise, it continues to run through the loop.

You can continue to nest control structures for many levels. For example, you could have a loop that contains an If/Then that contains another If/Then that contains a loop, and so on. Each control structure should be indented further than the one it is inside of, to help you identify what's going on in the program.

TIP   **If you nest several levels of control structures, it can be difficult to** tell what the code is doing at first glance. Include a comment to help yourself or another reader understand it at a later date.

Summary

This chapter took a detailed look at VBA control structures. They allow you to change the flow of a procedure by choosing whether certain parts of the code should run or not, and by allowing some code to be repeated many times. You learned how to use ElseIf with the If/Then statement to consider multiple conditions, and how to use the Select Case statement as an alternative to this. Several kinds of loops and their differences were discussed, and you learned which loops are suitable for which job, as well as how to exit a loop before it has performed all of its iterations.

Review questions

1 What are the two types of Do loops?

2 How can you consider several different cases with an If/Then statement?

3 If you wanted to enter a value in each cell in a range, which control structure would you use for the loop?

4 How do you exit a loop before it's reached the end?

5 How can you ensure that a Do While loop will run its code at least once?

6 What's the difference between Select Case and If/Then?

How can I use this in the real world?

Loops can also be nested inside other loops. For example, you could have a For/Next loop run through each month of the year. While a certain month value was in effect, you could start a Do While loop that would let you enter sales figures for that month until you indicated that you were done by clicking a button in a dialog box.

Exercises

1 Change the InviteGuests procedure so that a total of 150 guests can be invited.

2 Rewrite the DisplayPop procedure changing the beginning year to 1800. Make it so that it only looks at the census data for every 20 years, instead of every 10.

3 Add an Else clause to the Goldilocks procedure that will display a message box when the input is not one of the three bears.

4 Create a Do Until loop that prompts for a number and adds it to a running total until the total exceeds 500.

5 Write a For/Next loop that counts from 1 to 100. When it reaches 50, make it display a message box that says you're halfway there. (Hint: put an If/Then statement inside of the For/Next loop.)

6 Write a procedure that changes the name of all the worksheets in your workbook to MySheet1, MySheet2, etc.

11

How VBA Refers to Things in Excel

● **In this chapter:**

- ● Objects versus properties versus methods

- ● Learning the names for various objects

- ● OK, I've got an object, now tell me what I can do with it

- ● What it means when you see :=

- ● Use the Object Browser to find an object

Imagine trying to have a conversation without any nouns. Useful, aren't they? It's hard to talk about things—even in VBA—without knowing their names . . . .

A big part of learning to communicate is learning the names for things. In VBA, this means learning about Excel's objects and their properties and methods.

This is a big task, because there are hundreds of objects, properties, and methods in Excel. What's more, VBA is very unforgiving; if you don't use the precise name in exactly the right way, your code won't work.

This chapter is designed to give you an overview of how objects, properties, and methods are organized. The subject is far too big to be exhaustively covered in one chapter or even in one book. The way you'll *really* learn about them is to add them gradually to your programming vocabulary. After you've become comfortable with several objects, the organization and the rules of using them will become clearer.

The vocabulary of objects

There is an entire grammar of objects, properties, and methods. Just as there are rules for using adverbs and adjectives in a certain way in English, objects, methods, and properties have certain grammatical requirements.

However, just as you learned English by using language without knowing grammar (how many five-year-olds can tell you what a verb is?), you'll probably find that you're using many objects, methods, and properties without being completely informed about the rules of construction. This is the best way to learn!

It's nice to get an idea of what's going on, though. It will help you to apply a skill used with one object to another and give you a framework for under-standing what you're programming. This section gives you an overview of what objects, properties, and methods mean, so that you can better under-stand the things that you're probably already using.

Objects are the things in Excel you work with

Objects are the nouns of Excel. Think of some *thing* in Excel that you can point to. Chances are, it's an object. Commonly used objects include worksheets, menus, buttons, and ranges of cells.

To learn how to use Excel's online help, see Chapter 6, "VBA Information Online."

There are many, many objects in Excel. There is an object for every item on every menu, every button, and every worksheet in every workbook. You can see a complete list of the different kinds of Excel objects by looking up Objects in the Contents page of the Excel Help Topics dialog box. Figure 11.1 shows the first few objects.

Fig. 11.1
Excel's objects are all listed in the online help. Of course, you need to know what you're looking for to find anything useful that way.

Objects don't *do* anything. You do things *to* objects. To write a complete line of VBA code involving an object, you need to specify the object and then do something to it. Doing something to it involves using properties and methods. This is just like a noun in English. You can use a noun to specify an object, like "beachball." To use it in a sentence, though, you need to say something like, "Throw the beachball."

In VBA you specify an object with a **reference**. Often the reference consists of several different components, each one narrowing down the field of possible objects until a specific object is pinpointed. Each stage of narrowing down is separated by a period (.). For example,

```
Workbooks("Book2").Worksheets("Sheet1")
```

refers to a worksheet object. It's called Sheet1. To distinguish it from other worksheets called Sheet1 in different workbooks, the possibilities are first narrowed down by specifying Workbooks("Book2"), the book in which the desired sheet is located.

Note that this is not a complete VBA statement. You've just *specified* an object, not done anything with it. To make a statement, you need to do something with that object.

Properties are the attributes of objects

Certain attributes of objects in Excel are called **properties**. A button has a caption, a worksheet cell has a value or formula, and a menu has a name.

Properties describe an object, and you can change an object by changing its properties. If your object is a beachball, then you could describe its color, level of inflation, or price. These are all attributes of the beachball and similar to properties in Excel.

Sometimes different objects will have the same properties. A beachball and a car both have the color property. The car doesn't have the inflation level property, although its tires might.

In VBA, you specify the property of an object by giving a reference to the object and then adding a period (.) and the name of the property. For example, worksheets have a Name property. So, to refer to the name property of the worksheet object from the last section, you'd use

```
Workbooks("Book2").Worksheets("Sheet1").Name
```

This is not a full VBA statement. It's an expression that needs to be used as a part of a statement.

Methods do things to objects

If an object is like a noun, then a **method** is like a verb acting on that noun. The beachball object, for example, could have a throw method and a bounce method.

In VBA, using a method on an object happens in much the same way that you refer to a property of that object; you tack it on to the end of the reference with a period (.), separating it from the object. For example, a worksheet object has a delete method. As you might expect, using this method on a worksheet object will delete it. To use it on the worksheet described in the previous sections, you'd use

```
Workbooks("Book2").Worksheets("Sheet1").Delete
```

This is a complete VBA statement. It instructs VBA to delete a certain sheet, and it can stand on its own as a line of code.

Collections are groups of objects

Most objects belong to a group of similar objects. These groups are called **collections**. Your workbook could have three worksheets. Together, they form a collection called Worksheets. If you're using the drawing tools on a sheet, then all of the rectangles you draw belong to a Rectangles collection.

Collections are used in one of two ways. You can do things to a collection itself, like adding a menu to the Menus collection or closing all the workbooks in the Workbooks collection. Or, you can refer to the collection and pick out a certain member of the collection to work with. That's what

```
Workbooks("Book2")
```

does. Workbooks is the set of all open workbooks, and the ("Book2") part lets you pick out one of the objects in that collection to work with.

Specifying which object you want to work with

To do something with an object, you need to let VBA know exactly which object you've got in mind. With so many objects floating around, this is not always simple.

Refer to objects by.using.names.like.this

If you're telling someone where you live, the amount of detail you need to give depends on the context. For example, when speaking with someone who lives in the same city, you could give just the street address. But when talking to someone out of state, you'd need to give the street address, city name, and state. A similar situation exists when talking about objects in Excel. If you're referring to a cell, you may need to give information about the cell, the worksheet it's on, and which workbook the worksheet is in. Or, you might only need to mention where the cell is. It all depends on where you want the program to run and what sheet will be active when it happens.

When one object is inside of another object, the other object is called a **container**. For example, a workbook is a container for a worksheet, and a worksheet is a container for a range object. When you specify containers for objects, you start with the largest container on the left and list each smaller container until you get to the object you want, separating each entry with a period (.). For example, the following line of code refers to the cell B6 in the worksheet named Sheet1 in the workbook called MYBOOK.XLS:

```
Workbooks("MyBook.xls").Sheets("Sheet1").Range("B6")
```

By referring to an object this specifically (in this case a particular cell), you ensure that VBA won't accidentally perform an action in the wrong worksheet or workbook.

Sometimes, though, you'll want to refer to an object more generally. Perhaps you want to write code that does something to cell B6 in whatever worksheet is currently chosen. Then you must leave out the designations of which sheet and workbook containers are chosen and instead just use

```
Range("B6")
```

to refer to the object.

Objects that are currently active or selected

There are several convenient ways to refer to certain objects that are currently active or selected. They're formally known as **properties**, but they seem more like objects. They work by returning a reference to an object.

 Plain English, please!

To **return a reference** means that you're mentioning an object by describing it in some way. Often an object doesn't have a specific name, but you need to refer to it in order to work with it. There are several ways to refer to an object, using methods or properties which—when called upon—**return a reference** to the object you want. This phrase pops up all over the online help topics associated with Excel objects.

An example is ActiveCell. If a worksheet is the active sheet, then ActiveCell will return a reference to the currently active cell. So, if you're in a workbook and the active cell is C7, then ActiveCell and Range("C7") mean exactly the same thing. Any property or method that you could use on the Range object, you could use with ActiveCell instead. For example

```
ActiveCell.Value = 500
```

simply changes the value of the active cell to 500. Other "Actives" include:

Table 11.1 Properties that return references to active objects

Property	Object
ActiveWorksheet	Returns the sheet that is currently active. This can be a worksheet, dialog sheet, or module sheet
ActiveWorkbook	Returns the active workbook
ActiveDialog	Returns the topmost running dialog sheet (which may or may not be the same as the active sheet)

To learn about dialog sheets, see Chapter 20, "Creating and Using Dialog Boxes."

Another useful property is Selection. Selection will return the object that is currently selected—be it a range, a drawing object, or a button in a dialog box. Notice that Selection can return different kinds of objects.

The "Active" properties and Selection can be used to return an object and thus use a method or set, or read the value of the property. What you cannot do with these is to change which cell or sheet is active. To do that, you need to use the Activate method.

Q&A ***If cells are currently selected in my sheet, what's the difference between ActiveCell and Selection?***

Selection is whatever cells are selected in the worksheet. This can be a single cell or many cells. ActiveCell is always a single cell, even when many cells are selected. When several cells are selected, only one of them is the active cell. It's the one that is *not* highlighted in black as shown in the following figure.

Active cell —
Selection

Picking an object out of a collection

All of the sheets in a workbook comprise a collection called **Worksheets**. When you want to do work with one particular worksheet, you need to narrow things down. This can be done by using the Worksheets method, whose entire job is to pick a specific object out of the Worksheets collection.

 Q&A *Is Worksheets a collection or a method?*

It's both. There's a Worksheets collection. This is the set of all worksheets in a workbook. There's also a Worksheets method. That's a method used to pick out a particular worksheet.

The most common way to use the Worksheets method is with the name of the worksheet you want as an argument. To refer to a sheet called Budget, you would use `Worksheets("Budget")`.

There are many collections with accompanying methods like this. They include what's listed in table 11.2.

Table 11.2 Common Collections

Collection/Method	What It Refers to
Sheets	All the sheets in a workbook
Workbooks	All open workbooks
Menus	All menus in a menu bar
Buttons	All buttons on a dialog sheet

They all work the same way. To pick out a particular object in that collection, you use the name of the object in quotation marks with the method.

 TIP **Remember that these names are always pluralized. There is no** Worksheet or Sheet object name in Excel, although individual sheets are indeed objects.

Now that you know how to pick out an object from a collection, you still must do something with it.

```
Sheets("Module1")
```

is not a valid VBA statement because it just refers to an object and doesn't do anything with it. The section "Doing things to objects" later in this chapter talks about what you can do with an object once you've got it picked out.

By the way, you don't always want to pick out a particular object. Sometimes you want to do something to the whole collection, like counting all the sheets in a workbook or adding a menu to the Menus collection. Sometimes you'll omit a particular name and refer to the entire collection.

More ways to figure out the name of an object

Half the battle in VBA programming is to figure out what something is called. There are so many objects available, and the online help topics can often seem more complicated than helpful. Here, then, are a few tips on how to find that elusive object that you're looking for:

- Turn on the macro recorder and do something similar to what you want to do in your program. The code that gets generated will often show you how to refer to an object.

- Pay special attention to the code examples in the online help. It's easier to see how to refer to an object by example.

- Use the Object Browser (described later in this chapter in "The Object Browser").

For details on the Object Model, see Chapter 6, "VBA Information Online."
- Use the Object Model in the online help.

Objects are a big topic. This chapter is only designed to give you an overview of how they're organized. For ways to put objects to work, there are other chapters in this book that deal with using objects for specific purposes:

- Chapter 12 talks about ranges and other objects that involve getting data into and out of worksheets.

- Chapter 16 tells you more about menus, menu items, and menu bars.

- Chapter 17 gives you more info on toolbar-related objects.

- Chapter 20 talks about dialog box controls.

What kinds of things can I do to objects?

The whole idea of pinpointing an object is so that you can do something with it. "Doing something" can mean many different things, including:

- Changing an attribute, like the size of a font or the value of a cell

- Adding or removing an object

- Looking up the value of a property of an object (which doesn't change the object at all)

- Counting or sorting all of the objects in a collection

When doing something to an object, you're either performing a method on it or working with one of its properties. Sometimes it's hard to know what's a method, what's a property, and even what is the object being affected. You will find that you're able to do quite a lot without fully knowing which is which. After awhile, though, things will start to sort themselves out.

Changing the properties

Values can be assigned to properties the same way as variables: in an assignment statement. On the left side of the equal sign, you specify an object and the property you want to change. On the right is the value you want to assign to the property. This procedure changes a property for each of four objects.

```
Sub ChangeProperties()
    Worksheets("Sheet3").Name = "Stock Options"
    ActiveCell.Value = 25
    ActiveWindow.Caption = "Look up here"
    MenuBars(xlWorksheet).Menus("Data").Caption = "Lor"
End Sub
```

Each line in this procedure specifies an object and a property of that object, and then assigns a new value to it. `Worksheets("Sheet3")` refers to an object, and the Name property of that object is set to `Stock Options`. Similarly, the value of the active cell, the caption of the window, and the caption of the Data menu are all changed.

Each of the changes made in this procedure can be seen in figure 11.2.

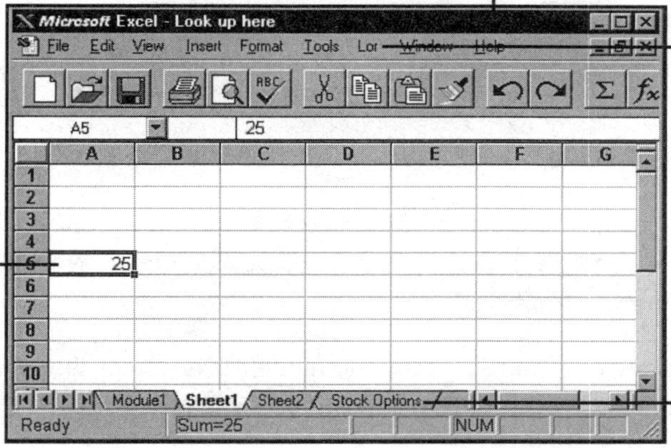

Fig. 11.2
You can see the effects of running the ChangeProperties procedure.

ActiveWindow.Caption property

Menu.Caption property

*ActiveCell.
Value property*

Worksheet.Name property

Q&A *How do I get my Data menu back to normal after running this procedure?*

Chapter 16 deals with resetting menus, but for now it will suffice to quit Excel. When you start again, your menus will be back to normal.

Many properties have unexpected syntaxes. For example, you might think that Font would be a property of a cell and that you could set this to Bold to change the style. Actually, though, Bold itself is a property of the Font *object* and you set the Bold property of a Font to true or false. This line of code makes the text in the current cell bold.

```
ActiveCell.Style.Font.Bold = True
```

TIP **Use the macro recorder to learn the names of properties. With the** recorder on, as described in Chapter 1, make a change in Excel. Then stop the recorder and see what was written in the module.

Reading the value of a property

You don't have to change the value of a property when you refer to it. In fact, some properties are **read only**, which means that they cannot be changed. What do you do with them then? You can look up the value of a property for informational purposes. A reference to a particular property is an expression whose value is the current value of that property. You can assign it to a variable, display it in a message box, or do anything else you would normally do with an expression.

This procedure looks up the value of two properties but does not change them.

```
Sub ReadProperties()
    x = Worksheets("Sheet1").Range("B6").Value
    MsgBox "This sheet is " & ActiveSheet.Name
End Sub
```

The expression `Worksheets("Sheet1").Range("B6").Value` returns whatever is entered in cell `B6` in `Sheet1` of the current workbook. This value is assigned to the variable `x`.

`ActiveSheet.Name` returns the name of the sheet that is active when the procedure is run. This expression, along with additional text, is displayed in a message box.

Using methods

Methods can be a hard concept to grasp. In their easiest form, they do things to objects or collections. For example, a worksheet object has Activate and Delete methods. This line of code simply deletes `Sheet1` from the current workbook.

```
Worksheets("Sheet1").Delete
```

Other methods do less obvious things or use a more complicated syntax.

Methods that take arguments

Just like procedures, methods can take arguments. In fact, some methods seem a whole lot like procedures. Some of them return a value and thus are

How can I use this in the real world?

Some macros are designed to work in a particular worksheet only. You might want to check that the active sheet is called "Budget Analysis" before running a macro designed to work only on that sheet.

To do this, you can use a reference to the name property of the active sheet in an If/Then statement. If the value of this property is equal to "Budget Analysis," then the macro will run. Otherwise, an appropriate message box can be displayed.

much like functions, while others just perform an action without returning a value and are more like subroutines.

Let's consider the Add method as an example. The Add method can be used with different object collections to add a new member to the collection. We'll consider it for adding a sheet to a workbook.

Here is a line of code that adds a new module sheet before the current Sheet2:

```
Sub AddNewSheet()
    Sheets.Add Sheets("Sheet2"), , , xlModule
End Sub
```

 `Sheets.Add` instructs VBA to add a sheet to the current workbook. `Sheets("Sheet2")` is the *before* argument of the Add method. Blank spaces separated with commas are left where the *after* and *count* arguments would go. The last argument, `xlModule`, specifies the *type* of sheet to be added—a module sheet.

Methods like Add that have several arguments are awkward to use. In the example above, all of those commas are needed so that the `xlModule` argument can be interpreted as being fourth in line, even though there is no second and third. Because of this, it is often standard practice to use named arguments when working with methods.

Speaking of *Add*

The syntax of Add for the Sheets collection is

```
Sheets.Add [before, after, count, type]
```

All the arguments for the Add method are optional. The arguments before and after allow you to specify where the sheet will appear. If you specify a sheet for *before*, the new sheet will be added to the workbook in front of the sheet specified. The default is to place the new sheet just before the active sheet. Use count to specify the number of sheets you want to add. The default value is 1. The value of type determines what kind of sheet should be added. Here you supply a VBA constant such as xlWorksheet, xlModule, or xlDialog to indicate the sheet you want to add. If you don't specify a type, then a worksheet will be added.

Plain English, please!

A **named argument** is one where the name of the argument is given right next to the argument itself. This identifies which argument it is. This is in contrast to **positional arguments** where the position of the argument identifies which argument it is. Although you haven't seen the name before, positional arguments are what you've been using throughout the other chapters of this book. **99**

By using named arguments, you don't need to worry about putting in commas for blank spaces or about keeping your arguments in a particular order. The Add line from the previous example would be written with named arguments as:

```
Sheets.Add Before:=Sheets("Sheet2"), Type:=xlModule
```

After `Sheets.Add`, the word `Before` indicates that what follows will be the value of the *before* argument. `Before` is followed by a colon and equal sign (`:=`). This is required when using named arguments. After the value for the Before argument is given, a comma is used to separate it from the next argument. Rather than going to the second argument of the add syntax, it skips right to the last one, `type`.

Note that you could reverse the order of these two arguments if you're using named arguments. The type argument could precede the before argument—something that would be impossible when using positional arguments.

With methods that take several arguments, it's common practice to use named arguments rather than positional ones. Since that's what you'll find in most of the online help examples, I'll mostly use named references for methods in this book as well.

 TIP If you prefer them, you can also use named arguments with your sub and function procedures.

A final word of advice about using methods with arguments—whether or not you enclose the entire argument list in parentheses depends on how you're using a method. When you use a method like a statement, you don't enclose its arguments in parentheses. When you use it like a function, you do. Ask yourself if the method is being used as an end in itself, such as

```
Sheets.add Type:=xlWorksheet
```

in which case, it uses no parentheses. Or, if it is being used to return a value that is a part of a larger VBA statement, then parentheses should be used around the arguments:

```
Sheets.add(Type:=xlWorksheet).Name = "Budget Analysis"
```

In this case, the Add method is used with parentheses around the argument. The return value is the new sheet, and it is immediately used to set the name property.

Catch the bug

I'm trying to enter a line of code that adds a worksheet to my existing workbook. By specifying a value for `After`, it should be placed right after `Sheet1`. Whenever I enter this line, however, I get an error message as shown in the following figure. What's wrong?

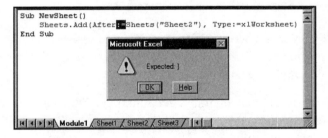

Answer: The Add method is being used like a statement. There's no need to enclose the argument list in parentheses. Instead, the line of code should read

```
Sheets.add After:=Sheets("Sheet2"), Type:=xlWorksheet
```

Methods that return objects

To select a specific sheet object from a workbook, you use code like the following:

```
Worksheets("Sheet1")
```

`Worksheets` is actually a method, and the thing it "does" is to pick an object out of a collection. You can choose to ignore the fact that `Worksheets` in this line of code is actually a method. It seems to make more sense to think of it as an object. However, if you rely on any kind of online reference (and you probably will need to when learning about new objects), you're going to encounter help topics like the one shown in figure 11.3 which describe the Buttons method. To refer to a button *object*, you'll have to use this *method*.

Fig. 11.3

It's disconcerting to see something called a method that seems like an object, but after seeing it a few times, you'll catch on.

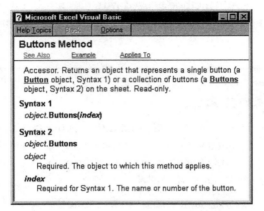

Whenever you see a help topic that uses phrases like: "Accessor" and "Returns an object..." you know that you're dealing with a method that can be used to refer to an object.

Methods like this are much like functions. They take an argument in parentheses. In the case of Worksheets, the argument was the name of the sheet you wanted to pick out of the collection. Their return value is an object which is a member of a collection.

Also like functions, they constitute an expression, rather than an entire VBA statement. You need to do something to it to change it into a statement. So, a complete line of code that uses the Workbooks method could be

```
Worksheets("Sheet1").Name = "My Worksheet"
```

It may help you to understand these methods as you think of them simply as the way to provide the name of a specific object.

Working with whole collections

Collections are a group of like objects. But, did you know that the collection itself is also an object? Again, this is one of those puzzling subtleties in the world of Excel objects. The important thing to keep in mind is that you can do things to an entire collection at once, rather than picking out a specific element. Some of the things you might do to a collection include:

- Counting all of the objects in that collection

- Adding an object to the collection

- Closing all members of the collection (closing all open workbooks, for example)

- Using a For Each loop to affect each object in the collection

Count and Add are common methods that are used on collections.

```
Sub AddAndCount()
    MsgBox "There are " & Sheets.Count & " sheets"
    Sheets.add
    MsgBox "There are " & Sheets.Count & " sheets"
End Sub
```

 This procedure displays a message box that gives the current number of sheets in a workbook. A sheet is then added, and a new message box appears with the revised number of sheets.

Why do I get an error saying a method failed?

A very common error message that appears is one saying that the method of an object failed. Usually this is caused by VBA's inability to find the object you're talking about. Consider the following procedure:

```
Sub ChangeName()
    Worksheets("Sheet1").Name = "Viken"
End Sub
```

If you type this into a new workbook, you'll be able to run it once. It will change the name of Sheet1 to Viken. If you try to run it again, though, it will produce a message box saying Worksheets method of Application class failed. This is because there is no longer a worksheet called Sheet1. You changed its name to Viken, so it won't be able to find it a second time (see fig. 11.4).

Fig. 11.4
When you get an error message like this one, it's often a sign that you got the name of an object wrong.

When you get messages of this sort, check to see if you've spelled the name right and if you've referred to the right object. Also make sure that VBA is looking for the object in the right place. If a different workbook is active, that may be the problem.

The Object Browser

To help navigate through the world of objects, Excel provides a tool called the Object Browser. You can use the Object Browser for two different purposes:

- To find out about objects, their properties, and methods

- To locate procedures in module sheets

The object browser is accessed by choosing <u>V</u>iew, <u>O</u>bject Browser while in a module sheet.

  TIP **You can also bring up the Object Browser by pressing F2** from within a module sheet or by clicking on the Object Browser button on the VBA toolbar.

Use the Object Browser for objects

You can use the Object Browser to find out what methods and properties are associated with a specific object. Once you've found a method or property that interests you, you can get help on that topic or paste the code of the method or property into a worksheet. This is particularly handy for methods that take several arguments since it also pastes the named arguments into the module.

Most objects are found in the Excel library of objects. Select Excel in the Libraries/Workbooks box at the top of the Object Browser. The left hand Objects/Modules box displays Excel's objects. The right hand Methods/ Properties box displays the methods and properties associated with whatever object is selected in the Objects/Modules box. For example, to find out about methods and properties of Sheets:

1 In a module sheet press F2 to bring up the Object Browser.

2 Choose Excel in the Libraries/Workbooks combo box.

3 Scroll through the Objects/Modules list until you find Sheets, then select it. Next, click on Add in the Methods/Properties list. The Object browser should now look like figure 11.5.

Fig. 11.5

Voilà! The properties and methods of the Sheets collection are at your disposal.

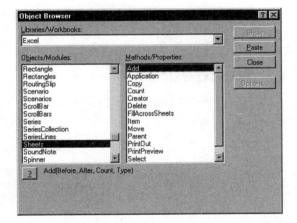

In figure 11.6, the Sheets object is selected, and its methods and properties are displayed on the right. Clicking on the ? button will bring up the help topic for the Add method.

Clicking on the <u>P</u>aste button will insert the code

```
Add(Before:=, After:=, Count:=, Type:=)
```

into the module sheet that was active when you brought up the Object Browser. This code gets inserted wherever the cursor was, even if it's in the middle of the word. You'll probably have to do some editing to get it to work correctly.

Every named argument must have a value, so if you're not going to specify an After value, you need to remove the `After:=`, part of the argument list. Also, if you're using the method like a statement, you'll need to remove the parentheses. Finally, don't forget that you need an object collection at the beginning of the line. The "cleaned up" version might be the following:

```
Sheets.Add Before:=Worksheets("Sheet1"), Count:=3
```

Use the Object Browser to find procedures

The Object Browser also lets you look through all of the modules in all the open workbooks. It displays any procedures you have written or macros you have recorded.

To look for a procedure, select one of the open workbooks in the <u>L</u>ibraries/Workbooks combo box of the Object Browser. All open workbooks, including hidden ones, are listed there. When you've selected a workbook, a list of all the module sheets in that workbook appears in the Ob<u>j</u>ects/Modules list box. Click on the module that you'd like to see the contents of. This causes the <u>M</u>ethods/Properties combo box to display all of the procedures in that module.

Clicking on a procedure name will make its name and description appear at the bottom of the Object Browser. To bring up the procedure so that you can look at it or edit it, click on the <u>S</u>how button.

You can also get lists of VBA's constants and other useful items

By selecting VBA in the <u>L</u>ibraries/Workbooks combo box, you can get lists of many of VBA's built-in terms. A list of all the VBA constants is available, and clicking on a specific constant will give you a little bit of information about what it is used for. You can also use this as a way to get to the help topic on that constant by clicking on the ? button.

Q&A ***Where are the constants that start with xl, like xlWorksheet?***

These are located in the Excel library, rather than the VBA library. Choose Excel in the Libraries/Workbooks combo box and select Constants in the Objects/Modules combo box.

Other things you'll find listed in the VBA category are a variety of built-in procedures organized by category. These include math procedures (like Cos and Exp), procedures that allow you to interact with the user (like MsgBox and InputBox), and procedures that work on text strings.

Summary

This chapter discussed the organization of Excel objects, properties, and methods. You learned how to refer to an object, read or change its properties, and use methods. The Object Browser is a useful tool for finding objects and their methods and properties, and also for finding procedures that you've created.

Review questions

1 What is a property?

2 What is a method?

3 Name some of the resources at your disposal for figuring out what a particular object is called.

4 What kinds of things can the Object Browser help you with?

5 How would you specify a workbook called BUDGET.XLS as an object?

Exercises

1   Change the first line of the ReadProperties procedure so that rather than looking up the value of cell B6 on Sheet1, it changes the value of this cell to 144.

2   Rewrite the AddNewSheets procedure so that it adds two sheets instead of just one.

3   Modify the AddNewSheets procedure you created in Exercise 2 so that it uses named arguments instead of positional arguments.

4   With the workbook you used for Exercises 2 and 3 still open, add a new workbook. Add a module sheet and then press F2 to bring up the Object Browser. Use the Object Browser to locate the AddNewSheets procedure and click on the <u>E</u>dit button to bring it up.

5   Write a procedure that changes the name of the active worksheet to the value written in cell A1 of that sheet. Try it out on a few worksheets.

12

Getting Information Into and Out of Worksheets

● **In this chapter:**

● **How do objects and methods work when I'm dealing with cells and ranges?**

● **I need to get information from my worksheet to VBA**

● **Now I need to send information from VBA to my worksheet**

● **How do I select different kinds of ranges with VBA?**

How do you get all that stuff from Excel into VBA and back? . . . .

On the one hand, you've got Excel's worksheets. In a worksheet, you work with ranges, cells, columns, rows, formulas, and data. On the other hand, you've got VBA's module sheets where you can write programs, perform calculations, store macros, and manipulate data. Is it possible to transfer information from one of these to the other?

VBA is so powerful and flexible that you can do just about anything with worksheet cells and ranges. With VBA, you can select, change, format, copy, and perform calculations on cells and ranges. To do this, though, you need to get pretty comfortable with the programming required to handle ranges.

This chapter gives you an in-depth look at how to pick out and manipulate ranges in Excel with VBA code. Once you've gotten used to these objects, your ability to write procedures that work directly with worksheets will improve dramatically.

How do I tell VBA which cells I want to work with?

Objects are the things in Excel that VBA can manipulate. So, it seems obvious that there would be a cell object. Actually, there is no such thing! Cells are lumped under the category of **range objects**, as are ranges, columns and rows.

To learn more about objects, properties and methods, see Chapter 11, "How VBA Refers to Things in Excel."

Range objects have useful properties and methods you can work with. But to do something to a range object, you need to first specify which one you want. Do you want a particular cell or all the cells on a worksheet? Maybe you want a range with a special name.

This is where things become complicated. Because so much of Excel centers around working with a cell or a group of cells (in other words, with various range objects), there are many different ways to specify a range. Specifying a range entails the use of a property or method that returns a range object. Here is a partial list of the tools that VBA provides for specifying a range:

- The Cells method lets you pick out one cell or all the cells in a worksheet.

- The Range method can return an individual cell, a rectangular range, or an irregular group of cells.

- ActiveCell is a property that returns the single cell in the workbook that is currently active.

- Selection returns the object that is currently selected. If it is a range that's selected, it returns a range object.

- The Column and Row methods can return an entire column or row, or a column or row of a smaller range.

Don't let all the choices scare you off! You can pick and choose as you need to specify different ranges. You don't need to understand every way perfectly to be able to use one way effectively.

Q&A ***What's the difference between a Range object and the Range method?***

The Range method is one of the ways you can specify a Range object. The Range method *returns* a Range object. So does the Cells method. But there is no Cells object. (Remember, VBA treats all cells like small ranges.)

Referring to a single cell

The Cells method and the Range method can return a reference to an individual cell. The difference between these methods is in the way that they are used. Once a cell is returned by one of these methods, VBA can't tell which method returned it. It's just a Range object. The first way to refer to a single cell is with the Range method.

Thus,

```
Worksheets("Sheet1").Range("A14")
```

Speaking of *Range*

The syntax for the Range method that returns a single cell is

```
object.Range("cell")
```

where *object* is an optional reference to the worksheet where the cell can be found, and *cell* is either the name or coordinates of the specific cell.

returns the cell A14 on Sheet1 of the active workbook. If no worksheet is specified, then Range will look for the cell in the current sheet. If the current sheet is not a worksheet, this method will fail.

One of the big drawbacks of Range is that you must give a specific reference to a cell. What if you want to use variables to specify the cell? That's one of the reasons you might want to use the Cells object.

There are two tricky parts to a Cells reference. The first one is that instead of using a letter to specify a column, you use a number or numeric expression. This is actually a big advantage, because it lets you use variables and other expressions that can be evaluated as numbers. It takes some getting used to, however. The second trick is that the row comes first. When talking about cell B7, the letter B refers to the column and the number 7 refers to the row, so you're used to seeing it the other way around: row first. Referring to the same cell using the Cells method looks like this:

```
Cells(7, 2)
```

VBA thinks of this as the cell in the seventh row, second column. You, can, by the way, get away with using letters for the column part of a cell reference and replace the 2 with a **"B"** (including the quotation marks). But then you couldn't create code like the following:

```
Sub MultiplicationTable()
    For rws = 1 To 10
        For cols = 1 To 10
            Cells(rws, cols).Value = rws * cols
        Next cols
    Next rws
End Sub
```

Speaking of *Cells*

The syntax for the *Cells* method that returns a single cell is

```
object.Cells(RowIndex, ColumnIndex)
```

where *object* is a an optional reference to the worksheet where the cell can be found, and *RowIndex* and *ColumnIndex* are numeric expressions for the row and column of the desired cell.

code This procedure fills in a 10 × 10 block of cells with a multiplication table. By using a nested loop, it systematically goes through each cell in the block. To understand how this works, let's first look at the middle line.

```
Cells(rws, cols).Value = rws * cols
```

This line take two variables, `rws` and `cols`, and uses them to specify a cell. If `rws` is currently equal to 2 and `cols` is equal to 3, then `Cells(rws, cols)` picks out the cell in row 2 and column 3, which is B3. The value of this cell is set at `rws*cols` or 6 in this case. Thus, whenever the middle line is reached, the product of the two variables is put into the corresponding cell.

Now, how do the nested For/Next loops work? The first `For` statement starts the variable `rws` out at a value of 1. The very next line starts `cols` out at a value of 1 as well. The next line is the middle line which works as discussed above. Then, the `Next cols` statement is reached. When VBA reaches this line, it returns to the `For cols` statement and increases the value of `cols` to 2. The variable `rws` is still at 1. The middle line is run again with `cols` equal to 2 and `rws` equal to 1. The inner loop keeps repeating until `cols` reaches 10, while each time `rws` is still equal to 1. This fills in the entire first row.

When the inner loop has been run 10 times, it exits. This means that VBA goes on to the next line

```
Next rws
```

When this happens, VBA increases the value of `rws` to 2 and jumps back up to the beginning of the `rws` loop. Then the `cols` loop happens all over again, 10 times in all, filling in the second row in all 10 columns. The `rws` loop continues until all 10 rows are filled.

To learn more about ActiveCell, see Chapter 11, "How VBA Refers to Things in Excel."

One more way to refer to a single cell is by using the ActiveCell property. ActiveCell returns the active cell of the current window. ActiveCell will fail if a worksheet is not the active sheet.

Catch the bug

This procedure was supposed to put the text hello into the first five cells of row 3 of my worksheet. Why did it only put hello into the first cell?

```
Sub SayHello()
    For a = 1 To 5
        Cells(3, "a").Value = "hello"
    Next a
End Sub
```

Answer: The variable a ranges from 1 to 5 during the iterations of the loop. For each value of a the middle line of code is run.

```
Cells(3, "a").Value = "hello"
```

This line is the source of the trouble. Rather than varying columns on each round of the loop, it keeps writing "hello" *in the first column. This is because the second argument of the Cells method is* "a" *instead of a. The quotation marks tell Cells that "a" is actually a column with the name "a". Instead, I should have written it without quotation marks to indicate that I wanted the column associated with the value of the variable a.*

Referring to many cells

Both the Cells and Range methods can return a reference to multiple cells. They are really different in this regard, though. Cells is something of an all-or-nothing proposition; without an argument, it will return all the cells in a worksheet. This can be useful if you need to do something to every cell, like changing the font. For example, this statement sets the bold property to true for all cells in Sheet1.

```
Worksheets("Sheet1").Cells.Font.Bold = True
```

The Range method has much more versatility. You can use it to select a rectangular block of cells, to select several individual cells, or a combination of the two. Rectangular blocks of cells are specified by using a starting cell and an ending cell and separating them with a colon. The following statement selects the cells shown in figure 12.1.

```
Range("B4:E6").Select
```

Fig. 12.1

Just give the top left and bottom right corners of a rectangular block of cells to the range method, and it will know you're talking about the entire range.

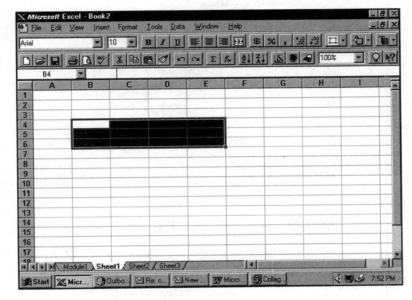

Another way to use the range method is to give different cells separated by commas. The line

```
Range("a1,b2,c1,d2").Select
```

selects four cells: A1, B2, C1 and D2. Notice that the quotation marks surround the entire list of cells, not each individual cell.

You can combine these two techniques to use the Range method to select any combination of rectangular ranges and individual cells. The following code selects the two different rectangular ranges shown in figure 12.2.

```
Range("A2:C4,D8:F:15").Select
```

Fig. 12.2
Range objects don't
have to be rectangular.
Any combination of
cells can be expressed
as a range object.

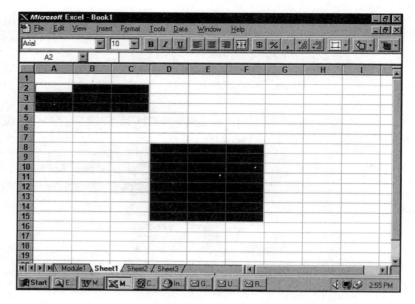

Rows and columns

A useful kind of range object is an entire row or column. Thus, there are methods designed to allow you to refer to them.

The Rows method allows you to pick out an entire row on a worksheet, or the row of a certain range. If you don't specify an object, then the Rows method will assume you're talking about the active sheet. If this isn't a worksheet, the method will fail. This statement

```
Rows(4).Select
```

selects all of row 4 on a worksheet.

Speaking of *Rows*

The syntax of the Rows method is

```
object.Rows(index)
```

where *object* is optional and can be a worksheet or a range, and *index* is the number of the row to be returned.

If a range is specified, then the method works a little differently. When counting rows, the first row is the one that's on top of the range. For example,

```
Range("B3:G7").Rows(2).Select
```

will select the second row of the range B3:G7. This turns out to be the range B4:G4, as shown in figure 12.3.

Fig. 12.3
Use the Rows method to specify an entire row from a worksheet or just a row within a selected range.

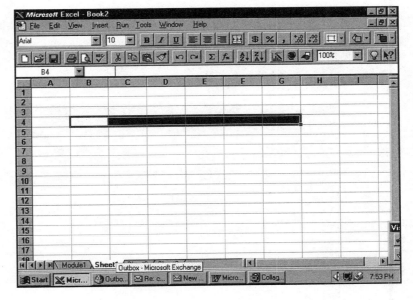

The Columns method works much like the Rows method. You can use a letter as the argument of the Columns method if you put it in quotation marks. So, to pick out the third column of a sheet you could use `Columns(3)` or `Columns("C")`.

Cells and ranges that have names

In Excel, you can name individual cells and ranges of cells. Once a cell or range is named, you can refer to it by name with the Range method. Just use the name where you would usually put the cell coordinates.

```
Range("Months")
```

returns a reference to the cell or range of cells called Months in the current worksheet.

You can name a cell or range of cells from a worksheet or in your code. To create a name from a worksheet:

1 Select the cell or range of cells that you want to name.

2 Choose Insert, Name, Define.

3 Type a name into the Define Name dialog box that appears and click on the OK button.

TIP **You can also define a name by selecting the cells and then** typing a name into the Name box. It's shown in figure 12.4; you can see Dannhardt, the name of the current selection. Make sure you press Enter after you type the name into the box.

Fig. 12.4
Select the cell or range you want to name, type a name for it in the Name box, and press Enter.

The Name box

How can I use this in the real world?

Often, cells get moved around in a worksheet. If you write a procedure that works with cell A3 and this cell gets moved to a different place on the worksheet, your procedure will still affect cell A3, even though it's no longer really the same cell. Named cells, on the other hand, keep their names if they are moved to a new place. If your code refers to them by name rather than by position, it will find them regardless of where they are in the worksheet.

Referring to a range's position relative to your current selection

We're back to the old relative references problem. What if you want your procedure to perform actions not on cells that are in a certain place, but rather in places relative to what is selected? You might want a macro that starts at the current selection and fills it and the next 11 cells in the column with the names of the months, and then goes on to put in values in the column next to it.

To learn about how to use relative references in your macros, see Chapter 1, "The Macro Recorder."

ActiveCell and Selection give you two ways to locate the current selection, but where do you go from there? That's where the Offset method comes in. The **Offset method** allows you to specify cells or ranges by saying how many rows and columns they are from a particular cell or range.

The offset numbers specify how far from the original range object the offset object should be. As a simple example,

```
Range("A3").Offset(1,1)
```

will return the cell B4, because it is offset one cell to the right and one cell below A3. You can also offset by negative amounts to offset to the left and above. Thus,

```
Range("D4").Offset(-2,-1)
```

will return the cell B3 which is two rows above and one column to the left. Here's a procedure that puts text in cells relative to the currently active cell. It needs to be run from within a worksheet.

Speaking of *Offset*

The syntax for the Offset method is

```
object.Offset(rowOffset, columnOffset)
```

A range object must be specified for *object* and numbers for *rowOffset* and *columnOffset*. The type of range returned by the Offset method is determined by the type of range provided as the *object*.

```
Sub UsesOffset()
    ActiveCell.Value = "Center"
    ActiveCell.Offset(1, 0).Value = "South"
    ActiveCell.Offset(0, -1).Value = "West"
    ActiveCell.Offset(-1, 1).Value = "Northeast"
End Sub
```

 This procedure starts by putting the text Center in the active cell. The following three lines put text in several of the cells surrounding the active cell.

Notice that the active cell remains constant throughout the procedure. The Offset method puts data into different cells, but these cells do not become the active cell. The one that was selected when the procedure started running remains active throughout.

You can also use Offset to specify several cells in a range. This line of code starts out with a rectangular range and then offsets it.

```
Range("A1:C5").Offset(5, 10)
```

The Range A1:C5 is a 15-cell range. The offset moves it down five rows and to the right by 10 rows. The resulting range is K6:M10.

What can I do with cells other than change the value?

There's no doubt about it—a cell's value is definitely its most popular property. However, there are other properties of cells and ranges that you will find useful:

- The Formula property can return the formula of a single cell or set the formula for a cell or a group of cells.

- The Row property of a cell will return a range object that is the entire row that the cell is in. You can also use this property with a multi-cell range to return the row that is the topmost of the range.

- The Column property returns the column of a cell or the left-most column of a range of cells.

To learn how to use the online help, see Chapter 6, "VBA Information Online."

You can find a complete list of the properties and methods of a range object by looking up **Range** in the VBA online help.

Q&A What's the difference between the formula and the value of a cell?

Suppose a cell contains a formula `"=A1+27"` and that the value of cell A1 is 4. The value property of this cell will return 31, whereas the formula property will return the actual formula used to compute this result: `"=A1+27"`.

Range objects are also containers for other objects, such as Font objects. A **Font** object has many different properties you can set, such as Bold and Underline. This procedure, run from within a worksheet, will make changes to the font object of the currently selected range.

```
Sub FormatCells()
    Selection.Font.Bold = True
    Selection.Font.Underline = xlDouble
End Sub
```

This procedure uses `Selection` to return a range object. Then `Font` returns the font object contained in that range object. Font has the properties `True` and `xlDouble`. These properties are assigned the values of `True` and `xlDouble`, respectively. The procedure takes the selected cells and makes the text in them bold with a double underline.

TIP **Using the macro recorder is a great way to find out about the** different properties and constants that are used to work with font objects.

To learn how to use Excel's online Help, see Chapter 6, "VBA Information Online."

To get more ideas about what you can do with range objects, have a look at the Object Browser and the Object Model. You can access both of these through the Index page of Excel's online help.

Summary

This chapter taught you the different kinds of methods and properties that you can use to refer to cells and ranges. By specifying a cell or range, you can bring the data into VBA to work with in a procedure, or use VBA to assign values, formula or formatting to cells and ranges.

Review questions

1 What kind of VBA object would you use to refer to a single cell?

2 What two methods could you use to return a single cell?

3 How can you select an entire row?

4 What method would you use if you wanted to specify a cell by using variables for its row and column?

5 How can you name a range?

6 If you wanted to do something to the cell that was four cells to the right of the active cell, how would you refer to it?

Exercises

1 Create a procedure that selects cell A5 using the Range method.

2 Create a procedure that selects cell A5 using the Cells method.

3 Write a macro that takes the value of the active cell, multiplies it by 5, and then puts the value in the cell directly below the active cell.

4 Design a procedure that will format the cells in the second row of the current selection as bold.

5 Use a For/Next loop and the Cells method to create a procedure that fills in cells A1 through A50 with multiples of the number 7.

6 With the InputBox function and the Cells method, write a loop that prompts you five times to supply a name and writes these names in the first five cells of row C of your worksheet.

13

Working with Lists of Things

● **In this chapter:**

- ● What's an array, and why would I want to create one?

- ● Use a loop to work with each element in an array

- ● Make an array grow and shrink as needed

- ● Can I use an array to work with a worksheet range?

Since VBA doesn't have cells to act as storage containers, you can create arrays to store lists of values . . . . ▶

Much of the information you work with falls naturally into lists. You can list the months of the year, the population of each state, what you need to do this afternoon, or the birthdays of everyone in the office.

Lists are an important part of programming, too. VBA has very useful tools for creating lists and dealing with the individual items. If you've got some category of items that you would like to work with in a program, then this chapter is for you.

What is an array?

Excel is great tool for working with lists. You can put a list in a single column and format all of the elements in the list together, or select the list and sort it. One of the reasons that Excel is a great place to work with lists is that it's already set up for them with rows and columns to store the items.

VBA can also work with lists. Since VBA doesn't have cells to act as storage containers, you need to create a place to store your list. You need an array.

 Plain English, please!

An **array** is a group of placeholders that can each take a value like a variable. All the placeholders are created together, but they can be used separately. **"**

Defining a simple array

To create an array, you must write a line of code just to declare it. With variables, you have a choice. You can declare them ahead of time, or just call them into existence when you need them. VBA isn't that flexible with arrays—you must declare them ahead of time. This can be done with a Dim statement.

Your declaration statement lets VBA know how many elements your array will have. This line creates an array with 14 elements:

```
Dim SalesReps(1 To 14)
```

In one line, you've effectively created 14 variables called SalesReps(1) up through SalesReps(14). You can now use these as you would any other variables.

You don't have to start at 1 in your array declaration. You can start at 0 instead. For example,

```
Dim Properties(0 To 5)
```

creates a **six-element array**. Properties(0) is the first element, then Properties(1), and so on.

TIP **If your array starts at 0, you can leave out the 0 and just give the** *End* **value. This line declares the same six-element array as above, with elements numbered 0–5:**

```
Dim Properties(5)
```

To learn how to declare local, module-level, and global variables, see Chapter 8, "VBA Procedures."

Like variables, *where* you declare the array determines where it can be used. An array can be declared within a procedure, in which case it is local; it can only be used inside that procedure. You can also declare it near the top of a module, above all your procedures. Then it can be used in any procedure in the module. Or, you can declare a global array that can be used from any module. Declaring arrays to be local, module-level, or global works just like declaring variables.

Speaking of *Dim*

When using Dim to declare an array, the syntax is

```
Dim ArrayName(Start to End) [As Type]
```

where *Start* and *End* are integers that determine the range of numbers used to identify elements in the array. *Start* and *End* must be numbers or numeric-valued constants. As *Type* is optional and allows you to specify which type of data will be accepted for each array element.

Catch the bug

What's wrong with this array procedure?

```
Sub BadArray()
    UpperLimit = 15
    Dim MyArray(1 To UpperLimit)
    MyArray(1) = 34.6
    MyArray(3) = "monkey"
End Sub
```

Answer: You can't use a variable in a Dim statement. Only integer-valued constants and integers can be used. Replace UpperLimit *with 15, or declare* UpperLimit *as a constant to fix the procedure.*

Assigning values to array elements

Once you've declared your array, each element is an independent placeholder for whatever value you'd like to store there. Here's a procedure that creates an array and assigns values to each of the elements in that array:

```
Sub SampleArrays()
    Dim FirstArray(1 To 5)
    FirstArray(1) = "Jerry"
    FirstArray(5) = "Cosmo"
    FirstArray(2) = "Elaine"
    FirstArray(4) = 256.46
    FirstArray(3) = FirstArray(1)
    MsgBox "The second element in this array is: " &
FirstArray(2)
End Sub
```

SampleArrays declares an array called FirstArray with five elements. The next five lines assign values to each of the array elements. Notice that these values aren't assigned in order and aren't even the same kind of data. One is a number, three are text values, and one element gets the value of another element assigned to it.

The message box in figure 13.1 appears, showing the value of the second element of the array.

Fig. 13.1
The second element of
FirstArray has the value
"Elaine".

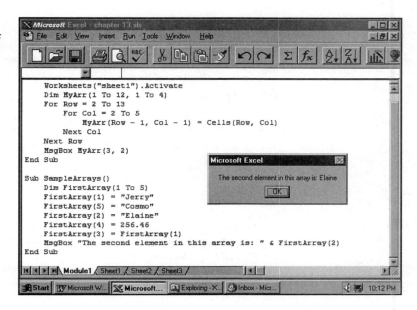

The `FirstArray` example assigned different types of data to each array element. Often, you'll know ahead of time that each array element will take the same kind of value. You might create an array that stores the gross sales of your company in whole dollars for each month of the year. Then the value of each array element will be an integer. You can specify the kind of data your array will accept the same way you would for a variable.

```
Dim GrossSales(1 to 12) As Integer
```

This declaration creates a 12-element array. Each element will accept an integer value.

Referring to array elements

When you declare an array, you effectively create many variables in one fell swoop. This is not the primary advantage of an array, however. What's really useful is the fact that you can refer to each of the elements of an array by its index number. What's more, you don't need to write the number itself, just provide an expression that has the value of the number you want.

Plain English, please!

The **index number** of an array element is the number in parentheses that specifies which element of the array you're referring to. In the expression Friends(2), the number 2 is the index. **,,**

This means that, when writing your code, you don't need to specify which element of the array you're talking about. You can use a variable that will determine the element.

```
Sub MyFriends()
    Dim Friends(1 To 4)
    Friends(1) = "Phoebe"
    Friends(2) = "Ross"
    Friends(3) = "Joey"
    Friends(4) = "Marcel"
    Answer = InputBox("Enter a number between 1 and 4")
    MsgBox Friends(Answer)
End Sub
```

The MyFriends procedure creates an array called Friends with four elements. A text string is assigned to each of the elements. Then an input box appears, prompting the user to enter a number between 1 and 4. The number entered is assigned to the variable Answer.

A message box appears. The text in this message box will be the value of one of the array elements. The one displayed will depend on the value of the variable Answer.

 I tried running the MyFriends program, and I got an error that said Subscript out of range. *What does that mean?*

If you enter a number that isn't in the range of values for the index of the array, then VBA will produce this error. If you enter something that isn't a whole number at all, you'll get a type mismatch error instead.

Remember that in the Dim statement, you *cannot* use a variable to specify the size of the array. You must use integers or integer-valued constants for both the *Start* and *End* values.

Loops and arrays work great together

Forget about arrays for a minute. Instead, suppose you wanted to create a program that displays an input box and stores the result the user enters 10 times. You need 10 variables, each one to store the user's input. What's more, you'll need to create 10 lines of code to collect the input, because there's no way to create a loop that will use a different variable each time.

Between the 10 variable declarations and the 10 assignment statements, you've got quite a long program on your hands, without having it do that much. Fortunately, you can use an array and a loop to achieve the same results with just six lines of code. What's more, the stored data is in a much more useful form.

```
Sub StoreTen()
    Dim MyArray(1 To 10)
    For n = 1 To 10
        MyArray(n) = InputBox("Enter the next value")
    Next n
End Sub
```

 The declaration statement at the beginning of this procedure creates an array with 10 elements. The loop that follows runs 10 times, one for each value of n between 1 and 10. On each iteration of the loop, an input box is displayed on the line:

```
MyArray(n) = InputBox("Enter the next value")
```

Whatever is typed into this box is assigned to one of the array elements. The array element depends on how many times the loop has repeated. On round one, MyArray(1) is assigned, on round two MyArray(2), and so on.

Assigning values to the elements of an array is only one of the uses for a loop. You can also perform calculations, find the member of the array that matches a certain criterion, or copy the information from the array into a range of worksheet cells. Whenever you need to do something similar to each element in an array, think about implementing a loop for the task.

What if I don't know the size of my array beforehand?

It can be hard to know ahead of time exactly how many items you're going to put onto a list. When you write a to-do list, for example, you want to keep adding items to the list until you can't think of any more. You don't know how many that will be. It could be five or 50.

Lists grow, too. You might know how many items are on a list to start with, but later you could find that you want to add more. To accommodate lists that don't have a fixed number of elements, you need a dynamic array.

 Plain English, please!

A **dynamic array** is simply an array whose size is not predetermined. To use it, you specify a size, and then it acts just like any other array. **"**

A dynamic array doesn't have a fixed size

A dynamic array is declared just like any other kind of array: with a Dim, Public, or Static statement. The only difference is that you put nothing in the parentheses where you'd usually specify the size of the array. Here's the declaration for a dynamic array called ShoppingList:

```
Dim ShoppingList()
```

With this line, you create an array but put off deciding how many elements the array will have. You will need to specify a size for the array before you can use it, but you can change this size several times throughout the program. This is done with a ReDim statement. For example,

```
ReDim ShoppingList(1 to 5)
```

sets the size of the array to five elements. You can also use a variable in a ReDim statement to set the size of the array. This is something that you cannot do in a Dim statement.

```
Sub Shopping()
    Dim ShoppingList()
    ListSize = InputBox("How many items do you want to buy?")
    ReDim ShoppingList(1 To ListSize)
```

```
For n = 1 To ListSize
    ShoppingList(n) = InputBox("Enter an item")
Next n
End Sub
```

The `Shopping` procedure declares a dynamic array called `ShoppingList` with the line

```
Dim ShoppingList()
```

This procedure does not specify how large this array is. Instead, the user is required to enter a value in an input box to size the array. This value is stored in the variable `ListSize` and the array is then sized with a `ReDim` statement:

```
ReDim ShoppingList(1 To ListSize)
```

Now the array can be used to store values. The For/Next loop runs through each element of the array and prompts the user to enter a shopping item with an input box. The number of times this input box appears is determined by the value of `ListSize`, and the value entered each time is stored in the corresponding array element.

Catch the bug

Why does this procedure provide a `Subscript out of Range` error message?

```
Sub BadShopping()
    Dim ShoppingList()
    ShoppingList(1) = "soy milk"
    ShoppingList(2) = "pickled herring"
End Sub
```

Answer: *You can't assign values to a dynamic array until you pick a size for it with the ReDim statement. You could fix this code by inserting the statement*

```
ReDim ShoppingList(1 to 2)
```

after the Dim statement. You can still change the size of the array later if you want.

How can I change the size of an array once it's set?

When you've declared an array as dynamic, you can use the ReDim statement on it many times. Each time, the ReDim statement will change the size of the array for you. The second time you use the ReDim statement to size an array, it can be done just like the first time. The following procedure creates a dynamic array, sizes it to 11 (from 0 to 10) elements using ReDim, and then sizes it to 21 elements using ReDim again.

```
Sub Resizer()
    Dim MyArray()
    ReDim MyArray(10)
    ReDim MyArray(20)
End Sub
```

When ReDim is used this way, it not only resizes the array but also erases any values that were stored in the array. If you had already stored anything in the array, it will be lost. To get around this, you can use the Preserve keyword in the ReDim statement. To resize an array from the above procedure without losing the values, you'd change the second ReDim statement to the following:

```
ReDim Preserve MyArray(20)
```

Preserve can only be used when you are enlarging the size of the array. Moreover, you can't use it when you're changing the start value of your array, only the end value. So you could not use it in the Resizer procedure like this:

```
ReDim Preserve MyArray (1 to 20)
```

because that changes the start index from 0 to 1. Only the end index may be changed, and then only to a larger number.

Here's an array that resizes every time the user adds a new element to it.

```
Sub KeepOnGrowing()
    Dim MyList()
    CurrentIndex = 0

    'get data from user for the array
    Do While MsgBox("Would you like to add another?",
    ➡vbYesNo) = vbYes
        ReDim Preserve MyList(CurrentIndex)
        MyList(CurrentIndex) = InputBox("Enter your
        ➡addition")
```

```
            CurrentIndex = CurrentIndex + 1
        Loop

        'display the values of the array elements
        For n = 0 To CurrentIndex - 1
            MsgBox "Item number " & n & " is: " & MyList(n)
        Next n
    End Sub
```

KeepOnGrowing creates a dynamic array called MyList and a variable called CurrentIndex which starts out at the value 0. The Do While loop is where values are assigned to the array elements. The test condition of the Do While loop is the return value of a message box. As long as the user keeps selecting the Yes button of this message box, the loop will repeat.

The first statement in the loop changes the size of the array to reflect the current value of the variable CurrentIndex. For the first iteration of the loop, this will be 0, creating a one-element array that starts and ends at the index 0. The next line displays an input box and assigns whatever is typed in it to the array element with the index CurrentIndex. This will always be the last element in the array—the one that was just added.

The value of CurrentIndex is then increased by one. VBA jumps back up to the first line of the loop. If the user selects Yes, the array is enlarged by one and the new element is assigned a value through the input box.

When the No button is selected by the user, VBA goes to the For Next loop at the bottom of the procedure. This runs through all the array elements from 0 to the last one that was created. A message box is used to display the value of each array element in turn.

If I'm not sure how many items there will ultimately be in my array, why not just make the array really big to start with to make sure I don't run out of room?

There are two reasons that this is often not a good idea. First of all, it's very convenient to know which items in your array are in use. In the KeepOnGrowing procedure, the second message box displays each of the elements in turn. If this were a 1,000–element array, you'd wind up with a lot of blank message boxes.

The other reason concerns computer resources. VBA must set aside memory for each array element. If your arrays are always much larger than they need to be, your programs will be slower and require more memory to run.

Multi-dimensional arrays

So far, the only arrays that have been discussed in this chapter have been **one-dimensional arrays**. This means that they consist of a simple list. You can think of a one-dimensional array like a line of cars. There's the first car, the second car, and so on up to the last car.

Now, suppose the cars are in a parking lot. The parking lot might have 10 rows with each row having 25 cars. Then, rather than talking about the first car, second car, and so on, you'd refer to a car as the first car in the first row, or the 15th car in the 7th row. This is what a **two-dimensional array** lets you do. One dimension is used to describe the row the car is in, and one dimension describes the position in that row. Two-dimensional arrays are also very much like worksheet ranges where the dimensions are the rows and columns.

You don't have to stop at two-dimensional arrays. Imagine parking your car in a multi-level parking garage. To locate it later, you'll need to know the level, the row, and the position on that row—a total of three dimensions.

These are just examples that show you how you might arrange data in categories. When you're creating multi-dimensional arrays in Excel, the arrays don't have to correspond to some physical reality. You could create a two-dimensional array where the first dimension relates to the month of the year and the second dimension is associated with a division of your company. Each array element will then by specified by a month and a division. An array element's value might consist of the sales for that month by that particular division.

Creating a multi-dimensional array

Suppose your company has four different divisions and each reports its monthly sales separately. If you want to write a program that deals with the sales figures from 1995, you can create a two-dimensional array where each element will store one month's sales for a particular division.

To create this array, you declare it with a second index:

```
Dim MonthSales(1 to 12, 1 to 4)
```

When you refer to an element of this array, you'll use one number to specify the month and one to specify the division. Thus, `MonthSales(4, 3)` would refer to the April sales of division 3. Each array element has its own value.

The MonthSales array can hold a total of 12×4 or 48 values: a value for each of four divisions in each of 12 months.

A three-dimensional array would be defined similarly, by adding another comma and index to the declaration statement.

Using arrays to work with ranges

For a worksheet, one of the most obvious uses of a two-dimensional array would be to work with a range of cells. If you want to preserve the original data in a range but manipulate the values in some kind of procedure, an array is a good way to do it. The worksheet in figure 13.2 shows the monthly sales by division.

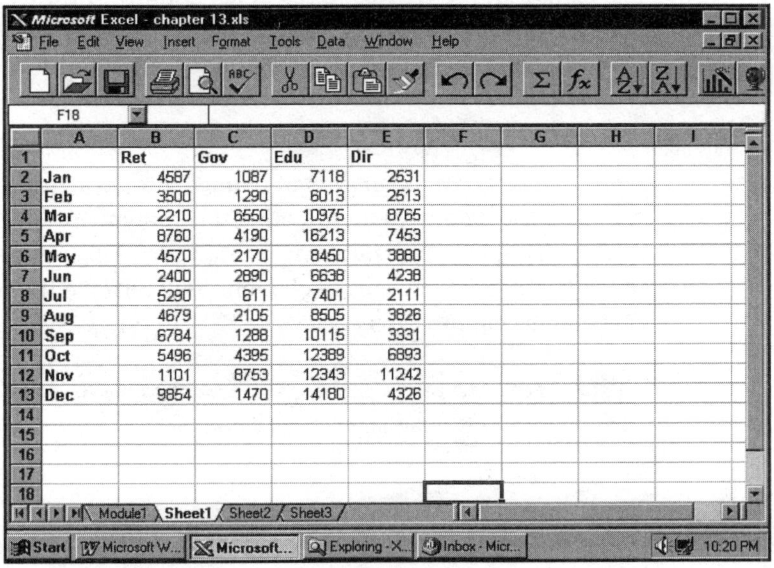

Fig. 13.2
The range B2:E13 contains data for monthly sales by division.

Here's a procedure that takes the values of cells and transfers them into array elements.

```
Sub ArrayMaker()
    Dim MyArr(1 To 12, 1 To 4)
    For Row = 2 To 13
        For Col = 2 To 5
            MyArr(Row - 1, Col - 1) = Cells(Row, Col).Value
        Next Col
    Next Row
End Sub
```

ArrayMaker creates a two-dimensional array. This array will store the values in the worksheet range B2:E13 in figure 13.2. Once the array has been declared, a nested loop goes through each of the cells in turn. The first loop starts

```
For Row = 2 to 13
```

so on the first iteration of the loop, Row will be equal to 2. The next line starts a second loop. On the first iteration of the loop, the first value of Col–2 will be used.

The next line uses the current values of Row and Col to assign the relevant cell values to the array elements. Notice that in the Cells method, the Row and Col values are used as-is. In the MyArr indexes, however, 1 is subtracted from each of these. This is to accommodate for the fact that you want the value in cell B2 to go into the array element MyArr(1, 1).

The loop repeats for each cell in the range.

Once you've got the contents of a range into an array, you can do what you like with the data without affecting the contents of the worksheet itself. For example, you might create a projection for 1996 by running another loop that used the value of each array element to determine the probable sales for that division in that month next year.

TIP You can also do things the other way around and copy the contents of an array into a worksheet.

What about changing the size of multi-dimensional arrays?

Arrays that are declared as dynamic can be single- or multi-dimensional. You can even change a single-dimensional array to a multi-dimensional one with another ReDim statement.

VBA is rather restrictive with the use of Preserve when resizing dynamic arrays. If you are only changing the last dimension of the array by increasing its end value, you can use Preserve to retain the array's values. Otherwise, the use of Preserve will cause an error.

```
Sub ChangeArrays()
    Dim MyArray()
    ReDim MyArray(1 To 4)
    ReDim MyArray(1 To 3, 1 To 4)
    ReDim Preserve MyArray(1 To 3, 1 To 7)
End Sub
```

The `Dim` statement creates a dynamic array. The first `ReDim` statement turns it into a one-dimensional array. The second `ReDim` statement turns it into a two-dimensional array. There were no values stored in the array between these two statements, but if there were, they would have been deleted.

The final `ReDim` statement enlarges the two-dimensional array by increasing the end value of the last dimension. `Preserve` is used in this statement, and if there had been any values in the variable prior to this line running, they would be maintained.

Summary

In this chapter, you learned that lists of things can be stored in VBA by using arrays. Arrays come in single and multiple dimension varieties, depending on the data needed to be stored. You can change the size of an array while a program is running, but you must take special steps to preserve the data stored in that array. Finally, you learned that since the elements of an array are numbered, loops are very useful for writing code that will affect each element of an array in turn.

Review questions

1 What is an array? An element? An array index number?

2 How many elements are in the array created by this Dim statement?

```
Dim HowMany(15)
```

3 When would you want to use a dynamic array?

4 If you have a dynamic array called LabData with 300 elements and you run this statement:

```
ReDim LabData(500)
```

what two things happen to the array?

To learn how to use the Cells method, see Chapter 12, "Getting Information Into and Out of Worksheets."

5 If you wanted to transfer the contents of a rectangular range of spreadsheet cells into VBA, how could you do it?

Exercises

1 Change the SampleArrays program so that it has six elements instead of five. Assign a value to the new array element you created.

2 Change the MyFriends procedure so that `Friends` is a dynamic array. (Hint: Don't forget to use a ReDim statement before you start assigning values.)

3 Write a procedure that creates a 25-element array. Use a For/Next loop to assign a value to each element. Assign the value of the square root of 1 to the first element, the square root of 2 to the second element, and so on.

4 Create a module-level, two-dimensional array for storing the names of the families that live in an apartment building. Let one dimension specify the floor of the building and the other the apartment number. Write a procedure that prompts the user for the floor number, then prompts the user for the apartment number, and then displays an input box to accept the name of the family that lives in that apartment on that floor.

5 Declare a dynamic array and then set its size to five elements. Use a loop and an input box to assign values to each of these elements, display a message box that asks whether to add another five elements to the array or not. If the answer is Yes, add another five elements to the array without destroying the original values.

14

Fixing Your Code: VBA's Debugging Tools

● **In this chapter:**

- **How to test a line of code before putting it in a macro**

- **How can I determine which line of my procedure is causing a problem?**

- **Figure out what values a variable has in the middle of a procedure**

- **Tracking expressions to see where things are going wrong**

- **Can I make my program pause in the middle so I can see what's happening then?**

You've written a program and it runs—but not the way you expected. Now what? . . . . ▷

I magine that you've written a program that calculates auto insurance rates. It collects information on age and driving record and then displays the insurance rate for such a driver. It never crashes, it's easy to use, and it looks great. There's just one, tiny problem. It keeps saying that 20-year-old male drivers with five tickets get the best insurance rates.

There are mistakes that VBA catches for you right away by generating a syntax error. These are usually easy to correct. You know exactly where they are, and when they're fixed, you can tell right away.

Another kind of problem is when VBA lets you enter each individual line but then produces an error when you try to run it. Usually, these aren't too bad, because you can get VBA to show you which line caused the problem.

The most insidious kind of programming problem is one that lets your code run but doesn't produce the results you expect, like the auto insurance program described above. As far as VBA is concerned, there is no problem. You instructed it to do certain tasks and it carried them out literally. VBA does what you say, not what you mean. Now you need to figure out exactly where your instructions were misleading. This is where VBA's debugging tools are really valuable.

Introducing the Debug window

The Debug window is the home turf of VBA's debugging tools. You can display the Debug window from within a module sheet by choosing View, Debug Window. Pressing Ctrl+G will also work.

The Debug window is divided into two panes. The lower one is called the **code pane**. It shows code from the current module sheet. The upper one can display one of two different panes, Watch or Immediate. You can switch between them by clicking on their tabs at the top of the pane. Figure 14.1 shows the Debug window with the Immediate pane active.

So what does this thing do? The Debug window is actually a combination of several powerful tools that allow you to closely scrutinize your code:

- The Code pane works like a module sheet. When no procedure is running, you can use it to enter and edit code. In addition, it can take you through a procedure line by line, showing you which statement will be run next.

Fig. 14.1
The Debug window displays your code in the bottom half of the window and the Immediate or Watch pane in the top half.

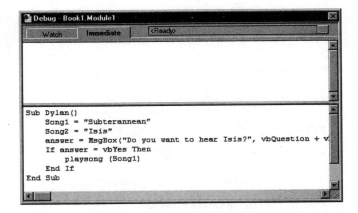

- The Immediate pane is a place to run single lines of code as a test, or to check the value of a certain variable. Things you type in the Immediate pane don't change your code as it is written in the module sheet, although they can affect the Excel environment or the value of a variable.

- The Watch pane lets you keep an eye on a value continuously. You can specify a variable or expression to watch, and its value will be updated in the Watch pane every time it changes.

There are a number of different ways that you can display the Debug window. The one you choose will depend on what you're using it for. For example, you can instruct your code to pause at a certain point and make the Debug window appear so that you can check out what's happening at that moment.

The Immediate pane

The Immediate pane lets you try out code without having to put it into a procedure. This is great if you want to try out a single line of code before having to use it in an entire procedure.

The code you type into the Immediate pane does not get put into your module sheet, but you can copy and paste code from the Immediate pane to a module sheet. So, if you had been experimenting with message boxes and found the right one, you could then copy and paste the line of code you'd written into a module.

You can't create procedures in the Immediate pane. You work one line at a time. If you try to use a Sub or Function statement, you'll get a message box explaining that it is invalid to do so in the Immediate pane. However, you can call subroutines and functions that exist elsewhere.

You can use the Immediate pane to:

- Test a single line of code to see if it works

- Check the value of a variable

- Make changes to Excel objects using properties and methods

- Run a function or procedure

Entering commands into the Immediate pane

Suppose you're not sure how the exclamation icon will look in a message box. You'd like to try it out without creating a whole procedure. Here's how you could do it using the Immediate pane:

1 From a module sheet, choose <u>V</u>iew, <u>D</u>ebug Window.

2 Click on the Immediate tab to bring the Immediate window to the front. The Debug window should now look more or less like figure 14.1, although there may be different code or none at all in the code pane.

3 Enter the code line

```
MsgBox "Test", vbExclamation
```

in the Immediate pane.

4 Press Enter. The code runs, and a message box with an exclamation icon appears.

If you want to run this line of code again, you don't need to retype it. You can put your cursor anywhere on the line, even in the middle of a word, and press Enter. It will run again. The lines in the Immediate pane are not in any particular order. They are run when you put your cursor on the line and press Enter. You can hop around from line to line and run them in whatever order you like.

Although the code you enter in the Immediate pane doesn't get saved to a module sheet, the values you enter there will stick around while the Debug window is active. Type **x=4** on a new line in the Immediate pane and press Enter. You don't see anything, but the value 4 was assigned to x. To see this, you can type **MsgBox x** on another line; it will display the value 4.

> **TIP**   **You can also run your subroutines from the Immediate pane.** Just type in the name of the procedure and arguments as you would on an ordinary line of code.

You can change the Excel environment from within the Immediate pane

The Immediate pane is a great place to experiment with Excel's objects. You can set properties and use methods from the Immediate pane. The effects will stay in place after the Immediate pane is closed (although they won't be saved when you quit Excel).

For example, the statement

```
Worksheets("Sheet1").visible = false
```

will hide the worksheet called Sheet1. You can bring it back easily: just go back up to the same line, change the word `false` to **true**, and press Enter.

How can I use this in the real world?

Sometimes it's convenient to be able to see code and a worksheet at the same time. You can use the Activate method on a worksheet to bring it to the front of the worksheets. For example, you can bring Sheet1 to the front of the workbook by entering

```
Worksheets("Sheet1").Activate
```

The Debug window will still be on top, but you'll be able to see the sheet behind it and to move the Debug window to the side to get a better picture of what's going on.

Displaying values

You can make the Immediate pane show you values of variables or properties. Previously, you may have been using MsgBox to do this, but sometimes it's quicker in the Immediate pane.

To display the value of a variable, use the Print statement. The statement

```
print y
```

will make the current value of y appear. If y hasn't had a value assigned to it, a blank line will appear.

> **TIP** Instead of using the Print statement, you can use a question mark (?). It does exactly the same thing.

Figure 14.2 shows a number of statements that have been run in the Immediate pane. Although it's not required to run them in order, these statements were run from top to bottom one after another.

Type in these two lines...   *...then this one appears automatically*

Fig. 14.2
In the Immediate pane, you can test out statements without having to run an entire procedure.

Now type in these two...

...and a new value for x is displayed

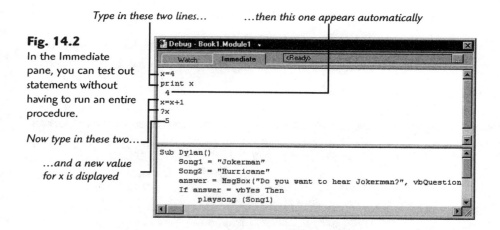

```
x=4
print x
 4
x=x+1
?x
 5
```

```
Sub Dylan()
    Song1 = "Jokerman"
    Song2 = "Hurricane"
    answer = MsgBox("Do you want to hear Jokerman?", vbQuestion
    If answer = vbYes Then
        playsong (Song1)
```

Later in this chapter, in the section "Step and use the Immediate pane together," you'll learn how to use the Immediate pane while a procedure is in the middle of running. This is often when you're most interested in the value of a variable. Somewhere, something is going wrong, and this is how you'll find out where.

Q&A *Can I use the Print statement in my module sheets, too?*

You can't print things from module sheets the way you do in the Immediate pane, but you can use the Debug.Print method to put a value into the Immediate pane. The statement

```
Debug.Print 5
```

in a module sheet will put 5 on a line in the Immediate pane, but you'll have to go there to look at it.

You can also display the value of a property setting. This can be the value of a cell in a worksheet or the name of a menu item. For example, the following statement will tell you what's in cell B5 of Sheet1 in the active workbook.

```
?worksheets("sheet1").range("b5").value
```

TIP **Another way to see the current value of a variable or** expression is with the Instant Watch feature. Select the variable or expression and then choose Tools, Instant Watch or click the Instant Watch button on the VBA toolbar. A dialog box will appear displaying the current value.

Go through your code one line at a time

Sometimes a procedure doesn't work the way you envisioned. It might encounter a problem and refuse to run, or maybe it runs but it doesn't work as you expected it to. Going through your procedures one line at a time and checking that each line works as expected can help you to determine where things are going wrong.

To try this out, enter a simple procedure into a module sheet. Normally, you run a procedure by choosing Start from the Run menu or pressing F5 or clicking the Run button on the VBA toolbar. Instead, position your cursor in the procedure you wish to step into and do one of the following:

- Choose Step Into from the Run menu.

- Press the F8 key on your keyboard.

- Click on the Step Into button on the Visual Basic toolbar.

The Debug window appears with your procedure in the code pane. A rectangle surrounds the first line of the procedure. This means that this line is the one that will be run next. VBA is ready to run your procedure one line at a time.

Fig. 14.3
The Debug window says, "You Are Here" by putting a rectangle around the current line of code.

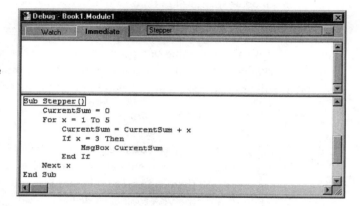

To run a line of your procedure, press F8 (or use the Step Into button on the Visual Basic toolbar). The statement that was outlined is run and the next one is outlined. Each time you press F8, another line will be run.

The Stepper procedure shown in figure 14.3 involves a loop. When VBA gets to the bottom of the loop, it keeps jumping back up to the top until x reaches the value 5. After the last line of code is run, the Debug window automatically closes.

TIP **Another way to step through a macro is to choose Tools, Macro** then select the name of the macro you wish to run and click on the Step button.

If you have a procedure that takes arguments, you won't be able to run it with the Step Into command. You can get around this by writing a macro that calls that procedure and then stepping into the macro.

For example, the macro

```
Sub RunsHypo()
    Hypo 5, 8
End Sub
```

simply runs a procedure called Hypo that takes two arguments. If you Step Into the RunsHypo macro, you'll be able to go through the Hypo procedure one line at a time with the values 5 and 8 passed to it.

Step and use the Immediate pane together

While you're stepping through a procedure, you can make use of the Immediate pane. You can use this to check the value of a variable or run additional lines of code while the procedure is running.

As an example, type this simple procedure into a module sheet:

```
Sub Message()
    x = 5
    MsgBox x
End Sub
```

Under normal circumstances, this procedure will produce a message box with the number 5 in it. With the Immediate pane, you can change the value that will be displayed right before it happens, by doing the following:

1 With the cursor anywhere in the Message procedure, press F8 to bring up the Debug window. A rectangle will be around the first line of the procedure, indicating that this is the next one that will be run.

2 Press F8 twice more. The first two lines of the procedure have been run, and the procedure is ready to display the message box.

3 Click your cursor in the Immediate pane. On a new line, type **?x** and press Enter. The Immediate pane will display the number 5, since that is the current value of x.

4 Type **x = "hello"** on a new line in the Immediate pane and press Enter. You've now changed the value of the variable x. Down in the code pane, the rectangle is still around the MsgBox line, waiting to run it.

5 Press F8. The MsgBox line will run, displaying the *new* value of x, the one you typed in the Immediate pane. The message box displays hello instead of 5.

While the Message procedure was running, you looked up the value of a variable and changed it. If there's a particular variable that you know you want to check several times over the course of a procedure, you can add a watch to it as described later in this chapter in the section, "Keeping an eye on a particular value."

Use Step Over when you know a procedure works

Many procedures call other procedures, such as this one:

```
Sub CallsOthers()
    x = 14
    y = AskForHeight
    Hypotenuse x, y
    MsgBox "The result has been calculated."
End Sub
```

The CallsOthers procedure calls a function and a subroutine that are defined elsewhere in the workbook. If you use the Step Into command to step through the CallsOthers procedure line by line, you'll wind up stepping through not only every line of the CallsOthers procedure, but also through every line of the AskForHeight function and Hypotenuse procedure. This may or may not be what you want.

You might be sure that AskForHeight works just fine. In that case, you'd like to run it all at once but still be able to step through the rest of the CallsOthers procedure. You can do this using the Step Over command.

 To step over the AskForHeight function, select Run, Step Over when the line calling the AskForHeight function has a box around it. You can also step over by pressing Shift+F8 or clicking the Step Over button on the Visual Basic toolbar.

Keeping an eye on a particular value

You can use Print statements in the Immediate pane to look at the value of a variable. However, you need to request the value of this variable each time you want to check it. This can be cumbersome if you want to check a variable several times or look at more than one variable at once. The alternative is to use the Watch pane of the Debug window. With the Watch pane, you can specify variables or other expressions that will have their values displayed at all times.

To select a variable to track using the Watch pane, select its name in your code. This can either be in a module sheet or in the code pane of the Debug window. Then choose Tools, Add Watch. The Add Watch dialog box appears.

Fig. 14.4

The Add Watch dialog box lets you select the expression you want to watch.

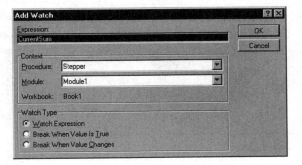

The Add Watch dialog box displays the name of the variable or expression you're going to keep an eye on, the procedure and module it's located in, and what type of watch you want. The Watch Expression type is the one you want. If you select the variable you want to watch before bringing up this dialog box, all of the choices should already be filled in the way you want them. Click OK to add the watch.

Here's a procedure that contains a loop.

```
Sub ElectionYear()
    FirstYear = 1992
    For n = 0 To 5
        Yr = FirstYear - 4 * n
        MsgBox Yr & " was an election year"
    Next n
End Sub
```

To add a watch to n (my counter variable) and to the variable Yr, do the following:

1 Enter the code into a module sheet.

2 Select Yr in the fourth line of the procedure and choose Tools, Add Watch. Select OK in the Add Watch dialog box.

3 Repeat step 2 for the variable n in the third line of the procedure.

4 With your cursor somewhere in the ElectionYear procedure, choose Run, Step Into.

Once you choose Step Into, the Debug window appears. If the Immediate pane is displayed, select the Watch pane so you can see the expressions for which you have set a watch. Figure 14.5 shows the Watch pane after the procedure has been through the loop twice.

Fig. 14.5
The Watch pane tells you the current value of watched expressions as you step through a procedure.

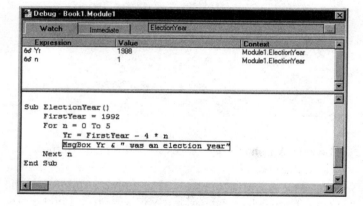

Step through the procedure as you normally would, by pressing F8 each time you want to go to the next line. As lines of code are run, you'll see the value of the variables changing in the Watch pane.

TIP **You can also add a watch to an entire expression. In the Election** Year procedure, you could add a watch to the expression Yr - 4 * n by selecting the entire expression and then choosing Tools, Add Watch.

Hold it right there! How to pause a procedure

The last tool in your bag of debugging tricks is a way to stop code in the middle of a procedure. Rather than using Step Into to go through each and every line of code, you can run a procedure right up to the place you wish to investigate and enter Break mode.

> 66 *Plain English, please!*
>
> **Break mode** is when VBA pauses in the middle of a program and displays the Debug window, waiting for you to take further action. 99

There are a number of different ways to enter Break mode:

- When you are stepping through a procedure, you're continuously in Break mode.

- Press the Esc key to stop a program that seems stuck and then click on the <u>D</u>ebug button in the dialog box that appears.

- When your program encounters an error and displays a message box like the one shown in figure 14.6, click on the <u>D</u>ebug button to enter Break mode.

Fig. 14.6
What better place to enter Break mode than right where an error has occurred?

All of these methods involve entering Break mode in a somewhat random place. Sometimes, you'll want to plan in advance where to enter Break mode. You might know where or about where your program is encountering difficulties and you want to direct VBA to hold up code execution at that point. This can be done by setting a breakpoint or using the Stop statement. These two methods of entering Break mode are discussed next.

Setting breakpoints

You can put a **breakpoint** into your code. When the code is run and Visual Basic encounters the breakpoint, it will enter Break mode and wait for further instructions.

To create a breakpoint, pick out the line where you want the procedure to stop running. All lines above this one will run, and then Excel will enter Break mode just before running the line.

 You set a breakpoint on a line by choosing <u>R</u>un, Toggle <u>B</u>reakpoint. Alternatively, you can set a breakpoint by pressing F9 or using the Toggle Breakpoint button on the Visual Basic toolbar.

When you do this, the line that has the breakpoint changes appearance by highlighting the line in brown and writing the text in white (if you have the default colors set). Figure 14.7 shows a procedure with a breakpoint set for the third line of code.

Fig. 14.7
Your breakpoints will stand out like sore thumbs: white text on a brown background.

```
End Sub

Sub Stepper()
    CurrentSum = 0
    For x = 1 To 5
        CurrentSum = CurrentSum + x
        If x = 3 Then
            MsgBox CurrentSum
        End If
    Next x
```

To remove a breakpoint, put your cursor on the line with the breakpoint and choose <u>R</u>un, Toggle <u>B</u>reakpoint again. Breakpoints also disappear when you close a workbook. Upon reopening the workbook, you'll find that your breakpoints are gone. If you want your breakpoints to stick around for a few sessions of Excel, try using the Stop command instead, as discussed in the next section.

Use the Stop command

Another way to enter Break mode is with the Stop command. When VBA encounters the Stop statement, it will stop running the procedure and enter Break mode with the next line of code outlined as the current one.

The difference between the Stop command and a breakpoint is that a Stop command will be saved with a workbook. If you are going to want to enter

Break mode at a certain point on a regular basis, it can be useful to use Stop so that you don't have to keep resetting your breakpoints.

Summary

In this chapter, you learned that there are a variety of tools in VBA that allow you to investigate your code closely. They are all available through the Debug window. The Immediate pane allows you to run single lines of code that aren't part of any procedure. You can check the value of variables or other expressions there. By stepping through code, you can run it one line at a time or you can use breakpoints or Stop statements to stop a procedure at a certain point. Once your procedure is halted, you can use the Immediate or Watch panes to investigate the current status of your code.

Review questions

1 What is the Debug window?

2 What are the three panes of the Debug window?

3 How can you run a line of code without putting it into a procedure?

4 Name two ways to check the value of an expression while a procedure is running.

5 Why would you use the Step Over command?

6 How can you tell your program to stop running at a certain point and wait for you to give it further instructions?

Exercises

1 Without running or stepping into a procedure, display the Debug window.

2 Write a macro that's at least four or five lines long and changes a variable value once or twice. Use Step Into to run the macro one line at a time.

3 Set a breakpoint in the macro from Exercise 2. Run the procedure, and when it reaches the breakpoint, check the value of the variable.

4 Add a watch to the variable in the macro from Exercise 2. Step through the procedure one line at a time while watching the value change in the Watch pane.

15

Change the Menus: No Programming Required!

● **In this chapter:**

● Why would I want to change Excel's menus?

● How to add new items to menus— or even whole new menus

● Can I do fancy stuff like add lines and underline letters in my menus?

● I only want my co-worker to be able to access certain menu items. How do I hide the others?

● Help! I need to go back to the way things were

The Menu Editor lets you revamp your menus entirely—all without writing a single line of code . . . . ⊘

By using the macro recorder or writing VBA code or both, you can create amazing, extensive automated procedures. These all amount to nothing if you can't access them. One of the best ways to provide access to your programs is through the menus.

Have you ever considered why they're called menus? In a restaurant, how do you know what's available? You look at a menu. In Excel, users look to the menus for exactly the same reason. Making your macros available through menus makes them easy to find, easy to run, and allows you to organize them by category. If others will be using your macros, putting them on the menu is practically a must!

The Menu Editor

 You can make extensive modifications to your menus without ever writing a word of code. The tool that lets you achieve this is the Menu Editor (see fig. 15.1). Open it by choosing Tools, Menu Editor while in a module sheet. You can use the Visual Basic toolbar to display the Menu Editor. If the Visual Basic toolbar isn't visible, select View, Toolbars and then put a check mark next to Visual Basic on the list. After you click OK, the Visual Basic toolbar will appear, and you can then press the Menu Editor button.

Fig. 15.1
With the Menu Editor, you can change the contents of menus and add new menus, all without writing a single line of VBA code.

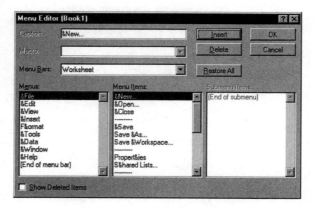

Q&A   ***Where is the Menu Editor? It's not in the Tools menu.***

Menu Editor only appears on the Tools menu when you're in a module sheet. You must either switch to a module sheet or use the Visual Basic toolbar to display the Menu Editor from within a worksheet.

With the Menu Editor, you can

- Add new menu items to existing menus

- Create new menus and contents for them

- Delete and hide menus (even the ones built into Excel!)

- Set up a macro to run when you choose a menu item

To learn how to affect menus with VBA code, see Chapter 16, "Using VBA to Work with Your Menus."

You can also add more functionality to your menus, such as putting check marks next to items to indicate whether or not they are active, or adding and removing menus and their contents during the course of a program. These extra features require VBA programming, however.

Some advice before you change menus

The great advantage of the Menu Editor is that it gives you extensive control over your menus without forcing you to learn new VBA programming. But power has its price! As useful as it is, the Menu Editor is not the best designed Excel component. It can be hard to understand and tricky to use correctly. There are also a couple of bugs in the Menu Editor that make it difficult to use. When you set up your menus the way you want them, everything will work well. But the route to getting there can be bumpy.

It is possible to use the Menu Editor to hide your existing menus, including the one that has the Menu Editor on it. Then what do you do? The picture looks bleak, but don't panic! There is a way out. The last section in this chapter discusses getting things back the way they were if something goes wrong. If you really go out of your way to make things difficult, you might need to read the next chapter to restore your menus to normal.

Don't let this scare you away from working with the Menu Editor, though. When you get the hang of its quirks, it'll be a great tool for customizing the Excel environment.

Here are some tips to help make things go smoothly:

- If you are the kind of person who likes to "wing it," consider following the step-by-step instructions in this chapter more closely than you normally do.

- Make a backup copy of your workbook before making changes to its menus. The changes are stored with the copy of the workbook. That way, if you want to get rid of all the changes you made, you'll have a "clean" copy of your work.

- Take your time and make changes gradually. Check out how one modification looks before adding another.

- Don't panic! Even if you delete every menu in sight and have no backup copy, the last section of this chapter and Chapter 16 tell you how to restore everything.

Where are changes stored?

When you change a menu using the Menu Editor, the changes are stored in the current workbook. Let's say you're working in a workbook called AUGUST.XLS. If you add a new item called Title to the Format menu, the new menu item appears there. But, it will also change the Format menu in all other open workbooks. The change is saved in AUGUST.XLS, and when you close that file, the changes in the other open workbooks go away. Open AUGUST.XLS, and the changes come back.

In other words, a customized menu in one workbook will affect the menus in all open workbooks. This can be a little disconcerting if you have special menu changes for one workbook that shouldn't apply to another workbook. If you have two different workbooks with different customized menus, you can get strange results as a combination of *both* sets of changes. Your best bet is to only open one workbook at a time with customized menus.

 TIP If you want to make menu changes that appear in *all* workbooks, make them in PERSONAL.XLS. Because it's always open (even though it's hidden), changes to this workbook appear in any workbook you open.

Another thing to remember is that there is a separate set of menus for different types of Excel sheets. Worksheets, charts, and modules all have their own set of menus. The File menu in a worksheet is similar to the File menu in a module sheet, but making changes to one doesn't make changes to the other.

You choose what menu category you want to affect in the Menu Bars dropdown list box of the Menu Editor.

 *Plain English, please!*

A **menu bar** is just the set of menu titles that appear in a particular type of Excel sheet. The Visual Basic Module menu bar, for example, consists of the File, Edit, View, Insert, Run, Tools, Window and Help menus. **99**

When you select the menu bar you want, the menus for that bar appear in the Menus list box. In figure 15.1, the Worksheet menu bar is chosen, and the Menus list box reflects the menus that appear when a worksheet is active.

I need to add an item to an existing menu

To learn how to add a menu item for a macro to the Tools menu, see Chapter 1, "Introducing Macros."

The simplest change you can make to a menu is to add a new item. You might already have been doing this by adding macros to the Tools menu, but you can add an item to *any* menu.

Often, when working in a worksheet, you'll want to display the Visual Basic toolbar. You can write a macro to do this.

How can I use this in the real world?

You can create a macro that prints a workbook at a particular laser printer in your office. This macro would be useful in any workbook, so store the macro in PERSONAL.XLS and add a menu item for it to PERSONAL.XLS as well.

Another macro might create a chart from data in a particular workbook. Because you don't want to use this macro on just any workbook, you should put into the workbook a menu item that controls this macro holding the data. Of course, if this workbook is open and you open a second workbook, the menu item will still be visible, but associating the menu item with the appropriate workbook helps the situation somewhat.

The following procedure will add a menu item for the macro to the View menu:

1 Choose Tools, Menu Editor, or click on the Menu Editor button on the Visual Basic toolbar. The Menu Editor dialog box appears.

2 Select Worksheet from the Menu Bars list box.

3 In the Menus list box, select &View (this is the menu you want to change). The meaning of the ampersand (&) is discussed in the section "Accelerator keys" later in this chapter. The contents of the View menu appear in the Menu Items list box.

4 To put the new menu item in, you need to insert a blank space in the menu. You're going to put it between the &Status Bar and &Toolbars items. To do this, click the &Toolbars item to prepare to insert a space. The Menu Editor should now look like figure 15.2. You have not yet made any changes to the menu, but you're about to.

Fig. 15.2
The Menu Editor is ready to make changes to the View menu.

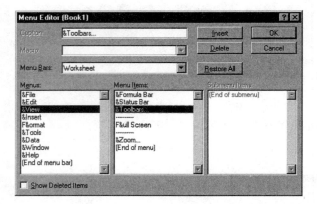

5 Click the Insert button. A blank space appears just above the &Toolbars item. This is where your new menu item will go.

6 Type **Visual Basic Bar** in the Caption text box.

7 Click OK. The Menu Editor closes (but it has noted your changes). A new item has been added to the View menu in your worksheets, as shown in figure 15.3.

Q&A *Why didn't my View menu change?*

Are you in a worksheet or a module sheet? The View menu you just changed is the one that appears when a worksheet is active.

Fig. 15.3
You can see the new Visual Basic Bar item on the <u>V</u>iew menu.

You've now added a menu item, but selecting it doesn't have any effect. The next few sections give you directions on making the new item functional and underlining a letter in the new menu item for a keyboard shortcut.

Separator bars

Take another look at figure 15.3 or at the <u>V</u>iew menu on your computer. There are two horizontal lines on the menu—one below the <u>T</u>oolbars item and one below the F<u>u</u>ll Screen item. These are called **separator bars**.

Separator bars are a good way to sort different types of menu items into categories. They are very easy to create. You do it by creating a phony menu item where you want the separator bar to go. Simply follow the procedure for inserting a new menu item, but give it a special name. In the Menu Editor dialog box, type a single hyphen (-) in the <u>C</u>aption text box. That's it. A separator bar will appear in that menu.

Cascaded menus

Figure 15.4 shows a cascaded menu that is a submenu of Cle<u>a</u>r. The cascaded part only appears when you select the Cle<u>a</u>r item. A triangle next to Cle<u>a</u>r is always present to indicate that a submenu is available.

Fig. 15.4
Cascaded menus let you combine several different commands under one general heading.

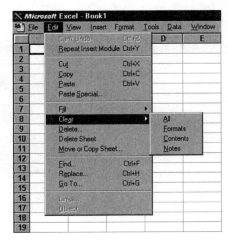

How do you create a submenu like the ones in figure 15.4? It's no big deal with the Menu Editor.

The first step to creating a cascaded menu is to create the original menu item (like the menu item Clear in fig. 15.4). Do this by following the same procedure used to create a new menu item earlier in this chapter. After you create the menu item, do the following:

1   From a module sheet, choose Tools, Menu Editor.

2   Select the same category you used for creating the original menu item in the Menu Bars list box (probably Worksheet, unless you got fancy).

3   Select the appropriate menu name in the Menus list box.

4   Your original item should appear in the Menu Items list box. Select it.

5   Click (End of Submenu) in the Submenu Items list box. This is where you will put all of the cascaded menu items.

Q&A   ***Why won't it let me click on (End of Submenu)?***

You probably haven't selected your own original menu item in the middle Menu Items list. You aren't allowed to add a submenu to one of Excel's built-in menu items.

6   Click Insert to put in a space.

7   Type the caption of your new menu item in the Caption text.

8   To add a second item to the submenu, repeat steps 5 through 7.

9   After you add all of the submenu items you want, click OK.

How can I use this in the real world?

If you have a number of macros that format a worksheet for different types of reports, create a menu item in the Format menu called Report. Have a submenu cascade from the Report menu, with items like Expense, Weekly, Monthly, and Annual.

Every menu name and every menu item should have an accelerator key. You'll thank me when you're trying to negotiate menus on the day your mouse dies!

Accelerator keys

 Plain English, please!

An **accelerator key**, sometimes known as a **hot key**, is an underlined letter in a menu or command name. This key provides a way to access that menu item or command name with the keyboard instead of the mouse.

Adding an accelerator key to a caption is simple. In the Caption text box of the Menu Editor dialog box, type an ampersand (**&**) before the letter you want to use as an accelerator key. That's it! Excel takes care of making this an underline and making it accessible from the keyboard. So, to create a menu item called Expense (with the letter x as the accelerator key), type **E&xpense** in the Caption text box.

 TIP   **Each menu item should have a *unique* accelerator key. If the first** letter of your item is already being used, pick another significant letter in its name.

Make the menu item do something

Menus with cascading submenus and accelerator keys are all very well and good, but they still don't do anything. To make your menus work, you need to attach code to them. The kind of code you're going to attach is a macro.

 Plain English, please!

Macro, as it is used here, means any VBA Sub procedure that does not require values to be sent to it. In other words, at the top of the macro's code, the parentheses are empty. All procedures created by the macro recorder fall into this category, but a macro can also be a Sub you wrote yourself in a module sheet.

You must first write or record your macro. When it's ready, run the Menu Editor. Select the menu bar, menu, menu item (and Sub item if necessary) to which you want to attach your macro. After you select the correct item, the Macro list box becomes active. This box only becomes active when you select a menu item you created. This prevents you from accidentally attaching a macro to one of Excel's built-in menus.

The Macro list box contains a list of available macros from all open workbooks. Select the macro you want to run when your menu item is chosen and press OK.

TIP **Select a macro from the current workbook or one from** PERSONAL.XLS to attach to your menu item. If you select one from another open workbook, Excel can't run that macro if the workbook containing the macro is later closed. Keep the menu item and its macro together!

Figure 15.5 shows the ShowVBBar macro being added to the Visual Basic Bar item created earlier.

Fig. 15.5
You create macros and menu items separately and then attach them in the Menu Editor.

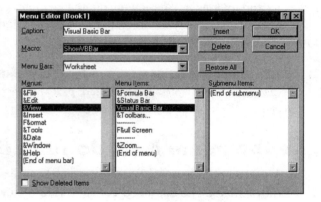

Make a new menu

You've created a small library of macros to use regularly. There are 15 that you would like to add to the menus, but where are you going to put them? Create an entirely new menu. Call it whatever seems appropriate. As usual, you can use the Menu Editor to do this with no programming required.

I don't know about you, but the first time I did this, I was very impressed. Here I am, creating my own menus and making my programs run just as if they were built-in to Excel. Figure 15.6 shows my menu, called Boonin, with several of my macros listed. These are macros I use in worksheets, so I made all the changes to the Worksheet menu bar.

Fig. 15.6
One way to organize your work is to make a menu that consists entirely of your macros.

Catch the bug

There's a hole in my menu! I was in the Menu Editor dialog box and I inserted a space on the F<u>o</u>rmat menu to put in my new menu item. I typed the name of the menu, **Buggy**, in the <u>C</u>aption text box and then clicked <u>I</u>nsert to put it in. When I checked the F<u>o</u>rmat menu, there was a hole above <u>B</u>uggy. Why did it do that?

A mysterious hole appeared in the Format menu.

Answer: In the Menu Editor dialog box, you click the <u>I</u>nsert button before you enter the name of a menu to create a space for it. Clicking the <u>I</u>nsert button after you type the caption inserts another space above the space created for the Buggy option.

You should click OK, but that has the unfortunate side effect of closing the Menu Editor dialog box. If you want to see your new item listed in place without clicking OK, try clicking a different item to see the changes before closing the Menu Editor.

The process for adding a menu is very similar to the process for adding a menu item. In the Menu Editor dialog box, perform these steps:

1 In the Menu Bars list box, select the category of menus you want to change.

2 Decide where you want your menu to appear (between what two existing menus). In the Menus list box, click the name of the existing menu you want your menu to precede.

3 Click Insert to put a blank space in the Menus list box for your new menu.

4 In the Caption text box, type the name for your menu. Make sure you include an accelerator key that's not used for any other menu in the list.

5 If you want to add menu items to your menu right away, then click the (End of Menu) item in the Menu Items list box. Then click Insert and proceed to add menu items as usual. You can do this step now or come back and do it later.

6 Click OK to accept the changes.

Here are some guidelines to help make your menus effective and easy to use:

• It's standard for File, Edit, and View to be the leftmost menu items, and for Window and Help to be the rightmost. Put your own menus somewhere between View and Window.

• If you're adding more than a few items to your menu, use separator bars to divide the items in your menu by category.

• Use cascaded menus sparingly. They can be difficult to navigate with the mouse, and they require an extra stroke when using the keyboard.

• Don't forget to use an accelerator key for each item in your menu and for each menu itself.

Removing and hiding menus and menu items

You've probably already noticed the Delete button in the Menu Editor dialog box. This button is both a powerful tool and a dangerous weapon. For something that important, Microsoft Excel hasn't done a great job of designing the feature. For example, if you inadvertently delete a menu you spent loads of time on, no message box appears to ask if you're sure. You can still press Cancel if you catch yourself in time, however. Also, although it seems like you can delete Excel's built-in menus, this isn't the case at all—they're just hidden. In the meantime, if you learn what's really going on with the Delete button, you can make judicious and effective use of it.

The procedure for hiding and deleting menus or menu items is to select the menu or menu item you want to hide or delete and then click the Delete button.

CAUTION The Restore All button puts menus back to the original state— that means you wind up with Excel's built-in menus only. All of your customizations are lost if you click Restore All.

Removing your own custom menus and items

In the course of working with the Menu Editor, you probably made some menu items or menus just as tests. Or, you mistakenly inserted a space where you don't want one. Remove the unwanted entry by clicking it and clicking the Delete button.

If you accidentally delete one of Excel's built-in menus and click on OK to accept the change, don't worry. You can easily get it back as described in the next section. If you accidentally delete one of your own menus or menu items and click on OK, then you'll have no such luck. However, any macros that were associated with this menu are unchanged. You only need to enter the menu items and attach the macros again. Whew!

Hiding Excel's built-in menus

If you click a built-in menu or menu item and click Delete, it will disappear. It hasn't actually been deleted, though. It's just hidden. To see the menu items and menu names that are hidden, select the Show Deleted Items check box. Any built-in menus you deleted are still there in gray text. To get them back, just click the item you want to bring back. The Delete button switches to Undelete. Click it to restore the item.

I once wondered what would happen if I changed the Visual Basic Module menu bar. I went ahead and deleted the Menu Editor item along with many other menu items. Then I closed the Menu Editor. Curiosity killed the programmer! Now what could I do? I couldn't get the Menu Editor back to restore the menu items because I'd hidden the menu item for the Menu Editor. This is a true story, and I spent a long time on the phone with Microsoft getting myself back on track.

To learn how to restore menus using VBA code, see Chapter 16, "Using VBA to Work with Your Menus."

This is about the toughest scrape you can get yourself into with the Menu Editor and even this one is reversible by entering the right VBA commands in a module sheet.

TIP   **If you get into trouble, always consider closing the file and going** back to your last saved version. You might lose some changes, but you'll also lose any problems that were caused by changes made since your last save.

Help! I want my original menus back!

In the Menu Editor dialog box is a tempting button called Restore All. It seems to promise a way back out of all difficulties. Let the clicker beware, though. Restore All will indeed return all of your menus back to the original state of Excel. But *all* menu customizations you made in this workbook—even if you made them months ago and saved them—will be deleted as well. If you were just fooling around with the Menu Editor and want to get rid of any and all changes you made, then this button is for you. But if you don't want to get rid of your custom menus, you can bring back all of Excel's built-in menus one at a time. Just select the Show Deleted Items check box, select the menu or menu item you want to restore, and click the Undelete button.

How can I use this in the real world?

Excel is a big program and it's easy for beginning users to get lost or confused. Often they wind up doing things inadvertently and don't know how to undo them. By hiding menu items that might lead users astray and providing them with your own ready-made macros, you can limit and control their environment. By protecting cells and ranges and hiding all but a few menu items, you can virtually assure that users will not lose or hurt important data or formulas in the sheet.

Summary

In this chapter, you learned how to add menus and menu items with the Menu Editor. You can attach any macro to a menu item you created and it will run automatically when you choose that item. You can create additional options with the Menu Editor, such as separator bars, accelerator keys, and cascaded menus. You also learned how to hide some or all of Excel's built-in menus and why you might want to do so.

Review questions

1 What is an accelerator key?

2 Can you permanently delete Excel's built-in menus and menu items?

3 How would you change the menus for your module sheets?

4 What kind of VBA code can you attach to a menu item?

5 If you open a workbook with changed menus, what happens when you open a new workbook?

Exercises

1 Add a menu item called Run Spot Run to the Run menu of the Visual Basic Module category of menu bars.

2 Add a new menu called Family to the Worksheet category of menu bars. Put it between the Format and Tools menus.

3 Add the names of the members of your family to the Family menu you created in Exercise 2. Put a separator bar somewhere on the menu.

4 Create submenu items for one of the family members you previously added. Take a look at the cascaded menu you created.

5 If you haven't already, create the Visual Basic Bar item in the View menu of your worksheets using the steps given earlier in this chapter. Record a macro that displays the Visual Basic toolbar and attach this macro to the menu item you created for it.

6 Delete all the menus you created in these exercises.

7 In the Worksheet category, use the <u>D</u>elete button to hide the entire <u>E</u>dit menu and some of the menu items of the <u>F</u>ile menu. Switch to a worksheet and look at the results. Go back to the Menu Editor and get the hidden items back one at a time (*without* using the <u>R</u>estore All button).

16

Using VBA to Work with Your Menus

● In this chapter:

- **You can *program* menu changes rather than use the Menu Editor**

- **How do I use VBA code to manipulate menus and menu items?**

- **Put a check mark next to a menu item when that feature is turned on**

- **How do I temporarily gray out an item on the menu?**

- **These two workbooks need to have different menus while they're open**

Using VBA to work with your menus will allow you to do things you couldn't accomplish with the Menu Editor alone . . . . . ⟩

Menus, menu items, and menu bars are all objects that can be controlled directly with VBA. Anything you can do with the Menu Editor, you can do with VBA—but you can also do much more. With the programming tools you're collecting, you can practically write your own application that rides on top of Excel.

Menus are the backbone of any application. If you are interested in pushing beyond the limits of Excel's traditional spreadsheet look, then this chapter is definitely for you.

What can VBA give me that the Menu Editor can't?

Using VBA to work with your menus will allow you to do things that you couldn't achieve with the Menu Editor alone. By using VBA you can:

- Make check marks appear next to menu items to show they're selected

- Have menu text appear as "grayed out" when the command is not available

- Change the caption of a menu or menu item during the course of a program

- Add and remove menu items in different contexts, such as when you activate a certain worksheet

- Create new menu bars

Another advantage of using VBA is that its results can be more predictable than those achieved with the Menu Editor. With the Menu Editor, customizing your menus in more than one workbook can cause confusion and mix-and-match menu schemes when more than one workbook is open. VBA gives you such precise control over your menus that you can have menu customizations appear only when a particular workbook is active. If it's open but another workbook is active, its menus can be ignored. This is impossible to do with just the Menu Editor.

How does VBA refer to menus and their contents?

Menus, their items, and the bars they are on are all Excel objects. To manipulate them in VBA you need to provide the right address for the object you want to work with. Every menu item is in a menu. Menus belong to a menu bar. Figure 16.1 shows the Worksheet menu bar with the View menu open so you can see the Full Screen menu item.

Fig. 16.1
A menu item is on a menu, which in turn is on a menu bar. The VBA code reflects this organization.

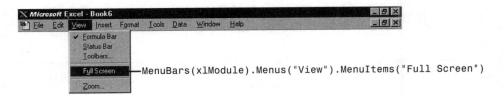

`—MenuBars(xlModule).Menus("View").MenuItems("Full Screen")`

To refer to the Full Screen menu item in VBA, use the following expression:

```
MenuBars(xlModule).Menus("View").MenuItems("Full Screen")
```

You specify menu bars by using Excel-defined constants. In the previous line of code, `xlModule` is a constant defined to be the correct value for the module sheet menu bar. The ones you'll encounter are shown in table 16.1.

Table 16.1   Excel's built-in menu bars

Menu Bar Constant	Context
xlModule	Appears when a module sheet is active
xlWorksheet	Appears when a worksheet is active
xlChart	Appears when a chart sheet is active
xlNoDocuments	Appears when no sheet is active (no documents are open)

To learn more about objects and collections, see Chapter 11, "How VBA Refers to Things in Excel."

You specify menus and menu items by their names, such as `Menus("View")`. Sometimes, you'll do something to the entire collection of menus or menu items, like adding a menu. In that case, leave off the name—you don't need to identify a particular menu when you are adding one to the collection.

Catch the bug

This procedure was supposed to add a menu to the module sheet menu bar, but it generates an error instead. What's the problem?

```
Sub AddMenu()
    MenuBars("xlModule").Menus.Add Caption:="Custom"
End Sub
```

Answer: *MenuBars are referred to by a constant, not by their name. The* xlModule *constant should not be in quotation marks. Remove the quotation marks, and the code will work.*

Adding and removing menus and their contents

The simplest menu changes involve adding and removing menus and their contents. You can do this with the Menu Editor, but not as well as you can with VBA. By writing code, you can add and remove menus dynamically—changing them in the context of the users' actions.

Speaking of *Menus.Add*

```
Menubars(menubar).menus.Add Caption:=menucaption
```

where *menubar* is one of the menubar constants, such as xlWorksheet or xlModule, and *caption* is a string designating the name of the menu to be added.

The following syntax is optional:

```
[, Before:=existingmenu][, Restore:=true/false]
```

You can append one or both of these optional syntaxes. Use Before to indicate which *existingmenu* it should precede. Use Restore:=True to restore a built-in Excel menu that you have deleted. The default for restore is False.

Adding and removing menus

When you add a menu, you need to specify which menu bar you're working on, then name the menus collection and use the Add method.

To learn about named and positional arguments, see Chapter 11, "How VBA Refers to Things in Excel."

Notice that named arguments are being used with Add instead of positional arguments. Because Add has several optional arguments, it's less confusing to specify the arguments by name, rather than worry about using the right number of commas.

To delete a menu, you must identify it by name. Notice the difference in the syntax between Add and Delete. Delete uses a name to specify a certain member of the menus collection, whereas Add does not.

Here's an example that adds a menu and removes it again. If you want to try it, run it in the module sheet because the menu bar it affects is the module sheet bar.

```
Sub AddAndDelete()
    MenuBars(xlModule).menus.Add Caption:="&Newmenu"
    MsgBox "Take a look at your menu"
    MenuBars(xlModule).menus("&Newmenu").Delete
End Sub
```

The first line of the body of this procedure adds a menu called <u>N</u>ewmenu to the Module Sheet menu bar. It gives no indication of where it should be placed, so VBA puts it in the default position—as the last menu before the <u>H</u>elp menu. The second line displays a message but will give you a chance to look at the menu bar before the third line is run. This line takes the menu away.

Don't be afraid to use the Delete method on built-in menus. You can't delete them permanently, even if you wanted to!

Speaking of *Menus.Delete*

```
Menubars(menubar).Menus(menuname).Delete
```

where *menubar* is one of the menubar constants and *menuname* is a string designating the name of the menu to be deleted.

Q&A *Why did I get an error message when I tried to delete a menu?*

To delete a particular menu, Excel needs to find it. If one part of your address for the menu is wrong, VBA can't find it to delete it. One common error is to enclose the name of the menubar constant in quotation marks. Or, if you ran the code that deletes the menu already, running it again will generate an error because that menu is no longer around to be deleted.

TIP **VBA creates accelerator keys for menus and menu items the same** way the Menu Editor does. Just type an ampersand (**&**) before the letter you want to underline when defining the caption.

Choosing where a menu winds up

You probably don't want all of your menus to be placed just before the <u>H</u>elp menu. Using `Before:=` with `Menu.Add` lets you specify where your menu will go. This line of code is the same as the one in the preceding example with the addition of `Before:=` to place it between the <u>I</u>nsert and <u>R</u>un menus.

```
MenuBars(xlModule).menus.Add Caption:="&Newmenu", Before:="Run"
```

Notice that to specify the Run menu, I used Run instead of &Run, which indicates the accelerator key. When you're identifying a menu, use of the accelerator key is optional. When you're creating a menu caption, you need to specify the accelerator key.

Use *Add* to restore a deleted built-in menu

You can use the delete method on a built-in Excel menu. However, just as with the Menu Editor, it's impossible to permanently delete these built-in menus. You can get them back with all of their contents intact by using the `Menus.Add` method.

There are a couple tricks to doing this successfully. If, for example, you delete your file menu and then type the following line of code:

```
MenuBars(xlModule).menus.Add Caption:="&File"
```

it will indeed put a menu called <u>F</u>ile on the menu bar. However, it won't be where you want it and it won't be the "real" <u>F</u>ile menu. Instead, it's just a customized menu that happens to have the same name as the original. It has no menu items, because none have been defined for it. To restore the original File menu and put it in the right place, the code you want is:

```
MenuBars(xlModule).menus.Add _
    Caption:="&File", Before:="Edit", Restore:=True
```

The `Restore:=True` part means that you're restoring a built-in menu. If you use this with a menu caption that is not a built-in menu or for a menu that hasn't been deleted, you'll get an error like the one in figure 16.2.

Fig. 16.2
You can't restore a built-in menu that hasn't been deleted yet!

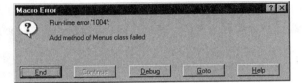

 TIP **Restore will bring back a menu and its contents, but you still need** to specify where to put it with `Before`. Otherwise, you'll wind up with the right built-in menu in the wrong place.

Adding and removing menu items

The VBA commands for adding and removing menu items are nearly identical to those for the menus themselves. The only difference is that the `MenuItems` collection is added to the statement.

Speaking of *MenuItems.Add*

```
Menubars(menubar).menus(menu).MenuItems.Add
    Caption:=menucaption
```

where *menubar* is one of the menu bar constants, such as `xlWorksheet` or `xlModule`, and *caption* is a string designating the name of the menu to be added.

The following syntax is optional:

```
[, Before:=existingmenu][, Restore:=true/false]
```

One or both of these optional syntaxes can be appended. Use `Before` to indicate which *existingmenu* it should be precede. Use `Restore:=True` to restore a built-in Excel menu that you have deleted. The default for Restore is False.

Notice that to add a menu item, the menu name was specified. Otherwise, how would Excel know where to put it? The name of the menu item is not given with the reference to the `MenuItems` collection, though. It's included as an argument at the end.

To delete a menu item, you need only refer to it specifically and then use the Delete method. Here's an example that deletes the <u>P</u>rint menu item from the <u>F</u>ile menu of the Worksheet menu bar:

```
MenuBars(xlWorksheet).Menus("file").MenuItems("Print...").Delete
```

Now make the menu items do something

Of course, you still need to attach code to the menu items you add to make them do anything. Just like with the Menu Editor, the idea is to write a macro (a Sub procedure that needs no values sent to it) that will run when a menu item is selected.

The best time to tell VBA what procedure a menu item will run is when you're creating the item. This is achieved by adding

> *OnAction:=*"*Procedure*"

at the end of the `Add` line where the menu item is created. *Procedure* can be any macro.

The following procedure only has one code statement in its body; it's just been broken into four lines, by using the underscore character (_).

```
Sub AddMenu()
    MenuBars(xlWorksheet).menus("View").MenuItems.Add _
    Caption:="&Visual Basic Toolbar", _
    Before:="Toolbars...", _
    OnAction:="ShowVBToolbar"
End Sub
```

This procedure adds a menu item to the View menu of the Worksheet menu bar. It gives it the caption <u>V</u>isual Basic Toolbar, positions it above the <u>T</u>oolbars item, and assigns it the procedure `ShowVBToolbar`. Whenever this menu item is selected, the procedure `ShowVBToolbar` will run.

Changing the look of menu items

While a program is running, it is sometimes helpful to change the way a menu item looks. Two simple and useful effects involve graying out items that are not currently available, and putting a check mark next to items that switch settings on and off.

Enabled

You can't use all commands at all times. Consider the Paste command. If you haven't cut or copied anything to the Clipboard, then there is nothing to paste. When this is the case, you don't want users choosing Paste in the Edit menu. To prevent them from doing this, you can disable the item. You make the item appear gray and not allow the user to select it. In figure 16.3, the last two menu items are disabled.

Fig. 16.3
Disabled menu items appear as faint gray text. Try as you might, you can't select a disabled item.

When a menu item is available for selection, like the Sort menu item in figure 16.2, it is **enabled**. Enabled is a property of a MenuItems object, which you can set to true or false. The default for this property is True. This line of code sets the enabled property of a custom menu item in the File menu to False:

```
MenuBars(xlModule).Menus("File").MenuItems("Backup").Enabled = False
```

To return the menu item to its normal enabled state, set the enabled property to True. If you reset the menu bar, this will also return the menu item to its original state.

You can only set the enabled property for custom menus. Excel takes care of whether its built-in menu items are enabled or not.

TIP   **If you want to make custom menu items temporarily unavailable** during a program, it's better to disable than to delete them. Users might become disoriented if menu items disappear altogether.

Check marks

Another easy feature to incorporate into your menu items is a check mark. Checked is a property of a MenuItems object (see fig. 16.4). Use a check mark for a menu item that switches something on and off, such as whether a toolbar is displayed. The check should appear when the setting is switched on and disappear when it's switched off.

Fig. 16.4
Check marks let you
see at a glance
whether a feature is
currently in use or not.

You can put check marks next to custom menu items or even next to built-in menu items. Run the following line to add a check to the File, Save menu item in the Worksheet menu bar:

```
MenuBars(xlWorksheet).Menus("File").MenuItems("Save").Checked=True
```

To remove it again, run a line of code that sets the property to False.

Notice that this changes the Save menu item in the File menu that appears in a worksheet. It will have no effect on the menus of a module sheet or other menu bar.

 ## How can I use this in the real world?

Do you have a custom toolbar you can display in Excel? If so, you can create a menu item for the View menu with the name of the toolbar. Selecting this menu item will display the toolbar if it is hidden or hide it if it is displayed. Whenever the toolbar is displayed, put a check next to the menu item. Remove it when the toolbar is hidden.

When and how many times do I change the menus?

You can issue a command to VBA to add a menu item. After you add this menu item, the menu item will appear unless you specifically remove it. If you save the workbook, close it and then open it again. The menu will still be there, just as if you'd added it with the Menu Editor.

Now suppose you run the command to add the menu item again. The menu item will be added a second time. You can wind up with multiple instances of the same menu item on a menu. Figure 16.5 shows the result of running such a line of code four times. It's probably not the result you want.

Fig. 16.5
Excel doesn't mind adding a duplicate menu item as many times as you care to run the code.

So, you need to think about where you're going to put a command that adds, deletes, or changes menus or menu items. It's okay to put these items in a piece of code that's run multiple times, just as long as you get rid of extra copies.

To learn how to make things happen automatically when a workbook opens, see Chapter 22, "Making Code Run Automatically."

One of the most common things you'll want to do when customizing your menus is to have a number of menu changes happen when a workbook is opened. For example, you might write a procedure that runs automatically when you open a workbook that adds a Macros menu with several items to your Worksheet menu bar. The first time you open your workbook, there's no problem. But what about the second time? The Macros menu will still be there from the first time you opened and saved it. If the code runs again, you'll get a second Macros menu.

There are several ways to solve this problem. One is to reset the menu bar.

Resetting the menu bar

Resetting a menu bar means eradicating any changes you made to it and going back to its original state. All of your custom additions will be taken out, and anything you might have deleted will be restored.

This example resets the Worksheet menu bar and adds a menu item called VB Toolbar to the View menu.

```
Sub AddVBBar()
    MenuBars(xlWorksheet).reset
    MenuBars(xlWorksheet).Menus("View").MenuItems.Add
Caption:="&VB Toolbar"
End Sub
```

If you run this procedure many times, you only wind up with one instance of the new menu item on your View menu. If, however, you delete the reset line and run it many times, each time will add another copy of VB Toolbar to the View menu.

Making menu changes specific to a single workbook

One of the really frustrating drawbacks of the Menu Editor is that a change you make to one workbook will affect any other open workbook. Again, there are a couple of different ways to solve this problem. The following code, when placed in one workbook for which you want to have custom menus, will solve the problem by making the menu changes only appear in that workbook. The workbook this code is in is called CUSTOMIZED.XLS.

Speaking of *Reset*

The general syntax of Reset for a menu bar is:

```
MenuBars(menubar).reset
```

where *menubar* is one of the Excel menu bar constants such as xlModule or xlWorksheet. Running this statement will reset all of the menus and their contents for the menu bar specified by *menubar*.

```
Sub PrepareBook()
  Application.OnWindow = "CancelChanges"
  Application.Windows("Customized.XLS").OnWindow="ChangeMenus"
End Sub

Sub ChangeMenus()
  MenuBars(xlModule).menus.Add Caption:="&Custom"
End Sub

Sub CancelChanges()
  MenuBars(xlWorksheet).Reset
  MenuBars(xlChart).Reset
  MenuBars(xlModule).Reset
  MenuBars(xlNoDocuments).Reset
End Sub
```

The first procedure, PrepareBook, is designed to be run whenever the book is opened. Its first line doesn't make any menu changes. Instead, it says that if at any time in the future a different window is selected, the CancelChanges sub should be run. The next line also doesn't make any changes to the menus, but says that if the CUSTOMIZED.XLS window is selected, then run the ChangeMenus sub. Chapter 22, "Making Code Run Automatically," discusses how to create code like this procedure and how to make it run on startup.

The ChangeMenus procedure adds a menu to the module sheet menu bar. You learn how to change this procedure to add or remove whatever menu items you choose. The CancelChanges procedure goes through each of the standard menu bars and cancels any changes made to the default settings.

How does it all work together? The first procedure should be set to run automatically on startup of the workbook. Then, any time a new window is selected after that (such as if another workbook is activated), appropriate action will be taken.

If a window other than the CUSTOMIZED.XLS workbook is chosen, then the CancelChanges procedure will be run, resetting all of its menus. If the CUSTOMIZED.XLS workbook is chosen, then the CancelChanges procedure will still run. However, it will be followed by the ChangeMenus procedure, which customizes the menus.

Summary

This chapter showed you ways to manipulate your menus beyond the capabilities of the Menu Editor. By writing code, you can create new menus and menu items, add special display features such as check marks, and make items disabled to prevent them being chosen when they are invalid. You also learned how to keep the changes to one workbook from affecting another. Finally, you learned how to reset menu bars, which will restore all menus to normal, regardless of what you might have deleted.

Review questions

1 Why would you make a menu item appear grayed out?

2 If you had a menu item called My Bar in the View menu of the worksheet menu bar, what code would you run to add a check mark to it?

3 In a line of code like this,

```
MenuBars(xlWorksheet).Menus("File").Delete
```

why do you use quotation marks when specifying the name of the menu, but not when for the menu bar?

4 What problem can you encounter if you write a procedure that adds a custom menu when you open a workbook?

5 What happens to Excel's built-in menus when you use the Reset method on a menu bar? What happens to your custom menus and menu items?

Exercises

1 Write a procedure that adds a menu called Test to the module sheet menu bar that. Put this menu between the Run and Tools menus.

2 Write a procedure that adds several menu items to the menu you created in Exercise 1. Attach a macro to at least one of these menu items.

3 Create a procedure that will change the state of a check mark. If a menu item is checked, it will uncheck it; if it is unchecked, it will check it.

4 In the section "Adding and removing menu items," an example was given of how to delete <u>P</u>rint from the <u>F</u>ile menu. Write a procedure that uses this statement, and then write another procedure that adds the <u>P</u>rint item back in.

5 Create a procedure that adds a menu item called <u>K</u>lemond to the <u>T</u>ools menu of the xlWorksheet menu bar. Make it so that the item will only be added if a menu item with this name doesn't already exist. (Hint: use a For/Each statement to look at each menu item.)

17

Toolbars

● **In this chapter:**

- **What's the advantage of using VBA with toolbars?**

- **Make toolbars look different in different workbooks**

- **How can I get my toolbars back to normal?**

- **Create your own toolbars**

- **How can I give a toolbar to someone else to use on another computer?**

Toolbars provide the ultimate mouse shortcut for running your macros. They're easy to use and enable you to run your programs with a single click. . . . . ▶

Excel didn't always have toolbars. But now it's hard to imagine Excel without them. It's not hard to see why they caught on the way they did. Toolbars give you an alternative to navigating menus and dialog boxes, often giving you access to something with a single click that could take quite a bit of searching to find otherwise.

If you're customizing your workbooks by adding macros, toolbars are one of the most effective ways to allow access to frequently used commands. You can use VBA to create and control toolbars and toolbar buttons, adding buttons that will run your macros. The programs you've created will be available at the click of a button.

You can also write programs to better organize the working environment. Toolbars you use for a certain situation can be limited to appearing only in that situation. You can control both Excel's built-in toolbars and your own this way.

Where are toolbar changes stored?

To learn how to customize menus, see Chapter 15, "Change the Menus: No Programming Required!"

When you make a change to a toolbar, whether you do it via VBA or using other methods, the change stays. You can close the current workbook and open another, or even close Excel without saving anything and run it again. The changes you made will still be present. This is very different from the way custom menus behave.

Toolbars are stored with your copy of Excel, rather than with a particular workbook. The nice part about this constancy is that on a single copy of Excel, it makes toolbars a little less confusing than menus. If you display a toolbar or add a button, it's not going to change unless you specify otherwise, regardless of which workbooks are open.

Changes do occur when you switch from one type of sheet to another. For example, if you activate a chart sheet, the Chart toolbar appears. Switch to another sheet, and it disappears. But, if you move the Chart toolbar and then close your workbook, the Chart toolbar will still be in its new position when you create a new chart the next day.

To learn how to make code run when a worksheet is activated, see Chapter 22, "Making Code Run Automatically."

One disadvantage of the constancy of toolbars is that if you want different toolbars to automatically appear in different situations, you'll have to create that functionality with special VBA programming. If you want a toolbar that is only displayed when a particular worksheet is active, you need to create VBA code that will display the toolbar when the worksheet is activated and will hide it when the worksheet is deactivated.

Another problem that arises is how to give a toolbar to someone else to use. Because toolbars are stored with Excel, not workbooks, when you put a copy of a workbook on another computer, its toolbars don't go with it. To include toolbars, you can attach them to a workbook by following a special procedure. There is a way to do it, but it takes more effort than associating menu changes with a workbook.

Working with existing toolbars

Excel has toolbars for many situations. The Toolbars collection includes Standard, Formatting, Chart, Visual Basic, and many other toolbars. You can add your own to the collection, as well. You can modify Excel's built-in toolbars and your own by adding, removing, or repositioning buttons or changing the position of the toolbar itself.

Using VBA to work with your toolbars, you can write procedures that do the following:

- Make toolbars appear or disappear
- Change the position of a toolbar by anchoring it to the top or bottom of the screen, or making it a "floating" toolbar you can drag around
- Change the buttons on a toolbar
- Have different toolbars appear in different situations
- Add custom buttons to a toolbar that run your macros

Some of these things, like adding and removing toolbar buttons, can be done without VBA. Using VBA, however, will provide you with more versatility and allow you to change the toolbars in context.

TIP **Use the Immediate pane, as described in Chapter 14, "Fixing**
Your Code: VBA's Debugging Tools," to experiment with toolbar changes.

Referring to a toolbar

To learn about collections and methods, see Chapter 11, "How VBA Refers to Things in Excel."

Each toolbar belongs to the Toolbars collection. Like all collections, there is a Toolbars method that allows you to specify a particular toolbar in this collection. You can do this by supplying the name of the toolbar as the argument for the Toolbars method. The Formatting toolbar, for example, would be referred to as Toolbars("Formatting").

You can see the names of all available toolbars by choosing View, Toolbars to display the Toolbars dialog box. Toolbars are listed in this box by name, including any custom toolbars you might have created. Figure 17.1 shows the Toolbars dialog box with the names of several built-in toolbars and the custom toolbar Sales Macros displayed.

Fig. 17.1
When you create a toolbar, Excel automatically adds it to the list in the Toolbars dialog box.

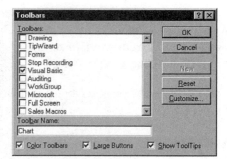

Toolbars also have a number associated with them. The Formatting toolbar, for example, is number 2. You can refer to it as Toolbars(2) or Toolbars("Formatting"). The macro recorder uses the number of a toolbar rather than its name.

 TIP **Use the name of a toolbar rather than the number when writing**
VBA code, because it will make your programs easier to understand.

Displaying and hiding toolbars

The Visible property of a toolbar determines whether it is displayed. Setting it to True or False displays or hides the toolbar.

```
Sub ShowDrawing()
    Toolbars("Drawing").Visible = True
    MsgBox "Now you see it"
    Toolbars("Drawing").Visible = False
    MsgBox "Now you don't"
End Sub
```

This procedure sets the Visible property of the Drawing toolbar to True. If the toolbar was not visible before the procedure was run, it becomes visible. If it was already visible, then no change occurs. A message box appears, which gives you time to take a look at the Drawing toolbar. After you click OK, the Visible property of the Drawing toolbar is set to False, which hides it, and a second message box appears.

Changing the Visible property of a toolbar achieves the same effect as removing the check mark next to the name of the toolbar in the Toolbars dialog box. Thus, if your code set the Visible property to True, a check mark will appear. Conversely, if you put a check mark in this dialog box, it will set the Visible property of the corresponding toolbar to True.

Positioning and sizing toolbars

If you've never tried it, you might be surprised to learn that you can move toolbars all over the screen. Figure 17.2 shows a worksheet with the Standard toolbar at the top of the screen, the Formatting toolbar on the bottom, the Visual Basic toolbar anchored to the side, and the Drawing toolbar floating in the middle of the worksheet.

 Plain English, please!

A toolbar is said to be **anchored** when it is aligned with one of the edges of the screen, like the Formatting or Visual Basic toolbars in figure 17.2. A **floating toolbar** is one that is not attached to a side of the window and can be dragged from one position to another like the Drawing toolbar in figure 17.2. **99**

Fig. 17.2

Excel won't let you anchor a toolbar to the side of the screen if it contains any wide buttons or controls.

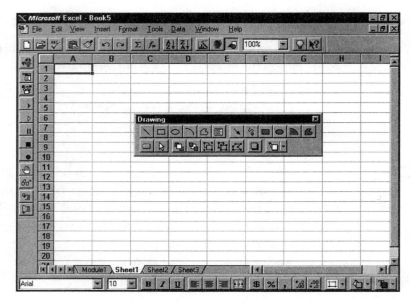

You can position any toolbar as anchored or floating. This includes toolbars like the Formatting toolbar, which you're accustomed to seeing anchored to the top of the screen. To change the position of the Formatting toolbar to a floating one, position your cursor over the toolbar so it isn't on a button or control. Click and drag the toolbar away from the edge of the screen.

Q&A *Why won't Excel let me anchor the Formatting toolbar on the left side of the screen?*

Most toolbar buttons are just squares with a picture or symbol in them. Some are more extensive controls, like the control in the Formatting toolbar that lets you change your font. You can anchor toolbars to the left or right side of the screen, provided they don't use any of these special toolbar buttons.

The position of a toolbar reflects the value of its Position property. There are Excel constants for each of the five possible positions: xlTop, xlBottom, xlLeft, xlRight, and xlFloating. This procedure displays the Visual Basic toolbar and moves it into several different positions.

```
Sub MoveToolbar()
    Toolbars("Visual Basic").Visible = True
    Toolbars("Visual Basic").Position = xlFloating
    MsgBox "Floating"
    Toolbars("Visual Basic").Position = xlBottom
    MsgBox "Bottom"
    Toolbars("Visual Basic").Position = xlRight
    MsgBox "Right"
End Sub
```

This procedure starts by setting the Visible property of the Visual Basic toolbar to True. Then its position property is set to xlFloating, xlBottom, and xlRight, each in turn. A message box follows each change in position to give you time to look at the new position before it changes.

There are several properties that determine where and how floating toolbars appear. The Top, Width, and Left properties are all given in increments of 1/72 of an inch. Top is how far from the top of the screen the toolbar appears, Left is how far from the left side, and Width is the width of a toolbar. The height will adjust automatically to accommodate all the buttons. This macro was recorded with the macro recorder. I turned on the macro recorder, then moved and resized the Standard toolbar until it looked like figure 17.3.

```
Sub Macro10()
    With Toolbars(2)
        .Position = xlFloating
        .Left = 300
        .Top = 180
        .Width = 291
    End With
End Sub
```

Use the With structure to perform several actions on the Toolbars(2) object. This is the Formatting toolbar. Since the macro was created with the Macro Recorder, the number was used for the toolbar instead of its name. The Position property of this toolbar is set to xlFloating. The Left and Top properties determine where to position the toolbar. By adjusting the Width property to 291, the toolbar is no longer wide enough to accommodate all of its buttons on a single line, so it changes its height automatically so that all buttons fit.

Fig. 17.3
Moving and resizing a toolbar affects its Left, Top, and Width properties.

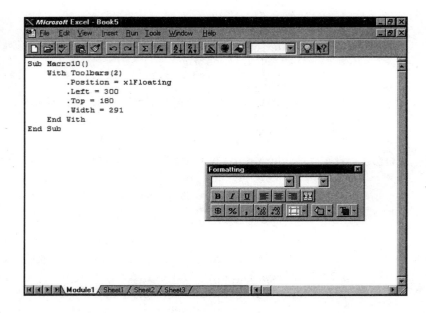

Affecting all toolbars at once

To learn how to use For Each loops, see Chapter 10, "Ways to Control the Flow of Your Programs."

You can refer to each toolbar in the Toolbars collection by using a For Each statement. The following procedure uses a For Each loop to hide all toolbars. Use another For Each loop to display the toolbars one by one until all possible toolbars appear on your screen.

```
Sub ShowAllBars()
    'hide all toolbars
    For Each tlbr In Toolbars
        tlbr.Visible = False
    Next tlbr

    'display toolbars one at a time
    For Each tlbr In Toolbars
        tlbr.Visible = True
        MsgBox "This is the " & tlbr.Name & " toolbar"
    Next tlbr
End Sub
```

The first For Each loop uses tlbr as the variable that will represent each of the toolbars in the collection. During each iteration of the loop, the Visible property of that toolbar is set to False, making it disappear from the screen.

The next For Each loop uses the same variable name and goes through the entire toolbars collection again. This time, the Visible property is set to True and a message box appears displaying the Name property of that toolbar.

After running this procedure, you'll wind up with every possible Excel toolbar displayed on your screen. You can get rid of them by choosing View, Toolbars, and removing the check marks from the ones you don't want to see.

Working with toolbar buttons

Toolbars are nothing without their buttons. The buttons of a toolbar do all the work; the toolbar is just where they live.

You can add and delete toolbar buttons to and from toolbars to suit your needs. If you create your own toolbars, you need to add buttons to it—they don't automatically appear.

To learn how to use the macro recorder to learn the names of objects, see Chapter 3, "Using the VBA Editor and the Macro Recorder Together."

You can manipulate toolbar buttons using VBA or non-programming methods. VBA provides much more flexibility, but the other methods can be very useful for making quick changes. You can also turn on the macro recorder and make these changes. Then, checking out the recorded code will give you the VBA code for the names of the objects and their properties.

How can I use this in the real world?

The Reset method is discussed later in this chapter in "Getting Excel toolbars back to normal." You can use it to return a built-in toolbar to its original state, thus erasing any added buttons and putting back any deleted buttons.

You can create a procedure that automatically displays a custom toolbar designed to work with a particular sheet. This procedure can run whenever the worksheet is activated. When it is deactivated, use a For Each loop to reset each toolbar with the Reset method. That way, the customizations will only appear when that worksheet is active.

Customizing toolbars without programming

You can make extensive changes to your toolbars without writing any VBA code by using the Customize dialog box. To display the Customize dialog box, choose View, Toolbars, and click Customize. The Customize dialog box appears as shown in figure 17.4. You can also open this dialog box by right-clicking any displayed toolbar and choosing Customize from the shortcut menu.

Fig. 17.4
Adding and removing toolbar buttons can be as simple as dragging and dropping when the Customize dialog box is displayed.

While the Customize dialog box is open, toolbar buttons are not operational. Clicking a toolbar button will not perform the action it usually does. However, now you can drag and drop buttons to move and reposition them.

To add a button from the Customize dialog box to an existing toolbar, just click the icon of the button you want and drag it to the toolbar. Excel automatically makes a place for it on the toolbar. If you want to reposition it, you can drag it to a new place on the toolbar.

 TIP **The buttons on a toolbar should be organized into logical groups.** Using spaces between different groups of related buttons is a big help in finding the right button.

The buttons in the Customize dialog box are organized by category. All except the Custom category are ready-made toolbar buttons. When you add them to a toolbar, they already have an action associated with them. Adding a button from the Custom category allows you to assign one of your own macros to the button to make it do something.

Adding buttons with VBA

The Customize dialog box provides an easy way to add toolbar buttons but, as usual, there are numerous advantages to using VBA to achieve the same thing. For one, you can change the way toolbars look based on the active worksheet or current workbook. For example, you can run code that customizes the toolbars when a worksheet is selected. Another less obvious, advantage is that a VBA procedure that changes toolbar buttons is a lasting record of changes.

If you configure a toolbar the way you like, with special buttons added, and then use the Reset method on that toolbar, it will revert to its original state in Excel. With a VBA program, you can simply run it again to reinstate the changes. The Reset method is discussed later in " Getting Excel's built-in toolbars back to normal."

Each toolbar has a ToolbarButtons collection. The way you refer to these buttons differs when you are adding and removing them. To add a button to a toolbar, you use the Add method. This method takes several arguments, which include the design for the button, its position, and what action it should perform when pressed.

You can look up the values for **button** in Excel's online help files. Use the Index page of the Help Topics dialog box and look under `ToolbarButton Objects`, `Available Buttons` and `Button IDs`. The Help topic on this subject shows all of the possible buttons and their ID numbers (see fig. 17.5).

Speaking of Add

The syntax for the Add method of the ToolbarButtons collection is

```
Toolbars("toolbar").ToolbarButtons.Add button, before
```

where *toolbar* is the name of the toolbar you want to add the button to, *button* is a number identifying the design of the button, and *before* gives the position the button should take.

Fig. 17.5

The entire selection of toolbar buttons and their ID numbers is in this online help topic—you'll have to scroll around to see them all.

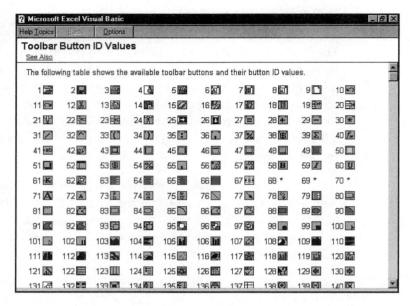

The value of *before* determines where on the toolbar the button should go. If you don't supply a value for this argument, your button will be placed at the end. The buttons on a toolbar are numbered. The one on the far left or top is 1, the next one is 2, and so on. Excel considers a gap between buttons to be a kind of button, too, so you need to count these as well. For example, the Visual Basic toolbar shown in figure 17.6 has Insert Module as Button 1, a blank space as Button 2, Menu Editor as Button 3, and so on.

By looking at the Toolbar Button ID Values in the online help, you can determine that the number corresponding to Cut is number 12. Thus the following line of code adds the Cut button to the Visual Basic toolbar, as shown in figure 17.7.

```
Toolbars("Visual Basic").ToolbarButtons.Add 12, 3
```

Fig. 17.6
Don't forget to count the blank spaces when you're positioning your toolbar buttons.

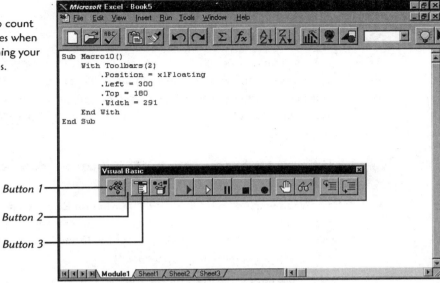

Button 1
Button 2
Button 3

Fig. 17.7
The Cut button has been added to the Visual Basic toolbar in position 3.

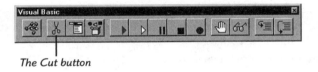

The Cut button

This statement added the toolbar button with ID 12 to the Visual Basic toolbar. It put it before the third button (counting the space after the first button as another button). Notice that now the Cut button is the third button, having replaced the Menu Editor button, which is now the fourth button.

TIP You can also add a space to your toolbar with VBA. Use the Add method with a button value of 0.

If you add a button that Excel usually uses for a certain action, like the Cut button, that action will be associated with the button. You can change it by assigning a new macro as discussed in the next section. Buttons that aren't usually used for other purposes will not have any action associated with them; you must assign it.

Running your macros
with toolbar buttons

Toolbar buttons can do one of two things: they can perform a default action defined by Excel, or run a macro you've created. This is true of all toolbar buttons, not just custom ones you add. If you assign a macro to a toolbar button that has a default action, the macro takes over and the default action is ignored.

Q&A *If I assign a macro to a built-in button, can I change it back later?*

Yes. When you reset a toolbar, all the buttons on Excel's built-in toolbars go back to their original state. Any association of macros with toolbar buttons will be deleted. Alternatively, you can set the OnAction property to an empty string as in the following statement:

```
Toolbars("Formatting").ToolbarButtons(1).OnAction = ""
```

This will remove any macro associated with the first toolbar button on the formatting toolbar and restore Excel's built-in action to the button.

You can assign macros to buttons with or without VBA. Here's how you do it without using VBA:

1 Display the toolbar you want to change.

2 Right-click anywhere on the toolbar and choose Customize from the shortcut menu. (The Customize dialog box appears, but you will not use it.)

3 Right-click the button you want to assign a macro to. (Click the button on the toolbar itself, not in the Customize dialog box.) Select Assign Macro from the shortcut menu.

4 The Assign Macro dialog box appears. Choose the macro you want for the button, and click OK to accept your choice.

Assigning a macro this way works as long as the button remains on the toolbar and you don't reset the toolbar. If you are creating a program that resets toolbars and adds buttons when a worksheet is open, assign your macro in the code. You can do this by setting the OnAction property to the name of the macro you want to run. For example, this statement assigns the macro called MyChartMacro to the sixth button on the Formatting toolbar:

```
Toolbars("Formatting").ToolbarButtons(6).OnAction _
= "MyChartMacro"
```

Removing buttons from a toolbar

You can remove buttons from toolbars by opening the Customize dialog box and dragging the icon of the button off the toolbar. You can also remove buttons in VBA code by using the Delete method. To delete the fifth button on the Standard toolbar, use this code:

```
Toolbars("Standard").ToolbarButtons(5).Delete
```

If you delete a built-in toolbar button, you can get it back by adding it to the toolbar or by resetting the toolbar (which restores it to its original state).

Notice that you refer to buttons very differently depending on whether you are adding or removing them. When you add a button, you refer to its unique ID number. When you remove it, you do so by using its position on the toolbar.

Create a custom toolbar

In addition to customizing Excel's built-in toolbars, you can add your own as well. You add toolbars to the Toolbars collection with the Add method. After you add them, you can work with them like any other toolbar—by using all the customization techniques described in this chapter. This procedure creates a new toolbar with four buttons and a blank space.

```
Sub CustToolbar()
    Toolbars.Add "Bridge Toolbar"
    Toolbars("Bridge Toolbar").ToolbarButtons.Add 221
    Toolbars("Bridge Toolbar").ToolbarButtons.Add 222
    Toolbars("Bridge Toolbar").ToolbarButtons.Add 223
    Toolbars("Bridge Toolbar").ToolbarButtons.Add 224
    Toolbars("Bridge Toolbar").ToolbarButtons.Add 0, 3
    Toolbars("Bridge Toolbar").Visible = True
    Toolbars("Bridge Toolbar").Position = xlFloating
End Sub
```

CustToolbar adds a new member to the Toolbars collection called `Bridge Toolbar`. The next four lines add buttons 221 through 224 to the toolbar. Because no argument is given for the position of these buttons, they are each added to the end of the toolbar in turn.

The next button that is added is not a button at all, but a space.

```
Toolbars("Bridge Toolbar").ToolbarButtons.Add 0, 3
```

The button ID given is 0, which is the ID value for a space. The *before* value is 3, which positions it before the third button. Thus, this line puts a space between the second and third toolbar buttons.

The Visible property of the toolbar is set to `True` and its `Position` is set to `xlFloating`. The finished product looks like the toolbar in figure 17.8.

Fig. 17.8
The CustToolbar procedure creates the Bridge toolbar and its buttons.

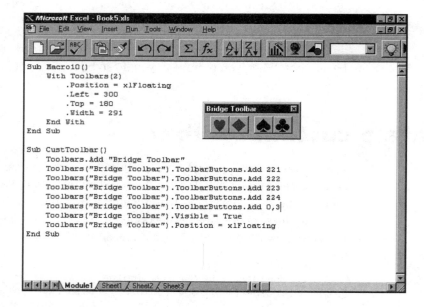

Attach custom toolbars to a workbook

If you create a toolbar that's designed to work with a particular workbook and then give that workbook to someone else to use, you'll want the toolbar to go with it. To do this, you need to specifically attach the custom toolbar to the workbook.

Here's how it works:

1 Open the worksheet you want to attach the toolbar to.

2 Activate a module sheet. (If none exists for that workbook, insert one.)

3 Choose Tools, Attach Toolbars to open the Attach Toolbars dialog box shown in figure 17.9.

Fig. 17.9
Once you attach a toolbar to a workbook, the toolbar goes where the workbook goes.

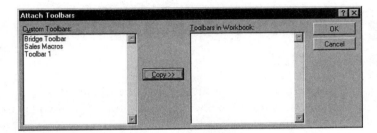

4 From the Custom Toolbars list, select the custom toolbar you want to attach to the workbook. Click the Copy button.

5 Repeat step 4 for any additional toolbars you want to attach and then click OK.

Now, wherever the workbook goes, the toolbar goes as well.

Deleting custom toolbars

You can delete custom toolbars in the Toolbars dialog box or in VBA code. In the Toolbars dialog box, there is a button that changes its caption based on whether a custom or built-in toolbar is displayed. When you select a custom toolbar in the Toolbars in Workbook list box, the caption is `Delete`. Clicking this button removes the custom toolbar.

You can achieve the same result in code with the Delete method. For example, this statement deletes a custom toolbar called My Toolbar:

```
Toolbars("Bridge Toolbar").Delete
```

CAUTION **Deleting a custom toolbar is permanent. If all you want to do is** put the toolbar away for awhile, set its Visible property to False.

You can't delete Excel's built-in toolbars. If you write a line of code that uses the Delete method on a built-in toolbar, VBA just ignores it.

Q&A *I deleted a custom toolbar but then I opened a workbook and it came back. What's going on?*

If you attach a toolbar to a workbook, deleting it via VBA or the Toolbars dialog box is not enough. You also need to display the Attach Toolbars dialog box, click the toolbar in the <u>T</u>oolbars in Workbook list box, and then click the <u>D</u>elete button.

Getting Excel's built-in toolbars back to normal

There are times you want to get your toolbars back to the way they were when you started. An obvious reason for this is if you got a little toolbar-happy and made all kinds of changes you never intended to be permanent, like removing all the buttons from your Formatting toolbar.

The Reset method returns a built-in toolbar to its original state. The Reset method has no effect on custom toolbars.

```
Sub ResetToolbars()
    For Each tlbr In Toolbars
        tlbr.Reset
    Next tlbr
End Sub
```

This procedure uses a For Each loop to go through all the toolbars and reset each one. This procedure does not affect custom toolbars.

How can I use this in the real world?

Another time you might want to reset toolbars is when code is running that customizes the toolbars. When a workbook opens, you can have it automatically run a procedure that modifies the toolbars in a way that's useful for that particular workbook. When you close the workbook, you'll want to set the toolbars back to normal so the changes won't be in effect for other workbooks.

Summary

In this chapter, you learned how to create and modify toolbars with VBA and non-programming methods. You also learned how to write procedures that handle displaying, hiding, and customizing toolbars so you can change your toolbars to fit the context.

Review questions

1 What is a floating toolbar?

2 How can you make a custom toolbar button do something?

3 If you change a toolbar and then quit Excel without saving the workbook, what happens to your changes?

4 How can you give access to your toolbars to someone using a different computer?

5 How can you tell what ID number goes with what toolbar button?

6 What can you do to make a toolbar appear only in one workbook?

Exercises

1 Write a procedure that displays the Forms toolbar and anchors it to the right side of the screen.

2 The ResetToolbars procedure only affects built-in toolbars. Add code to it so it will delete all custom toolbars as well. (Hint: Remember that VBA will ignore any instructions to reset a custom toolbar or to delete a built-in toolbar, so you can delete and reset all toolbars.)

3 Using VBA code, add the button with a smiley face on it to the Forms toolbar. Put this button just after the Edit Code button.

4 Write a macro that toggles the position of the Forms toolbar between floating and anchored to the right side of the screen. Attach this macro to the button you created in Exercise 3. (Hint: The statement

```
If Toolbars("Forms").Position = xlRight Then
```

will help determine what position you should assign.)

5 Create a custom toolbar, add several buttons to it, attach macros, and attach to a workbook.

18

Ready-Made Dialog Boxes

● In this chapter:

- Add icons and titles to the message boxes

- How can I use different buttons in my message boxes?

- Once the buttons are there, how can I make my programs react to the button that was selected?

- An easy way to let the user enter text

- Is there a way to display Excel's normal dialog boxes as part of my programs?

These easy dialog boxes can get you through many program-ming situations, just like a simple phrasebook can get you through many conversations in a foreign language . . . . . . ❯

Have you ever thought about the derivation of the term *dialog box*? A dialog is a conversation, and in dialog boxes we converse with our computers. There are dialog boxes that display information—that's the computer talking to us—and ones where we provide information for the computer—we're talking to it.

Conversations between the user and the computer can be very complicated and can involve all kinds of different controls. Text boxes, option buttons, and scroll bars can all be added to dialog boxes to add functionality and improved communication. But before you take on the task of learning how to have complicated conversations, you can start having simple ones right away. There are several kinds of dialog boxes that can be created with a single line of code. They can get you through many programming situations that require getting information to and from the user, just like a simple phrasebook can get you through many conversations in a foreign language.

Message boxes

The simplest dialog boxes are **message boxes**. These are dialog boxes that give the user a message and provide one or more buttons for the user to choose among. In VBA, these are created by using MsgBox.

I've made heavy use of MsgBox in many of the examples in this book because it's one of the easiest ways to display information about what's happening in your VBA code. However, these examples only scratch the surface of what MsgBox is capable of. MsgBox can also:

- Display an icon like an exclamation point or question mark within the message box

- Have any title (rather than the default one of Microsoft Excel)

- Display several buttons and perform actions based on the button that the user selects

The great thing about MsgBox is how easy it is to add to your VBA programs. Building entire dialog boxes from scratch is a lot of work. Fortunately, for many situations MsgBox will do the trick.

MsgBox as a statement lets you display information

In its simplest form, MsgBox is used as a statement with a single argument—the message that it is to display. For example, this line of code produces the message box shown in figure 18.1.

```
MsgBox "This is a message box."
```

Fig. 18.1
With just a single line of code, you've created an entire dialog box.

This is the form of message box that you'll see peppering examples throughout the book. You can also use MsgBox to display a numeric value.

```
Sub ShowValue()
    Amount = 10
    MsgBox Amount
End Sub
```

The variable Amount is assigned the value 10. On the next line, MsgBox is used to display Amount. Notice that there are no quotation marks around Amount, since it's the value of the variable you want to display, not the word "Amount."

If you want to combine text and values or need to use two separate text strings together in a single message box, you can use the concatenation operator (**&**).

 Plain English, please!
Concatenation is the programming term for sticking two things together.

The following procedure uses the concatenation operator to put two text strings in a single message box.

```
Sub SayGoodNight()
    FirstName = "Gracie"
    MsgBox "Say good night " & FirstName
End Sub
```

The string "Gracie" is assigned to the variable FirstName. In the MsgBox line, a text string "Say good night " is supplied. It's followed by & FirstName which tells MsgBox to append the value of the variable FirstName to the "Say good night " string.

TIP **One way to make a procedure pause is to put in a message box.** When you run the code, VBA will get to the message box, display it, and then wait for you to click OK.

What options are available for MsgBox?

MsgBox can take several arguments. Only one of them is required: the prompt. You can, however, use optional arguments to insert an icon and to change the title (see fig. 18.2).

Fig. 18.2
Icons and a customized title make your message boxes more helpful and informative.

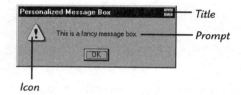

Put an icon in

A very easy way to customize your message boxes is by adding an icon. There are four icons available for message boxes. Each one has a particular numeric value that needs to be supplied as an argument to MsgBox. Rather than using the number, however, you can use specially named constants that are built into VBA. They're much easier to remember. You just type in the name of the constant, and VBA converts it to the number when running the code.

The available icons and their constants are shown in table 18.1.

Table 18.1 Message box icons

Display	Constant	When do I use it?
ℹ	vbInformation	When the message just tells the user something that doesn't require an answer
?	vbQuestion	When the message box is used to ask a question
⚠	vbExclamation	When the message box explains something important
✕	vbCritical	When alerting the user that something bad has happened or is happening (use very sparingly!)

To use an icon with your message box, you supply the constant for the icon as the second argument. The following line of code will display a message box with the Exclamation icon.

```
MsgBox "You just set a new high score!", vbExclamation
```

How can I use this in the real world?

Sometimes, users generate errors in the normal course of events. Unfortunately, the error messages that VBA generates are rather cryptic and intimidating. In Chapter 23, "Making Your Programming User-Friendly," you learn how to intercept an error before VBA does and create your own error message.

For example, you may have written a macro that will run only if a worksheet is the current sheet. Add code to this macro at the beginning that will look to see what kind of sheet is the active sheet. If it's not a worksheet, then display a message box with an exclamation icon explaining that the macro can only be run in a spreadsheet. Then exit the procedure without running the part that will generate an error.

Change the title

The third argument that MsgBox can take is for a title. If you don't supply this argument, then your message box will automatically get the title `Microsoft Excel`. This line of code creates a message box shown earlier in figure 18.2.

```
MsgBox "This is a fancy message box.", vbExclamation, _
    "Personalized Message Box"
```

The title needs to be the third argument, after the prompt and the icon. So, if you don't want to use an icon, you must leave a blank space between the commas for the second argument. For example, to produce the message box from figure 18.2 without an icon, you could type the following:

```
MsgBox "This is a fancy message box.", , "Personalized Message Box"
```

Catch the bug

What's wrong with this procedure? It's trying to create a simple message box with a title, but instead generates a type mismatch error.

```
Sub WontWork()
    MsgBox "This is my prompt", "This is my title"
End Sub
```

Answer: The title is always the third argument given to MsgBox. Even though you don't want to use an icon, VBA interprets the second argument as the icon but doesn't know what to make of it. It's expecting a numeric value (usually a constant) but is getting a text string instead.

To fix this procedure, change the line of code to

```
MsgBox "This is my prompt", , "This is my title"
```

The extra comma puts in a place for the second argument. Then VBA knows that the string `This is my title` *is actually the third argument.*

You can use the MsgBox function to ask the user questions

Guess what? MsgBox is a function!

This might seem a little weird because all along you've been using MsgBox as a statement. Actually, though, any function can be used like a statement if you don't care about its return value. That's what the first part of this chapter showed you how to do—use the MsgBox function in a way that just presents information and doesn't generate a return value.

Well, if MsgBox is indeed a function and can return a value, what kind of value would it return and how would you use this value? The answer is that MsgBox can return a value corresponding to the button a user presses.

One of the options available for message box is to change the buttons it displays. Here's a message box that is probably very familiar to you. It appears when you try to exit Excel while you still have unsaved changes in your document. The message box has three buttons.

Fig. 18.3
Message boxes are a good way to alert a user to a potentially undesired outcome—like quitting Excel without saving changes.

You select a button, and Excel will do something *based on the button chosen*. To do this, Excel is getting the information about which button you selected from somewhere. That's how a message box is used as a function. You present the message box to display information and ask a question, and the user selects one of the buttons available. Information about which button was pressed is automatically generated, and you can write code to take appropriate action based on this information.

Use MsgBox as a function

Using MsgBox as a function is a little different from the way you've been using it.

When used as a function, MsgBox does not constitute a complete statement. Rather, it is an expression that must be used as a part of a statement. One of the most common uses of the MsgBox function is to assign the return value to a variable. This procedure uses MsgBox twice: once as a function and once as a statement.

```
Sub Message()
    Answer = MsgBox("hello", vbYesNoCancel, "A New Title!")
    MsgBox "The number of the button selected was " & Answer
End Sub
```

The first use of MsgBox in this procedure is as a function. One of the ways to distinguish how it is being used is by the parentheses that surround its argument. There are three arguments given to MsgBox: a prompt, a constant to set which buttons are displayed, and a title. When the message box is displayed and the user clicks one of the buttons that appears, a value corresponding to this button is assigned to the variable Answer.

The next line of code uses MsgBox as a statement; no parentheses are used around its arguments this time. MsgBox is only given one argument—a prompt—and it displays the value of the button that was selected.

Speaking of *MsgBox*

The general format for the MsgBox function is

```
MsgBox(prompt[,buttons][,title])
```

Prompt is the only required argument. Supply a string value for the text of the message box.

If you want to change the title appearing at the top of the message box, supply a text string for *title*. If none is supplied, the default title Microsoft Excel will be used.

By changing the value of *buttons*, you can affect which buttons are displayed. The value of *buttons* also controls whether an icon appears with the message box.

Change the buttons you display

Which buttons you choose to display depends on what kind of answer you're looking for. Do you want to ask the user a yes or no question? Maybe OK and Cancel would be more appropriate.

Each combination of buttons has a numeric value. For example, using 3 displays the OK and Cancel buttons. However, it's much easier to use the built-in VBA constants instead of a numeric value. Rather than having to memorize that 3 is for OK and Cancel, you can use the constant vbOKCancel. Here are the button combinations, their constants, and when you'd use them.

Table 18.2 Button combinations

Display	Constant	When do I use it?
OK	vbOKOnly	When the message box doesn't require the user to make a decision
OK Cancel	vbOKCancel	When the message box explains an action that's about to happen but will let the user opt out with the Cancel button
Yes No	vbYesNo	An alternative to vbOKCancel when it seems to make the message box easier to understand
Yes No Cancel	vbYesNoCancel	For situations such as quitting or closing files without saving, like the one described earlier and shown in figure 18.3
Abort Retry Ignore	vbAbortRetryIgnore	When responding to disk or file errors
Retry Cancel	vbRetryCancel	When responding to disk or file errors

If you don't specify which buttons are going to appear, then the default of the OK button is supplied. It's up to you to pick the right button for the job.

Interpreting the button that *is* selected

You display a message box with certain buttons and the user selects one of them. Now what?

Here's where we'll make use of the return value of the MsgBox function. By looking at the value that was returned, appropriate action can be taken in your program. Each of the buttons produces a numeric value that is assigned to the return value of MsgBox. Rather than memorizing the values, though, you can use the built-in constants. The constants are all of the same form: the name of the button preceded by vb. So, the constant for the OK button is vbOK and the constant for the Yes button is vbYes.

This all is a little easier to understand in the context of an example.

```
Sub WhichButton()
    Answer = MsgBox("Do you want to hear a beep?", vbYesNo)
    If Answer = vbYes Then Beep
End Sub
```

 The MsgBox function is used with two arguments. The first is a prompt that asks the user a question. The second is the constant that displays the Yes and No buttons. The value of the button selected is assigned to the variable Answer.

On the next line, the procedure looks to see if the value of Answer is equal to the constant vbYes. If it is, then a beep is produced. Thus, when you run this program, selecting the Yes button will produce a beep, but selecting No will not.

So how do I change the buttons AND use an icon?

The *button* argument of the MsgBox function does double duty. It is where you specify whether you want an icon displayed and also which button combination you want displayed. How to specify one or the other has been discussed earlier in the sections "Put an icon in" and "Change the buttons you display." What if you want to specify both?

Catch the bug

This procedure is supposed to get a yes or no response from the user and beep if yes was chosen. There's a problem, though. Can you find it?

```
Sub WillItBeep()
    Answer = MsgBox("Yes or no?", YesNoCancel)
    If Answer = vbYes Then Beep
End Sub
```

Answer: *The problem lies in the argument of the MsgBox function. The constant I wanted is called* vbYesNoCancel, *but I left out the first two letters.*

OK, you've found the problem, but what will happen if you run the code as is? Will it run? What will it display?

Answer: *A message box will be displayed with only an OK button. This is because VBA thinks that* YesNoCancel *is a variable and is using the value of this variable instead of the numeric constant that I wanted. Because the variable has never had a value assigned to it, its default value is zero. Zero happens to be the value of the* vbOKOnly *constant, so an OK button appears.*

To add an icon and specify the button combination, give an argument that is the sum of the constants for the appropriate option. In other words, just write the button combination plus the icon choice.

```
Sub IconsButtons()
    Answer = MsgBox ("Voila!", vbOKCancel + vbExclamation)
End Sub
```

By using vbOKCancel + vbExclamation for the *button* argument of the MsgBox function, the OK and Cancel buttons are displayed as well as the Exclamation icon.

Notice that although the return value of MsgBox is assigned to `Answer`, no use is made of it. You could replace the line of code with

```
MsgBox "Look, an icon and buttons", vbOKCancel + vbExclamation
```

and get the same result while leaving `Answer` out of it altogether. In this case, no parentheses are present because MsgBox is being used like a statement.

Input boxes

On with the dialog. So far in this chapter, you've done most of the talking and have only asked limited questions of the user. Sometimes, you'll want to get more extensive information than a message box can handle. You might want to ask users to type in their names, for example. That's where input boxes come in (see fig. 18.4).

Fig. 18.4
Message boxes only let you record which button was pressed. An input box can get much more specific information from the user.

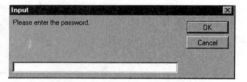

Speaking of InputBox

The InputBox function has the following syntax:

```
InputBox(prompt[, title])
```

The *prompt* is a required argument for which you supply a text message to the user. The *title* is optional and if omitted a default title of `Input` is used.

The return value of the InputBox function is whatever text the user types into the text area of the input box. Here, the user is prompted for a name which is assigned to the variable `UserName`.

```
UserName = InputBox("Type in your name, please.")
```

*To learn about If/
Then statements, see
Chapter 10, "Ways
to Control the Flow
of Your Programs."*

InputBox is a function and as such must be used as an expression. The following example uses InputBox as the conditional expression in an If/Then statement.

```
Sub WhoIsIt()
 If InputBox("Who's there?", "Knock, knock") = "Lika" Then Davan
 End If
End Sub
```

The If statement creates an input box with the prompt `"Who's there?"` and the title `"Knock, knock."`. When the user types in a text string, it is compared to the string `"Lika."`. If they are the same, then the subroutine `Davan` runs.

My prompts are too long to fit on one line

If the information you want to display in an input box or a message box is too long to fit on a single line, you need to break it into several lines. To do this, you must use a special character called the **linefeed character**. To indicate the linefeed character in VBA, type **Chr(13)**.

How can I use this in the real world?

If you want to solicit a list of names from the user, you can create a loop (see Chapters 5 and 10) and make an input box appear on each iteration of the loop. Every name the user enters can be stored in a spreadsheet cell (see Chapter 12), or in an array (see Chapter 13).

Simply put, when you tell VBA to display Chr(13), it will skip down to the next line. Any subsequent text will appear on the new line. This line of code produces the message box in figure 18.5.

```
MsgBox "This prompt became" & Chr(13) & "too long for one line."
```

Fig. 18.5
If your text becomes too long to display comfortably, divide it into several lines.

Notice how the linefeed is used. It's not inside of the quotation marks for the prompt. Instead, it is sandwiched between two text strings, with the concatenation operator (&) attaching them to each other.

By the way, using the underscore character (_) in a line of code will allow you to break the code up into multiple lines in your module sheet. However, it has no effect on how it is displayed in a dialog box.

TIP **Try to keep your message and input box prompts short and sweet.** You should only occasionally need multiple lines.

Displaying Excel's normal dialog boxes in special situations

To learn more about the Show method, see Chapter 19, "Creating and Using Dialog Boxes."

To learn about objects and methods, see Chapter 11, "How VBA Refers to Things in Excel."

If you're re-creating the working environment of Excel, chances are you'll still want to use many of Excel's built-in dialog boxes. For example, you might get rid of the menus and make a big button in the middle of the screen that says Open File. When the user selects this button, the dialog box that you'd normally get by selecting File, Open can appear. You can manage this by referring to the dialog you want as an object and using the **Show method**.

The code required to display the File, Open dialog box is

```
Application.Dialogs(xlDialogOpen).Show
```

If this code is run, the dialog box will appear and will work just as if the user had selected Open from the File menu. To display a different dialog box, you need to replace the constant xlDialogOpen with the constant for the dialog you want to display.

To learn about using Excel's online help, see Chapter 6, "VBA Information Online."

A list of all the constants can be found in the online help under the topic **Built-In Dialog Boxes**. They all follow the same naming format of xlDialog*Something* where *Something*, is usually the name written at the top of the dialog box.

Summary

This chapter showed you a number of ways to create dialog boxes with a single line of code. The MsgBox keyword can be used as a statement for explaining things to the user or as a function to solicit an answer in the form of a button selected. Either use of MsgBox allows you to customize the icon displayed, the title, and the prompt. InputBox is always used as a function and allows you to get text entries from the user. You can also display one of Excel's built-in dialog boxes by using the Show method.

Review questions

1 What icons can be displayed in a message box?

2 Why would you want to use message box as a function?

3 What must you do with your code to use MsgBox as a function rather than a statement?

4 How can you break a prompt into several lines?

5 Assuming that it's like most other constants of its type, can you guess the name of the constant for Excel's built-in Save As dialog box?

Exercises

1 Change the SayGoodNight procedure so that the message box instead asks "Is it time for bed?" and displays a question mark icon.

2 Edit the WhoIsIt procedure so that if the name entered is yours, it will display a message box that says `hello`.

3 Write a procedure that uses a message box with a critical icon and warns the user that proceeding will destroy data. Ask if the user wishes to continue. Provide yes or no buttons for the user to select. If the user selects no, make the computer beep.

4 With two different input boxes, ask for the user's first and last names. In a message box, display the first and last names on separate lines.

5 Create an If/Then statement that compares the return value of MsgBox to vbYes as part of the conditional expression. (In other words, write a line of code that says: `if the return value of MsgBox is vbYes then....`) The message box should ask if the user wants to print and display a question icon and Yes and No buttons. If the user chooses Yes, then display Excel's built-in Print dialog box.

19

Using Dialog Box Controls

● **In this chapter:**

● **What is a dialog box control, and why would I want one on a worksheet?**

● **What's the difference between all those kinds of boxes and buttons?**

● **How these controls affect data in a worksheet**

● **Create a sheet that a coworker can enter data on but can't mess up**

It's amazing that something as simple as adding dialog controls and linking them to cells can dramatically improve the way you work with your sheets. . . . . ●

Dialog box controls are the various buttons, boxes, and other gadgets you normally see on dialog boxes. This chapter doesn't talk about dialog boxes, though. Instead, it shows you how to put these controls right onto a worksheet.

Without doing any programming, you can completely change the way data is entered into a worksheet. Users can point and click and choose from lists, rather than typing in data. As you grow more comfortable creating these controls, you can add customized programs that are run when the controls are used.

Putting dialog controls on a worksheet

Dialog controls can be used right on a worksheet or on a separate dialog sheet. By putting dialog controls directly onto a worksheet, you can provide the user with an alternate way of entering data into the worksheet. There are a number of advantages to this:

- Dialog controls are easier to understand for users who are not proficient with spreadsheets.

- You can use dialog controls to restrict the kind of information that a user enters in a cell, such as making the user select an item from a list.

- Controls can also limit the range of values that a user enters—for example, restricting the value to a whole number between 1 and 100.

- You can protect a sheet in such a way that the user can only change its contents via the dialog controls, thus protecting your formulas and permanent data.

How much you do with controls on a worksheet is up to you. You can just include a button that performs a macro when pressed, or you can completely restrict the user to dialog controls for entering information, not allowing any direct editing of worksheet cells.

Dialog controls are created by using the Forms toolbar to select a control and then dragging to create the control on the form. Figure 19.1 shows the Forms toolbar and each of the dialog controls it can create.

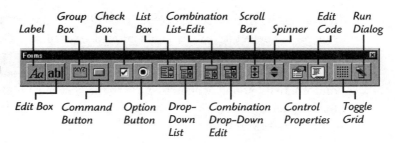

Fig. 19.1
Pick the dialog control you want, and draw the control right onto a worksheet.

Dialog boxes and their tools are discussed in Chapter 20, "Creating and Using Dialog Boxes."

The last four items on the Forms toolbar are not dialog controls at all, but tools that you'd use when working with dialog boxes.

The first thing you need to do to work with a dialog control is to add it to a worksheet. As an example, here's how you'd add an option button:

1 Open up a new workbook and with a worksheet active, choose <u>V</u>iew, <u>T</u>oolbars, and put a check mark next to the Forms toolbar. Click OK.

2 Click on the Option Button button on the Forms toolbar. See figure 19.1 if you're not sure which one that is.

3 The shape of your cursor has changed. Position your cursor at the top-left corner of cell C5. Press and hold the mouse button and drag your cursor to the bottom-right corner of cell D6. You've just added an option button to your worksheet.

 Q&A *I tried to add a control to my worksheet and I couldn't click on the button on the Forms toolbar. What's going on?*

Some of the dialog controls on the Forms toolbar can only be added to actual dialog sheets, not to worksheets. Try it again with the Option Button button or one of the other controls discussed in this chapter.

Selecting, moving, resizing, and deleting controls

Clicking on a check box tells Excel to put a check in it. Similarly, clicking on other dialog controls means to use the control in its unique way. Thus, when you want to select a control to move, resize, or otherwise change it, you need to use another technique.

By holding down the Ctrl key on your keyboard and then clicking on a control, you select it. Now it can be moved, resized, or deleted. To move a control, first select it and raise your mouse button. Then move the pointer over the control until it looks like an arrow you'd use to select a menu. For some controls, you may need to point to the very edge of the control to get your pointer this way. Then, click and drag the mouse to reposition the control where you want it.

Q&A *Why do I keep getting copies of my dialog controls when I try to move them?*

If you hold down the Ctrl key and then click and drag a control, Excel creates a copy for you. To move a control, you need to release the mouse button when you are selecting the control, and then click and drag to move it.

Dialog controls are resized by first selecting them and then dragging the resize boxes that are around the edges of the selected control. To delete a control, simply select it and press the Delete key on your keyboard.

Another method for selecting controls uses the right mouse button. By pointing to a control and clicking on the right mouse button, you both select it and display the pop-up menu associated with that control. You can select a number of different options for the control from the pop-up menu. If you press Esc instead, the pop-up menu will disappear but the control will remain selected.

TIP When you first create a control, it is already selected so that you can modify it.

The name and caption of your control

As controls are added to your worksheet, Excel assigns each of them a name. If the first control is an option button, it gets the name `Option Button 1`; if the second is a list box, it gets the name `List Box 2`. Even though it's the first list box on the worksheet, it's still the second dialog control.

Some controls, like option buttons, command buttons, and check boxes, have text that appears next to the control. This is the **caption**.

To change the caption of a control:

1 Select the control by holding down the Ctrl key and clicking on it.

2 Move your cursor over the caption of the control. Your cursor turns into an I-beam text editing pointer.

3 Select the entire text of the caption and type the new caption you want to use.

4 Click elsewhere in the worksheet to accept the changes you made.

Q&A ***What's the difference between the name of a control and its caption?***

The caption is the text that appears next to a control. Its name is how Excel knows what it is. The name of a control is used when you're programming the control to do something.

When Excel creates a control with a caption, it sets the caption to the name of the control. In other words, controls often start out with their name and caption the same. An exception to this is when you copy a control. The copy will have the same caption but a new name. Names of dialog controls are unique, so your VBA code can describe exactly which one it's working with. Generally, you change the caption of a control. This does not affect the name.

Setting up your controls

The size, position, and caption of a control are modified by working with the control itself. There are other features of dialog controls that are available through the Format Object dialog box. Figure 19.2 shows the Format Object dialog box that appears when the object selected is a check box.

Fig. 19.2
The Format Object dialog box varies slightly for different controls.

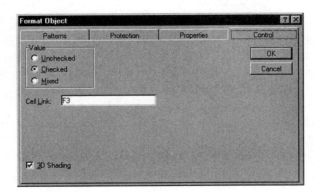

You can access the Format Object dialog box by clicking on the control with the right mouse button and then selecting Format Object from the pop-up menu. Format Object is a tabbed dialog box. What pages it contains depends in part on the dialog control you selected. Except for command buttons, all of the dialog controls have a Control page. The Control page for a check box is shown in figure 19.2. The Control page is where you specify links to your worksheet and values that the control will display.

All dialog controls have a Properties page in the Format Object dialog box. On this page, you can select whether a control should be included when you print the worksheet and whether the control gets moved or resized when the cells it's placed on top of is moved or resized.

The dialog controls that have a Control page will have an option button allowing you to choose a 3D shading effect for the control. For some controls, like check boxes, this doesn't show up so well on the white background of a worksheet. For other controls, like scroll bars, it makes a huge difference: using the 3D Shading option looks much nicer. By changing the background color of the cells in your worksheet, you can make the 3D effect look like it does in dialog boxes. This technique is described later in the section, "Option buttons."

 TIP Removing the grid lines from a worksheet improves the appearance of dialog controls.

The different kinds of controls

When I first used a computer that had different fonts, I went a little crazy. I created memos that used three or four different fonts. The effect was flashy, tacky, and not terribly easy to read. In my enthusiasm for new choices, I had forgotten that the reason behind using different typefaces was to communicate more effectively. The same is true of dialog controls. There are many to choose from, and your choices should be based on what you think will make your worksheets easier and more efficient to use.

Each dialog control has a different kind of use. Table 19.1 lists the various kinds of controls and the type of work they're suited for.

Table 19.1   Dialog controls

Control name	Use
Check box	Toggles the state of a setting between true and false, or between on and off.
Combination	Combine the features of a list box and edit box into one control. Only available in dialog boxes.
Command button	Issues a command to Excel to perform an action.
Drop-down list	Presents a list of pre-defined choices to the user. Used rather than a list box when there is limited room on-screen for a scrolling list box.
Group box	Surrounds related controls to help organize them. Used extensively with option buttons to identify them as a group.
Edit box	Allows the user to enter freeform text. Alternatively used to display text that cannot be changed by the user, but changes according to the status of the program. Only available in dialog boxes.
Label	Creates text for explanations and titles. Generally used in dialog boxes, not on worksheets.
List box	Presents a list of pre-defined choices to the user. The list can be quite long.
Option button	Always used in groups of two or more. Lets the user choose among several mutually exclusive options.
Scroll bar	Controls a numeric value. Often the value is associated with a setting, such as volume or the position in a document.
Spinner	Similar to scroll bars but with less versatility for making large changes to the numeric value.

Each of the controls available for use in worksheets is discussed in the following sections.

Command buttons

Command buttons are used to issue instructions to Excel. This is accomplished by assigning a macro to a command button. When you add a command button to a worksheet, a dialog box appears which lets you select an existing macro to associate with your command button. If you don't want to assign one right away, you can click Cancel. The button is still there; it just doesn't do anything if you click it.

You can later assign a macro by selecting the button and then choosing Tools, Assign Macro to bring up the Assign Macro dialog box.

Check boxes

Check boxes are used for setting true and false or yes and no values. You can put a check box on a worksheet and link it to a cell. Putting a check mark in the check box will cause the value True to appear in the linked cell. Removing the check changes the cell value to False. A check box can also be shaded gray, indicating the value is neither true nor false. This changes the value in the linked cell to #N/A. The check boxes in figure 19.3 are linked to the cells on their right.

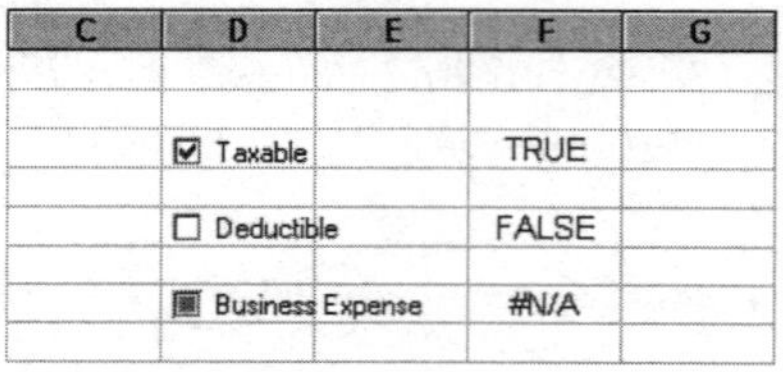

Fig. 19.3

Change the state of the check box, and you change the worksheet cell to True or False.

C	D	E	F	G
	☑ Taxable		TRUE	
	☐ Deductible		FALSE	
	▣ Business Expense		#N/A	

Here's how the check boxes in figure 19.3 were created:

1 Click the Check Box button on the Forms toolbar, and add a check box to the worksheet by dragging the cursor across cells D3 and E3. By dragging the cursor the width of two columns, you'll have enough room to type in the caption of the check box.

2 Change the caption of the check box to **Taxable**.

3 With the right mouse button, click on the check box and choose Format Object from the pop-up menu.

4 The tabbed Format Object dialog box appears. Select the Control tab.

5 Put a check in the 3D Shading box.

6 Put your cursor in the Cell Link box. Type in **F3**. Alternatively, you can just click on cell F3 (moving the dialog box if you need to). Click OK.

7 Repeat steps 1 through 6, adjusting the name and position for the other two check boxes.

The link between a check box and its cell goes two ways; changing the value in the cell will cause the check mark to appear, disappear, or be grayed out to indicate a mixed value. If you enter text into the cell that Excel doesn't associate with True or False, then the state of the check box will remain the same as it was before the text was entered. However, remember that Excel treats all non-zero numeric values as True and zero as False. So, you may get surprising results if you enter numeric values in the linked cells.

Option buttons

Option buttons are used in groups, usually between three or five option buttons per group. They represent mutually exclusive choices, so only one can be selected at a time.

To group option buttons together, you can create a **group box**. This is a box with a caption that surrounds other dialog controls. Figure 19.4 shows a group box with three option buttons. To get the full 3D effect, I changed the shading of the cells the controls are on to look like the normal gray tone of a dialog box.

Fig. 19.4
Putting option buttons together inside of a group box not only makes them look nicer, but also makes them work together properly as well.

	A	B	C	D	E	F	G
1							
2			Account Manager				
3			○ Tina Pavelic			2	
4							
5			● Ancil Nance				
6							
7			○ Pete Reagan				
8							
9							
10							
11							

How can I use this in the real world?

If your company divides the U.S. into three regions, you might use option buttons to select the region in which a customer is located.

To group the buttons together, you'd create a group box with the caption Regions and then create three option buttons labeled East, Central, and West. By putting the option buttons together in a group box, Excel will make sure that exactly one of the buttons is selected at any given time.

If you don't use a group box, Excel will treat all your option buttons on a worksheet as if they were in the same group. Selecting one deselects any others that are on. By using a group box, you can have several sets of option buttons, each set having one button selected.

When you link one option button to a worksheet cell, all of the buttons in that group are linked to it as well. The value of the cell will be a number associated with the option button. If there are three option buttons, the cell will have the value 1, 2, or 3 depending on which button is selected. The option buttons are numbered based on the order they were added to the worksheet. This number has nothing to do with the name or caption of the button. The option buttons in figure 19.4 are linked to cell F3, which displays the number 2, since the second option button is currently selected.

Here's how the option buttons in figure 19.4 were created:

1 Click on the Group Box button on the Forms toolbar. Add a group box to your worksheet that covers cells C2 through F8. Change its caption to **Account Manager**.

2 Click on the Option Button button on the Forms toolbar and add an option button that covers cells D3 and E3.

3 Change the caption of this button to **Tina Pavelic**.

4 Right-click on the option button and choose Format Object from the pop-up menu.

5 The tabbed Format Object dialog box appears. Select the Control tab.

6 Put a check in the 3D Shading box.

7 Put your cursor in the Cell Link box. Type in **F3** (or click on cell F3). Click OK.

8 Repeat steps 1 through 6, adjusting the name and position for the other two option buttons. Do not repeat step 7. The link only needs to be created for one of the option buttons.

9 Now you need to refine the 3D effect of your controls. Select the range B2:G10. Choose Format, Cells and the click on the Patterns tab in the Format Cells dialog box. Choose the shade of gray that matches the background color for your normal dialog boxes. You may have to experiment to find the right one.

Listing information

To learn how to affect the items in a list box with VBA code, see Chapter 20, "Creating and Using Dialog Boxes."

List boxes are somewhat more involved than other kinds of dialog controls. With a list box, you need to specify the different items that are listed. This can be done either with VBA code or by associating the list box with a range of cells that contain the contents of the list box.

There are several different kinds of controls that list information. List boxes themselves come in two different styles, **standard list boxes** and **drop-down list boxes**. The difference is that the drop-down kind only shows the currently selected item, whereas a standard list box shows several items, the exact number depending on how large the list box is.

Figure 19.5 shows two list boxes. The one on the left is a drop-down. The one on the right is a standard list box. They both have the same items in their lists, but with the drop-down you can only see the current selection. The other selections can be seen by clicking the arrow button. In the standard list box, you can see five of the list items, and more can be seen by using the scroll bar.

Fig. 19.5
Drop-down lists are great space savers. Standard lists let you see several different list items at all times.

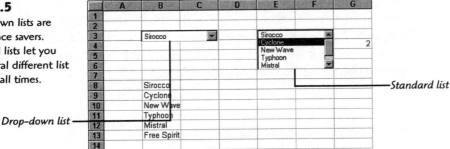

Here's how the standard list box in figure 19.5 was created:

1 In cells B8 through B13, type the following names, one per cell: **Sirocco**, **Cyclone**, **New Wave**, **Typhoon**, **Mistral**, and **Free Spirit**.

2 Click on the List Box button in the Forms toolbar and create a list box that covers cells E3 through F6.

3 Right-click on the list box you just created and choose Format Object from the pop-up menu.

4 In the tabbed Format Object dialog box, choose the Control tab.

5 Click in the Input Range box. You could type in the cells for the range, but instead move the Format Object box to the side so that you can see the cells you edited in step 1. Select this range with your cursor, and the cell references will be automatically entered in the Input Range box. The cell references determine the items that will get listed in your list box.

6 In the Cell Link box, enter **G4**. Click OK.

Now the items from the range B8:B13 appear in the list box. When you select one, a number corresponding to its position on the list appears in cell G4.

Scroll bars and spinners

The last two types of controls that you can use in your worksheets are **scroll bars** and **spinners**. Both of these are used to allow the user to input numeric data without actually typing the number. Instead, the user clicks on the buttons of the control to affect the value of a cell.

Scroll bars and spinners are created like any other dialog controls. Select the desired control from the Forms toolbar and drag on the worksheet to create the control. Scroll bars can be oriented either horizontally or vertically. This is done automatically depending on the relative height and width of the control. Spinners are always oriented vertically. Figure 19.6 shows a scroll bar in a horizontal orientation and a spinner.

Fig. 19.6
Scroll bars and spinners are both used to change numeric values. Scroll bars can represent this value in the position of the control, but spinners need to be linked to a cell to work properly.

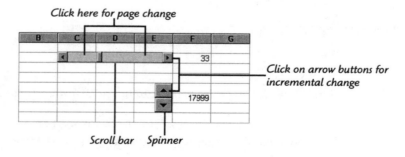

Set up your scroll bars and spinners on the Control page of the Format Object dialog box. Scroll bars and spinners share many of the same properties. They each have a maximum and minimum value. When using the control to affect the value of a number, it won't go beyond these values. They also have an Incremental value setting. This setting indicates how much the value changes by when the up or down button of the control is clicked. This is useful if you want to restrict the user to entering certain numbers, like multiples of 5 or 10.

Scroll bars have a property that is not shared by spinners: the Page Change value. This is the amount that the scroll bar will change when you click on the area indicated in figure 19.6.

Once an item is selected, how do I respond?

If you create a cell link for a group of option buttons or a list box, you get a number in the linked cell. The number refers to which item in the list or group was selected. So what good is this number? Who cares that the user picked out the third item in the list box?

You can use VBA code to put this number to good work. However, even without any programming, Excel's built-in INDEX worksheet function gives you a way to make this number useful.

INDEX takes two arguments. The first is a reference to a range of cells; the second specifies which cell in that range should be returned. You can use the linked cell from a list as the second argument. The first argument—the range—can be the original range that was used to set up the list box, or it can be another range.

For example, the list box created earlier is shown again in figure 19.7. Cell G4 is the linked cell. The second item in the list is selected, so 2 appears in this cell. The items in the list box come from the range B8:B13. The range right next to this gives the prices for each of the list objects. Here's where INDEX gets put to work. The selected cell, E10, contains the formula =INDEX(C8:C13,G4). The first argument of INDEX tells it to return one of the values from the range C8:C13, the prices. The second argument, G4, tells it which item in that range to return based on a cell reference. The cell it refers to changes every time you select a new item. So, the price that corresponds to the item is automatically updated each time an item is selected in the list box.

Fig. 19.7
With the INDEX worksheet function, you can make your lists actually look up values.

	A	B	C	D	E	F	G	H	I
1									
2									
3					Sirocco				
4					Cyclone		2		
5					New Wave				
6		glider:	price:		Typhoon				
7					Mistral				
8		Sirocco	$3,200						
9		Cyclone	$4,100						
10		New Wave	$2,500		$4,100				
11		Typhoon	$1,100						
12		Mistral	$400						
13		Free Spirit	$1,500						
14									
15									

Checks / Options / Lists / Scroll \ Lists (2)

TIP **Naming your ranges can make them easier to work with and make** your formulas easier to read. If you gave the name Prices to the range C8:C13, your formula could be written as =INDEX(Prices,G4).

Making code run when a control is used

When you create a command button, you're prompted to assign a macro to it right away. That's because command buttons are really designed to do one and only one thing: run macros. However, you can assign macros to *any* dialog control. The code will run when the control is used. What it means to use a control depends on the control you're talking about. In the case of a list box, it means that the selection has changed. In the case of a scroll box, it means that the position of the bar has changed.

You can write a macro beforehand and assign it to a control. Create the macro and then click on the control with the right mouse button. Select Assign Macro from the pop-up menu. The Assign Macro dialog box appears. Choose the macro you want and click OK.

You can also use the Assign Macro dialog box to create a macro, either by recording it or typing it into a module sheet. When the Assign Macro dialog box appears, type in a name for your macro and click Edit to type it into a module sheet, or Record to create it with the macro recorder.

To learn more about these automatically named macros, see Chapter 20, "Creating and Using Dialog Boxes."

There's also a button called Edit Code on the Forms toolbar. Figure 19.1 at the beginning of this chapter identifies this button. To use this button, you must first select a dialog control. If the control already has a macro associated with it, this button will bring you right to the macro so you can work with it. It's a very handy way to find the right macro quickly. If the control doesn't yet have a macro associated with it, this button will create one, by typing the first and last lines of a specially named macro into a module sheet. Then you can put in the middle lines of code.

Designing the sheet to protect the user

You can design your sheet so that the user can only work with the dialog controls and cannot affect the contents of the cells themselves. That way, the user won't destroy important formulas and is also guided into entering the right kind of data.

Both worksheet cells and dialog controls are locked to start with. Locking doesn't go into effect until a sheet is protected. So, when you protect a sheet, every cell and every dialog control that you don't specifically unlock will be impervious to change.

To protect a sheet, choose <u>T</u>ools, <u>P</u>rotection, <u>P</u>rotect Sheet. The Protect Sheet dialog box appears. You have the option of using a password to protect the sheet. If you choose to use one, you will be required to supply it again when unprotecting the sheet. Click OK to protect the sheet.

 *CAUTION* **If you use a password to protect a sheet, be careful you don't** forget it. If you do, you're stuck.

The values of locked cells and controls can't be directly manipulated by the user. However, cells that make calculations will still be able to do their thing.

How can I use this in the real world?

You might have a list box that displays various items that your company manufactures. You can write a macro to run whenever you select a new item in the list box. The macro will fill in a range of cells with the different parts and supplies that are used to manufacture that product. Then you can enter the month's costs for these parts and supplies.

The one exception to this is the cells that are specified as the <u>C</u>ell Link for dialog controls. If your scroll bar affects the value in cell A3, then this cell must be unlocked for you to be able to use the scroll bar. Another cell that makes a calculation based on A3 can be locked, but A3 itself must be unlocked. So, before you protect your sheet, unlock all the cells that are links to dialog controls.

 TIP **If you don't want the user to inadvertently change the values in** these unlocked cells, put them all in one column and change the column width to 0. When the sheet is protected, the user won't be able to access this column.

To unprotect a sheet, choose <u>T</u>ools, <u>P</u>rotection, Un<u>p</u>rotect Sheet. If you used a password when you protected the sheet, you'll be prompted to supply it in order to unprotect it.

Summary

In this chapter, you learned how to place dialog controls on a worksheet. Once put onto a worksheet, these controls can be used to affect the value of certain cells and to run macros. You learned how to use these controls to provide an alternate method of data entry, and to protect your formulas and other worksheet contents from being changed.

Review questions

1 What are command buttons used for?

2 How do you select a dialog control that's already on a worksheet?

3 Why would you want to use dialog controls on a worksheet?

4 What is the difference between a check box and an option button?

5 How do you associate a procedure with a dialog control?

6 How do you keep worksheet cells from being modified?

Exercises

1 Create a list box like the one in figure 19.7 by changing the list items to the days of the week.

2 Add a command button to a worksheet, and attach a macro to the button so that it will automatically run when the button is pressed.

3 Add a spinner control to a worksheet that allows you to change the value of cell C2 to a number between 10 and 100.

4 Change the spinner control from Exercise 3 so that clicking on the control changes the value by 5 at a time: 10, 15, 20, and so on.

5 Add a check box and a scroll bar to a worksheet. Each control should be linked to a cell and able to affect its value. Protect the sheet so that using these controls is the only way to affect any cell in the sheet.

6 Invent five product names and list them in cells A1 through A5. Invent corresponding prices and list them in cells B1 through B5. Create a drop-down list box that displays the product names. Create a formula in a cell that will automatically show the price of the selected product. (Hint: Use the INDEX worksheet function.)

20

Creating and Using Dialog Boxes

● In this chapter:

- How do I create custom dialog boxes?

- Is there a difference between putting controls on dialog boxes and on worksheets?

- Using the information that is provided by the user in the dialog box

- Make a dialog box show current information

- What do I do if the user presses Cancel?

Dialog boxes pave the way for extensive communication between your program and the user. . . . .

Sometimes, it's easier to do something for a coworker than to explain how it should be done. Perhaps someone wants to know how to add data to a complicated spreadsheet you've designed. It might seem easier to do it yourself than to risk the inadvertent mistakes that could result from an inexperienced user interacting with your worksheet.

But this is hardly an effective use of your time. Instead, why not create a custom dialog box that will replace the normal interface of Excel? Then you can provide easy-to-use dialog controls that are guaranteed to enter the right data in the right places.

In this chapter, you learn how to create, display, and use the information entered in custom dialog boxes. This is the high-end of VBA programming. You can modify the environment to the point that no one need even know that Excel is running behind your dialog boxes.

Getting acquainted with dialog sheets

Dialog sheets are a type of Excel sheet used for designing original dialog boxes. Like module sheets, you need to add them to your workbook specifically—none are created when you open a new workbook. To add a dialog sheet to a workbook, choose Insert, Macro, Dialog. A dialog sheet like the one in figure 20.1 appears. It includes a frame with a title bar and two command buttons—OK and Cancel.

Dialog sheets are a little different from worksheets in that you only use them for design purposes. Later, if you want to display the dialog box you created, you use VBA code to show the dialog box. The sheet itself doesn't appear.

 To see what will appear when the dialog box is displayed via a program, you can use the Run Dialog button on the Forms toolbar. That way, you can test the dialog box from within a dialog sheet.

Fig. 20.1
Adding a dialog sheet
to the workbook gives
you a ready-made
dialog box, complete
with OK and Cancel
buttons.

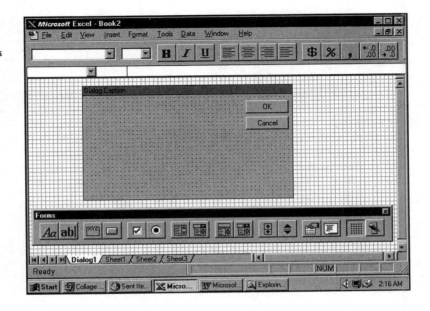

What's the difference between a dialog box and a dialog sheet?

A **dialog sheet** is a kind of VBA sheet where dialog boxes are designed. Dialog sheets have sheet tabs at the bottom, just like worksheets or modules. Each dialog sheet contains the design-mode version of a dialog box; this is called a **dialog frame**. You can make changes to it in the dialog sheet. Once you've finished work on the sheet, you can hide the sheet and still display the dialog frame it contains.

When you display a dialog box, it pops up alone without the surrounding sheet. No sheet tab will appear at the bottom of the workbook associated with a dialog box. You can't add new buttons directly to the dialog box; you must go to the dialog sheet where it is stored to change it. In a way, dialog sheets are where dialog boxes live when they're not in use.

Changing the dialog frame

The **dialog frame** is what actually becomes the dialog box when you run it. The rest of the sheet is just empty space. There is one frame per dialog sheet. When you create a dialog sheet, it provides a frame with two buttons and a caption. You can change the size of the frame, remove one or both of the two buttons, and provide a new caption.

To change the size of the frame, which changes the size of the displayed dialog box, first select the frame by clicking on its title bar. Then resize it by clicking one of the resize handles that appear around the edges (see fig. 20.2).

Fig. 20.2
How big you make your dialog box all depends on what you want to put in it.

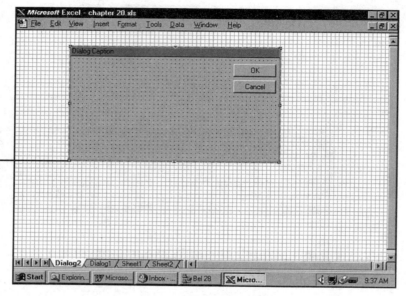

Click and drag one of the resize handles to change the size of the dialog box

Dialog boxes should have a descriptive title. When you create a new dialog sheet, a default title of `Dialog Caption` is created. You can change this by clicking on the dialog box's title bar to select the frame, and then editing the text on the title bar.

TIP If you're making a dialog box that will appear when a button or menu item is selected, then the caption of the dialog box should be the same or as close as possible to the name on the menu or button.

Working with controls on dialog sheets

Controls are added to dialog sheets in the same way they are added to worksheets. Select the control you want from the Forms toolbar and drag the mouse across the place you want to put it.

When you're in a dialog sheet, clicking on a dialog control will select it. This is different from worksheets where you need to hold down the Ctrl key while clicking on a dialog control to select it.

To make it easier to line up controls and make them the same size, there is a grid in the background. While the grid is turned on, controls are moved and resized in increments of this grid. You can turn this feature off by clicking on the Toggle Grid button on the Forms toolbar. When the feature is turned off, the small dots and lines that represent the grid disappear from the dialog sheet. Figure 20.2 on the previous page shows a dialog sheet with the gridlines turned on.

Naming controls

As controls are added to a dialog sheet, they are given a unique name for that sheet. The name consists of the type of control it is and a number. So, if the fifth control you add to a dialog box is an option button, its name will be given as `Option Button 5`.

Don't confuse the name of a control with its caption. The caption of a control is what is displayed when the dialog box is shown. Its name is how it is referred to in VBA. The name of a control can be seen by selecting the control and reading its name in the name box. Figure 20.3 shows a check box whose caption is `Bold` and whose name is `Check Box 5`.

Fig. 20.3
There's a big difference between the name and caption of a control. The name of this check box is `Check Box 5` and its caption is `Bold`.

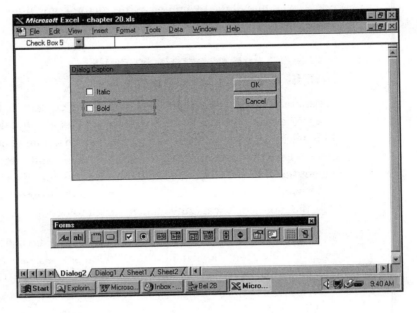

You can change the name of a control to make it easier for you to remember. To change the name of a control:

1 Click on the control to select it. Its current name will appear in the Name box to the left of the formula bar.

2 Select the current name and type a new one.

3 Press Enter to accept the new name. (This is important. If you don't press Enter, the name will not be changed.)

If you're going to change the names of your controls, you should do it when you first add them to a dialog sheet. The problem with changing the names later is that you'll have to change any VBA code you've written that refers to that control. If you write a procedure that refers to Option Button 4 and later change the name of that button to `MyOption`, VBA won't know what to do with the code referring to Option Button 4 and will produce an error.

Programmers commonly use names beginning with a prefix that describes the type of control they are naming. So an edit box that is for inputting an address might be called `edtAddress`, and the OK command button would be `cmdOK`. In some of the examples in this chapter, you'll find these kinds of names in use.

Should I link controls to cells, just like on a worksheet?

In general, it is *not* a good idea to link a dialog control that's in a dialog box to a worksheet cell. You usually won't want changes to take place immediately when the user selects the control. Instead, a dialog box is usually a place where the user enters one or more choices and then chooses OK to accept the choices. Most dialog boxes have an OK and a Cancel button. You don't want the changes to go into effect until the user selects OK. If Cancel is selected, you won't want any changes at all to occur.

There are exceptions. Sometimes a dialog box will be used in a situation that doesn't really seem like a dialog box. You might be replacing the normal interface of Excel with a dialog box in certain situations. Or, you might have a control that displays the value in a certain cell and cannot be changed by the user. Then there's no harm in linking it to that cell.

In the majority of cases, though, you'll have to make changes when the OK button is pressed. Thus, you will not want to link the controls to cells.

Instead, you'll write code to be run when the OK button is pressed that puts the changes into effect.

Where do I put the code that makes a control do something?

Each control has a typical action associated with it: a button is clicked, an item from a list box is selected, a scroll bar's value is changed. It might seem like a daunting task to be able to figure out when something like that happens and to make an action occur. In fact, the framework required to achieve all of this is already built into Excel. The typical action for each control has a special kind of procedure that can be automatically generated.

To see an example of this, select the OK button on a dialog sheet. Now click on the Edit Code button on the Forms toolbar. A module sheet is active with a procedure stub already created for you, like the one shown in figure 20.4.

> ❝ *Plain English, please!*
>
> A **procedure stub** is the skeleton of a procedure: the first and last lines. When Excel creates a procedure stub for you, all you need to do is fill in the contents. ❞

Fig. 20.4
The procedure stub is ready and waiting with first and last lines prepared. All you need to do is write some code to go in between.

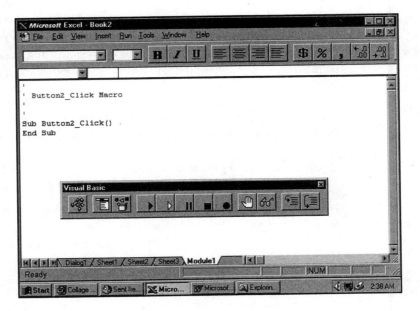

The stub is specially named for automatic detection of clicks on that particular button. You should leave the name of the procedure as-is. However, you can add code to the stub. For example, add a Beep statement to the procedure stub from figure 20.4.

```
Sub Button_2_Click()
    Beep
End Sub
```

That's all you need to do to make the OK button beep when it is clicked. The task of detecting the click and finding the right procedure to run is taken care of for you. Try it out by activating the dialog sheet and clicking the Run Dialog button on the Forms toolbar. When you click on the OK button, the computer will beep.

The OK button is where you'll wind up putting most of your code. If you have a dialog box that lets the user change some Excel settings, then you'll want these settings to be implemented when the OK button is selected. That way, if Cancel is selected, nothing will happen.

There are a few things that you might want to have happen when a particular dialog control is used, though. For example, consider a dialog box that allows you to change the billing address for customers in your database. A list box might contain the name of the customer, and then several edit boxes would display the address. When you select a different customer in the list box, the edit boxes should update to show the address for that customer. You're not changing any permanent data, just what's being displayed in the dialog box.

This could be done by writing code associated with changing the value of the list box. To do this, select the list box, click on the Edit Code button, and then enter code into the procedure stub that was created for you.

Q&A ***Why do I get a* Reference is not valid *error message when I click on the Edit Code button?***

This is a really silly design problem in Excel. If you delete a procedure stub associated with a particular control, then Excel still looks for it when you click on the Edit Code button for the same control. To fix the problem, right-click on the control and then select Assign Macro from the pop-up menu.

In the Assign Macro dialog box, a macro will be listed in the <u>M</u>acro Name/ Reference box at the top. Delete the reference to this macro and click OK.

The problem was that the control was associated with the procedure stub that you deleted.

To avoid having this problem, don't delete procedure stubs. You can take out all the internal code so that it does nothing at all, and just leave the first and last lines.

How do I specify a control?

To learn about objects and collections, see Chapter 11, "How VBA Refers to Things in Excel."

Each type of dialog control has a collection. An edit box is a member of the EditBoxes collection, and an option button is a member of the OptionButtons collection. You specify a particular control by using the collection's method and the name of the control as the argument. For example,

```
OptionButtons("Option Button 4")
```

specifies a particular option button.

Like all objects, you need to give full information on where the object is located. If the dialog box will be active when the code is run, you can use ActiveSheet. If not, you need to specify the sheet as well. In either case, you do need to first give a reference to a sheet, and then to the dialog control. This statement sets the state of a check box in the sheet Dialog1 to unchecked:

```
Sheets("Dialog1").CheckBoxes("Check Box 4").Value = xlOff
```

Displaying your dialog boxes

A dialog box is displayed by specifying the appropriate sheet and using the Show method. Thus, a dialog sheet named Dialog1 would be displayed by the line of code:

```
Sheets("Dialog1").Show
```

It will remain on-screen until the user presses the OK or Cancel button. You can also get rid of the dialog box by using the Hide method. Not surprisingly, running the statement

```
Sheets("Dialog1").Hide
```

will hide the sheet that was displayed above.

Notice the difference between the Show method, which runs a dialog *box*, and the Activate method, which makes the dialog *sheet* the active sheet with a statement like the following:

```
Sheets("Dialog1").Activate
```

The Show method displays the dialog box in "working" mode; the sheet the dialog box was created on is nowhere to be seen, and the dialog controls are ready to be used. With Activate you see the dialog box in "design" mode as part of the dialog sheet. The dialog sheet is brought to the front, and the controls can be selected and modified.

TIP **Once you've finished designing your dialog box, hide the dialog sheet.** You can still use the Show method on the sheet to display the dialog box, but the sheet itself will be hidden from the user and thus protected from inadvertent tampering.

As you can see, the code required to display a dialog box—i.e., the Show method—is pretty straightforward. It's where you decide to put this code that makes things interesting. There are many different situations where you might want to display a dialog box. The procedure to run it will look pretty much the same whether you attach it to a menu item, a button, or make it run automatically.

...when a menu item is selected or a button is pressed

To learn more about making procedures run automatically, see Chapter 22, "Making Code Run Automatically."

When you choose File, Save As, Excel displays its built-in Save As dialog box. By writing a macro that displays a dialog box and creating a custom menu item to run that macro, you can make your own menu items that bring up your custom dialog boxes.

Another common way to display a dialog box is in response to a command button being pressed. The command button might be on a worksheet or on another dialog box. An example is shown in figure 20.5. There is a New Purchase Order button on the Purchase Orders worksheet.

Fig. 20.5
The three dots on the New Purchase Order button are a giveaway; clicking on this button will bring up a dialog box.

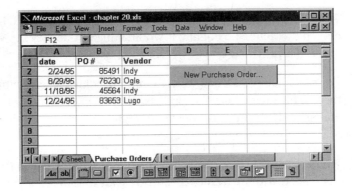

Menu items and command buttons that display dialog boxes when selected have an **ellipsis** (…) after the caption. The corresponding dialog box should have the same name as the menu item or button, but without the ellipsis. Thus, a menu item called <u>A</u>dd Customer… would bring up a dialog box with the caption Add Customer.

…when the user enters Excel

You can create a dialog box that automatically appears when Excel is run or when a particular workbook is opened. Excel is a pretty complicated program. With dialog boxes, you can guide the user through appropriate choices. Here are some of the things you might do with a dialog box that appears automatically when Excel is run:

- Limit the user to opening one of several existing workbooks.

- Present the user with descriptions of a number of different kinds of new worksheets that can be created. Based on the user's choices, load an appropriate template.

- Ask the user to enter a name and password and then automatically open the workbook that belongs to that user.

Don't forget to initialize the dialog box

Suppose you create a dialog box that allows the user to add a new customer name and address to a database. Each time the dialog box is displayed, you want the edit boxes to be blank to accept new information. However, the default behavior for dialog boxes is to display the information that was entered there the last time you used it. In other words, if I entered the name

John Smith into my Add Customer dialog box, clicked OK, and then displayed the dialog box again, it would still say John Smith where I had entered it previously.

For this reason, you will want to initialize dialog boxes when you display them. This means that you specify the values of certain properties for the dialog controls. For instance, you might want an option button to be checked or an edit box to display a particular value.

When a dialog box is displayed, it will automatically run the procedure associated with its frame. By putting your initialization instructions into this procedure, they will be run each time you display the dialog box. Adding code to this procedure is just like adding code to any other dialog control.

Here's an example of a dialog box with an edit box. Each time you display the dialog, it clears the edit box. To create this dialog box, do the following:

1 Open a new workbook and insert a dialog sheet by choosing Insert, Macro, Dialog.

2 Add an edit box to the sheet.

3 Click on the title bar of the dialog frame to select the entire dialog box.

 4 Click on the Edit Code button on the Forms toolbar. A module sheet appears with the first and last lines of the DialogFrame1_Show procedure created for you.

5 Between these two lines, type the statement

```
ActiveSheet.EditBoxes("edit box 4").Text = ""
```

To try it out, select the dialog sheet and click on the Run Dialog button on the Forms toolbar. Type some text into the edit box and click on the OK button. Now run the dialog again. The text box will be clear.

Initializing your dialog box doesn't necessarily mean making sure all of the controls are blank. You might want to initialize a control to a particular value. For example, you could enter the value of the current cell into an edit box. Or, you could specify that an option button be selected to reflect the most common choice.

Handling dialog controls with VBA

The primary direction of information is *from* dialog boxes *to* other parts of Excel. Thus, the user will change the value of controls in a dialog box, and your procedures will react to these controls by making changes to worksheets or running certain VBA procedures. So, you need to know how to get information that's been entered in a dialog box.

It can go the other way, too. You can change the state of a control in a dialog box with VBA code. This is usually done by changing the value of one of the object's properties. Which property you work with will depend on the control. With a check box, you might want to change the value property to determine whether it appears as checked or not, but for a list box, you can change the Index property that selects which item from the list is currently chosen.

The subject of working with various dialog controls could fill an entire book. Rather than try to cover the topic in great detail for every control, let's look at two kinds of controls: check boxes and edit boxes.

An example using check boxes

What is represented by a check in a check box in the language of VBA? Check box objects have a `Value` property. Whether this property is equal to `xlOn` or `xlOff` determines if the box is checked. A third setting of `xlMixed` is allowed when the check box is grayed.

Figure 20.6 shows a dialog box that allows the user to make some very simple formatting changes to a selection by changing the value of the two check boxes.

When I created this dialog box, I changed the names of the controls so that they would be easier to remember when I wrote the program that controls them. The check boxes are named `chkBold` and `chkItalic`. The OK command button is named `cmdOK`. Here's the code that runs when the OK button is clicked.

Fig. 20.6
Checking the Bold and Italic boxes will change the format of the text in the selected cells.

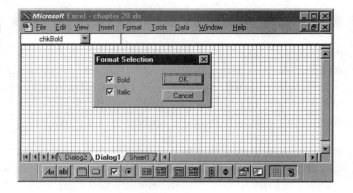

```
Sub cmdOK_Click()
    If Sheets("Dialog1").CheckBoxes("chkBold").Value = xlOn Then
        Selection.Font.Bold = True
    Else
        Selection.Font.Bold = False
    End If

    If Sheets("Dialog1").CheckBoxes("chkItalic").Value = xlOn Then
        Selection.Font.Italic = True
    Else
        Selection.Font.Italic = False
    End If
End Sub
```

This procedure consists of two If/Then/Else blocks. The first one looks at whether a check mark exists in chkBold. If a check is present, then the current selection's font is made bold. If no check is present, then the bold is removed from the current selection.

The second If/Then/Else block does exactly the same thing for the chkItalic box and the italic property of the font in the selection.

An example using edit boxes

Edit boxes have two properties that you'll commonly want to work with. The Text property reflects the text in the edit box. The following line of code takes the text that's in an edit box called Edit Box 4 and stores it in a variable called NameEntered.

```
NameEntered = ActiveSheet.EditBoxes("Edit Box 4").Text
```

The Enabled property affects whether the contents of an edit box can be changed. By setting the enabled property of an edit box to False, you can display data that the user cannot change. This is useful if you want to reflect some current state of the workbook that the dialog box cannot alter.

Here's an example that makes use of both the Text and Enabled properties of edit boxes. The dialog box shown in figure 20.7 is displayed when the user wants to generate a new purchase order.

Fig. 20.7

A new purchase order number is automatically added in the PO Number edit box whenever this dialog box is displayed.

The following two procedures are used in conjunction with this dialog box. The first one is run when displaying the dialog box. The second updates Excel when changes have been entered in the dialog box and the OK button is selected.

```
Sub dlgPO_Show()
    CurrentPO = 45294
    Sheets("PO Dialog").EditBoxes("edtPO").Text = CurrentPO
    Sheets("PO Dialog").EditBoxes("edtPO").Enabled = False
    Sheets("PO Dialog").EditBoxes("edtVendor").Text = ""
End Sub

Sub cmdOK_Click()
    CurrentVendor = Sheets("PO
Dialog").EditBoxes("edtVendor").Text
    CurrentPO = Sheets("PO Dialog").EditBoxes("edtPO").Text
    AddPO CurrentPO, CurrentVendor
End Sub
```

The dlgPO_Show procedure is the one that is automatically run whenever the dialog box is shown. It creates a variable called CurrentPO and assigns it the value 45294. In a more realistic situation, the CurrentPO value might be found on the worksheet or by looking at the value of a global variable.

The next line puts the current PO number in an edit box. This edit box has its Enabled property set to False on the following line. Thus, the user can only read the number of the current PO, not alter it in the dialog box. Finally, the value of the second edit box is set to an empty text string, so that when the dialog box appears, this edit box will be empty. Thus, when the dialog box is displayed, it will look like the one in figure 20.7.

The second procedure, cmdOK_Click, is run when the OK button is selected. This procedure creates variables called CurrentPO and CurrentVendor and assigns them values by retrieving the text that was entered into the two edit boxes in the dialog box. One of these values, CurrentVendor, was entered by the user. The other one was entered by the dlgPO_Show procedure.

The last line calls a procedure called AddPO with two arguments. Presumably, this is a procedure that will store the vendor name and the PO number on the worksheet.

Summary

In this chapter, you learned how to add a dialog sheet to your workbook and how to add controls to the sheet to create a useful dialog box. The dialog box is used by running the Show method on the dialog sheet object. You learned the difference between using controls on a dialog sheet and on a worksheet, and how to react to the information that users enter in dialog boxes.

Review questions

1   What's the difference between a dialog sheet and a dialog frame?

2   How do you run a dialog box with VBA code?

3   Name three things that could trigger the display of a dialog box.

4   Why is it generally a bad idea to link controls in dialog boxes to worksheet cells?

5   How can you specify how dialog controls should look when the dialog box is displayed?

6   How can you design a dialog box that will only make changes when the OK button is selected and will ignore any changes if the Cancel button is selected?

Exercises

1   Add a dialog sheet to a workbook. Then create a command button, an edit box, and an option button on the sheet.

2 Change the caption of the dialog box created in Exercise 1 to My Dialog. Display the dialog box using the Run Dialog button on the Forms toolbar.

3 Create a dialog box with an edit box control that is blank whenever the dialog box is run.

4 Using the dialog box created in Exercise 3, create a procedure that takes the text entered in this dialog box and puts it into the active worksheet cell if you choose the OK button, but makes no changes if you choose the Cancel button.

21

Integrate Your Program with Excel

● **In this chapter:**

- **Get rid of the *PERSONAL.XLS!* that appears in front of macro names**

- **Hide VBA code where it can't be found accidentally**

- **I'd like my coworkers to be able to choose to install certain customizations without getting lost or hurting my programs**

- **Is there an easy way to copy programs to other computers?**

If you create an add-in, other users might never know that the features you provide are not a built-in part of Excel . . . .

A friend of mine had a scare with Excel not too long ago. She was accustomed to using a built-in function called EDATE that allows you to calculate what the date will be a certain number of months from a particular start date. She installed a new version of Excel and typed a formula using EDATE into a worksheet cell but got a #NAME? error. It seemed like EDATE had been removed from the new version of Excel.

Actually, EDATE was never part of the core Excel program. It is stored in a special kind of file called an **Excel add-in**. Functionality that is stored in these files is so seamlessly integrated with Excel that you might never know that they are not built into Excel itself. My friend had put a new copy of Excel on her machine and needed to reinstall the add-in that contained this function. This required only a few mouse clicks, and she got her EDATE back.

It's a simple task to create your own add-ins. Then your customizations can fit so seamlessly into Excel that they'll seem like they are a part of the program itself.

What's an add-in?

Add-ins are special files that contain added Excel functionality. They can be installed into Excel so that they seem to be a built-in part of the program.

You can easily create an add-in by converting a worksheet to an add-in file. On your computer, add-ins are stored as a special kind of Excel file. The file extension for an add-in is usually XLA, although some add-ins that come with Excel have the extension XLL or XLT. You can see a list of all available add-ins by selecting Tools, Add-Ins.

Available add-ins can be installed or uninstalled. In figure 21.1, the check mark beside the names of some of the add-ins indicates that they are currently installed.

Fig. 21.1

Pick from the list of add-ins that come with Excel and ones that you create yourself.

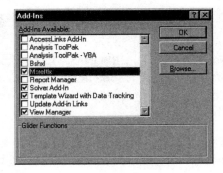

A simple add-in might consist of some user-defined worksheet functions you've created. By installing them in an add-in, they'll appear on the list in the Functions dialog box, regardless of which workbook is open. A more complicated add-in might consist of a whole new look for Excel with custom toolbars, menus, dialog boxes, and formatting.

The add-ins you make will start out as workbooks. Thus, your add-in will be able to do many of the things that a customized workbook does. However, an add-in is always hidden. You can't access its modules or worksheets. In fact, it's a good idea to remove all the worksheets from a workbook before you turn it into an add-in. You won't be able to use them, and there's no sense in keeping the sheets there since removing them will make the add-in take up less room in memory.

Putting your VBA programs, dialog sheets, menus, and toolbars into an add-in and installing it is like putting them into the PERSONAL.XLS file. They will be available from all workbooks at all times. The difference is that the add-in will be integrated seamlessly with Excel. There will be no special workbook open. The add-in cannot be unhidden like the PERSONAL.XLS workbook, and your macros and functions will not need to have PERSONAL.XLS! in front of their names when you use them.

Why would I want to make an add-in?

Much of what can be done with add-ins can be done with other techniques as well. You can put programs in the PERSONAL.XLS workbook and make them run automatically. Or, you can create document templates and store them in the XLSTART directory. Why, then, would you choose to create an add-in over one of these other methods?

Add-ins provide a higher degree of integration with the existing Excel environment. Here are a few of the advantages of an add-in over the existing Excel environment:

- Macros and functions that are stored in PERSONAL.XLS must be called using the name of the workbook as well. A macro called Budget stored in PERSONAL.XLS appears in the Macro dialog box as `Personal.xls!Budget()`. Put the macro in an add-in, and it will appear simply as `Budget()`.

- PERSONAL.XLS is just like any other workbook. If the user unhides this workbook, it can be edited or closed. This can cause problems if the user inadvertently unhides PERSONAL.XLS. Add-ins cannot be displayed in Excel.

- With an add-in, the user can choose whether or not to install the added functionality through the Add-Ins dialog box. PERSONAL.XLS automatically loads regardless of the circumstances.

- Add-ins provide a method for transporting customization from one computer to another without having to replace the existing PERSONAL.XLS file.

Creating a sample add-in

One use for add-ins would be to give better access to your user-defined worksheet functions. Figure 21.2 shows a workbook that contains a single module sheet. (All of the worksheets have been deleted.) The module contains two functions that can be used as user-defined worksheet functions.

Fig. 21.2
Strip your workbook down to the bare minimum and BACK IT UP to a separate file before converting it to an add-in.

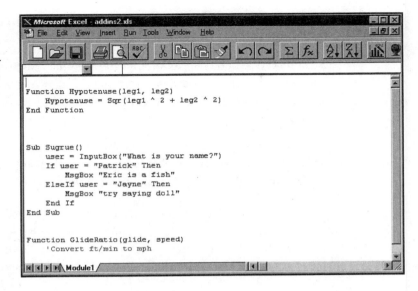

```
Microsoft Excel - addins2.xls
File   Edit   View   Insert   Run   Tools   Window   Help

Function Hypotenuse(leg1, leg2)
    Hypotenuse = Sqr(leg1 ^ 2 + leg2 ^ 2)
End Function


Sub Sugrue()
    user = InputBox("What is your name?")
    If user = "Patrick" Then
        MsgBox "Eric is a fish"
    ElseIf user = "Jayne" Then
        MsgBox "try saying doll"
    End If
End Sub


Function GlideRatio(glide, speed)
    'Convert ft/min to mph
```
Module1

Here is how you would go about converting the workbook in figure 21.2 into an add-in:

1 Choose File, Properties to bring up the Properties dialog box. Select the Summary tab. The Summary page is shown in figure 21.3.

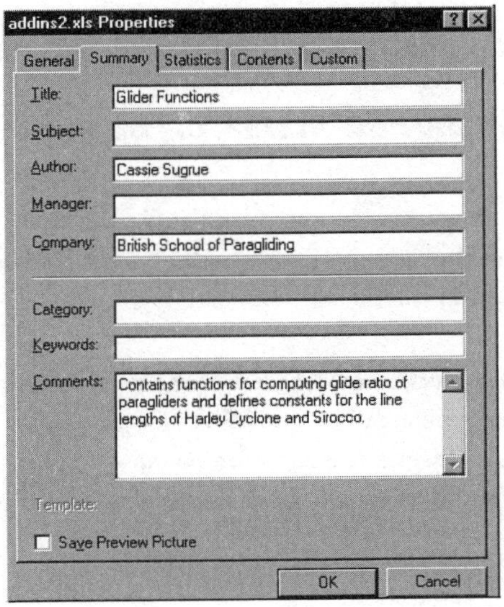

Fig. 21.3
The Summary page of the Properties dialog box lets you set the Title and Comments for your workbook. These will appear later in the Add-Ins dialog box.

addins2.xls Properties

General | Summary | Statistics | Contents | Custom

Title: Glider Functions

Subject:

Author: Cassie Sugrue

Manager:

Company: British School of Paragliding

Category:

Keywords:

Comments: Contains functions for computing glide ratio of paragliders and defines constants for the line lengths of Harley Cyclone and Sirocco.

Template:

☐ Save Preview Picture

OK   Cancel

2 Save the workbook so that you'll have an XLS file to work with after you convert this workbook to an add-in.

3 Enter a title and description into the Summary page of the Properties dialog box. The title and description you give will control how your add-in is listed in the Add-Ins dialog box. Click OK to accept your title and summary.

4 Choose Tools, Make Add-In. The Make Add-In dialog box appears. This is similar to the Save As dialog box. You can change the directory where the add-in will be saved or the name of the add-in file.

That's it. You've created an add-in. What that means is that you've saved a workbook in a special format that cannot be used like a workbook. It can only be accessed by choosing it through the Add-Ins dialog box, whereupon its customizations and code will be available to all workbooks.

Why isn't the Make Add-In menu item on the Tools menu?

This item only appears on the Tools menu when a module sheet is active. Activate a module sheet and check again.

If you created a title in step 3, the name of the file will not affect the name that is displayed in the Add-Ins dialog box. Add-ins are usually stored in the Library subdirectory of the Excel directory, although this is not required.

Why isn't my add-in showing up in the Add-Ins dialog box?

The first time you use your add-in, you'll have to locate it for Excel. This is described in the next section. After that, your add-in will appear along with all the others in the dialog box.

CAUTION **Always save your workbook before you convert it into an add-in.** If you save it, there will be an XLS version (a normal workbook) and an XLA version (the add-in). You can't modify an XLA file. If you ever want to change it or add to it, you'll need a copy of the original workbook.

Installing an existing add-in

Once an add-in exists, there are two more steps necessary to install it: adding it to the list in the Add-Ins dialog box, and selecting it from this list.

To put your add-in on the list, select the Browse button in the Add-Ins dialog box. This brings up the Browse dialog box which will let you look through folders until you locate your add-in. In the Browse dialog box, you're looking for a file name. For an add-in file that you created this will normally be an XLA file. Find the file, and click on OK.

Once you've done this, your add-in will appear on the list in the Add-Ins dialog box. The entry on the list will not appear by file name. Instead, the title you supplied in the Summary page will be used. If you didn't create a title on the summary page, then the file name will be used instead. Once your add-in is on the list, simply put a check mark in the corresponding box to install it. Figure 21.4 shows the Add-Ins dialog box after the worksheet shown in figures 21.2 and 21.3 is added to the list.

Fig. 21.4
The first time you use an add-in, you need to locate it for Excel. After that it appears in the Add-Ins dialog box automatically.

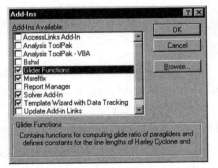

Removing an add-in

Removing an add-in consists of two steps. First, remove the XLA file that contains the information for the add-in. You can delete the XLA file if you no longer want it, or you can move it to another directory. Either way, Excel will not be able to find it the next time it looks. Then to get it off the list in the Add-Ins dialog box, select the add-in that you just deleted or moved. Since Excel can't find it, an error message is produced like the one in figure 21.5. Click on the Yes button to remove it from the list.

Fig. 21.5
If Excel can't find an add-in, it gives you the option of removing it from the list.

Changing add-ins

Add-ins can't be changed directly. You need to make your changes to the workbook that you used to create the add-in and then use that workbook to create a new add-in. Then you can replace the old version with the new one.

Remember to save your workbooks before converting them into add-ins. Once you've converted them, you won't be able to view the code and change it. Your only recourse is to change the original file and create a new add-in.

Using VBA code to work with add-ins

Excel has an AddIns collection, and each add-in is a member of that collection. You can use VBA to name add-ins, install them, and add new add-ins to the collection.

You can use VBA code to automate the installation and removal of add-ins. This is particularly useful for distributing your programs to other computers.

Referring to a particular add-in

The AddIns method returns a reference to an add-in object. The AddIns method can take the name of an add-in as its argument. For example,

```
AddIns("Analysis ToolPak")
```

refers to the Analysis ToolPak add-in that comes with Excel. Notice that the argument of the AddIns method is the name that gets displayed in the Add-Ins dialog box. It is *not* the name of the XLA file associated with this add-in.

An add-in object has several useful properties. The Installed property can be set to True or False reflecting whether or not the add-in is currently checked, and thus installed, in the Add-Ins dialog box. The Name property returns the file name of the add-in. This is different from the Title property, which is the way the add-in is displayed in the Add-Ins dialog box. The value of the Comments property is the text that is displayed when the add-in is selected in the Add-Ins dialog box. This procedure uses the AddIns method to refer to the Report Manager add-in and then reads and changes several of its properties.

```
Sub SetAddins()
    'Check with user about install
    answer = MsgBox("Install the Report Manager?", vbYesNo)
    If answer = vbYes Then
        AddIns("Report Manager").Installed = True
    ElseIf answer = vbNo Then
        AddIns("Report Manager").Installed = False
    End If

    'Show file of Report Manager
    MsgBox AddIns("Report Manager").Name & " " _
        & AddIns("Report Manager").Comments
End Sub
```

This procedure asks whether the user wants the Report Manager installed or not. Based on the user's answer, the Installed property of this add-in is set to True or False.

After this is done, the name of the file that contains the actual add-in and the comments is displayed. This message box appears in figure 21.6.

Fig. 21.6
The Name and Comments properties are just like any other object properties and can be used as text strings in a message box.

Adding an add-in to Excel with VBA

The Installed property of an add-in can only be set to True once the add-in appears on this list in the Add-Ins dialog box. How does it get onto this list? The list displays the members of the AddIns collection, so you must add an add-in to the AddIns collection. This is accomplished by selecting the <u>B</u>rowse button in the Add-Ins dialog box and locating the file, but you can also do it with VBA code by using the Add method.

Add is a method of the AddIns collection, and you must provide the name of the file to be added as the argument. Unlike the AddIns method where you used the title of the add-in, now you need to use the actual file name including its path. This statement adds the MATHMACROS.XLA file to the collection of add-ins.

```
AddIns.Add ("c:\Excel\My Add-Ins\Mathmacros.XLA")
```

When you use the Add method like this, Excel will automatically take care of putting the appropriate title and description into the Add-Ins dialog box (assuming you created them in the Summary page of the Properties dialog box).

Summary

In this chapter, you learned how to create and use add-ins, a special kind of Excel file that integrates your VBA programs and other customizations into the Excel environment. You also learned how to write VBA code that can create, install, and set the properties of your add-ins.

How can I use this in the real world?

If you want to distribute your add-ins to other computers, you can put your XLA file on a disk along with another workbook. The other workbook can contain a procedure that runs when the workbook is opened and installs the add-in on the new computer.

Chapter 22 talks about making code run automatically. When the workbook is opened, a procedure that steps the user through a series of dialog boxes can run. If the user indicates he wishes to install the add-in, code can be run to copy the add-in file to the hard drive and install the add-in.

Review questions

1 In terms of files on your computer, what is an add-in?

2 How can you tell if an add-in is installed or not?

3 Why is it important to save your workbook as an XLS file before you convert it to an add-in?

4 If you create a user-defined worksheet function called MyFunction, how will it appear in the Function Wizard if it is stored in PERSONAL.XLS? What if it is part of an add-in?

Exercises

1 Create a workbook with a user-defined worksheet function or macro in it. Give it a title and comments. Save it, then convert it to an add-in.

2 In the Add-Ins dialog box, browse to find your add-in and then install it. Now try running a macro or a function from your add-in while in another workbook.

3 Uninstall the add-in by unchecking it in the Add-Ins dialog box. Then find the XLA file you created in step 1 and delete it.

4 Remove the add-in you created in step 1 from the Add-Ins dialog box.

22

Making Code Run Automatically

In this chapter:

- Write programs that run without requiring the user to select them

- How do I make a dialog box appear when my program starts?

- Is there a way to make menu and toolbar changes apply to one particular worksheet or workbook?

- Other kinds of actions that can trigger programs

Why wait for the user to tell a macro to run? You can put Excel on the lookout for appropriate situations and run your macros automatically. . . . . >

There are a lot of lights in my car. When I put my key in the ignition, a light appears telling me to put on my seatbelt. If I put it on, the light goes off. If my gas level gets low, another light goes on. When I open the door, the dome light goes on, and when I close the door, the light shuts off again.

All of these lights turn on and off in response to something that happens. They are all controlled very differently from my headlights. The headlights I specifically switch on and off by turning a knob. These other lights are controlled indirectly by other things I do. Somehow, they're keeping an eye on the current state of affairs in my car. They turn on and off automatically in the appropriate situation or in response to other actions.

Like my car, Excel can tell when certain things are happening. Similar to how my car can tell if my seatbelt is on, my gas is low, or my door is open, Excel can tell when a sheet is selected, a file is opened, or a time is reached. You don't have to press a button or use a menu command to run a macro; you can make it run automatically based on the situation at hand.

Making a workbook open automatically

Most customization that you can do in Excel is stored in workbooks. This includes VBA code, menu changes, and dialog boxes. Only toolbars and changes stored in add-ins are not associated with a particular workbook. So, if you want your customizations or programs to run automatically, you need the appropriate workbook to open automatically.

You're already used to having one workbook open automatically: PERSONAL.XLS, the Personal Macro Workbook. The reason that it opens automatically is not because it's a special workbook in any way. PERSONAL.XLS opens automatically not because of *what* it is, but because of *where* it is. You'll find it on your hard drive in XLSTART, a subdirectory of your Excel directory.

Workbooks stored in the XLSTART directory always open when Excel is run. If they are hidden, like PERSONAL.XLS, you won't see them, but their effects will be felt nonetheless. You can have several workbooks in the XLSTART directory and make them hidden or visible. In the next section, you learn how you can automatically run a procedure when a workbook is opened. Because the workbooks in XLSTART are opened automatically, you can create procedures in these workbooks that you want to have run whenever Excel itself is started.

Usually, PERSONAL.XLS suffices for hidden workbooks. There's not much you can do with two hidden books that you can't do with one. But, you may want to add another book to the XLSTART directory that isn't hidden. If most of the work done on the computer is in a particular workbook, it makes sense to load this automatically. Or, you might want to load several different sheets and provide a toolbar that lets users click a button to move between them.

Procedures that run when a workbook is opened or closed

VBA has two special kinds of procedures that can be associated with a workbook. They will run whenever the workbook is opened or closed by the user. These procedures are identified by their names: Auto_Open and Auto_Close. Just giving a macro one of these names will cause it to run automatically when its workbook is opened or closed.

Some of the uses for this kind of procedure are obvious. If you want to display a dialog box whenever a certain workbook is loaded, you can put this

How can I use this in the real world?

You can create dialog boxes of your own to replace Excel's interface. By automatically loading a workbook that contains your dialog sheets and then putting in a procedure that displays the first dialog box automatically, your interface will go directly into effect as soon as Excel is opened.

You achieve this effect by creating a workbook with an Auto_Open procedure (described in the next section) that displays that startup dialog box. Store this workbook in the XLSTART directory, and whenever Excel is started, it will open the workbook that will in turn display the dialog box.

command into the Auto_Open procedure. Or, you might run a program that prompts the user to back up a file to floppy disk whenever a workbook is closed.

Excel includes built-in password functionality. Here is a program that makes things a little more refined by controlling password protection on a single sheet in a workbook. Because it is an Auto_Open procedure, it runs whenever this workbook is opened.

```
Sub Auto_Open()
    ReadOnlyPW = "jmb1118"
    ReadWritePW = "nzb0224"
    password = InputBox("Please enter your password")
    Select Case password
        Case ReadOnlyPW
            Worksheets("Sheet1").Protect password:=ReadWritePW
            MsgBox "You may view the contents of this sheet."
        Case ReadWritePW
            Worksheets("Sheet1").Unprotect
            MsgBox "You have full read/write permission."
        Case Else
            MsgBox "Sorry, that is an invalid password"
            Worksheets("Sheet1").Visible = xlVeryHidden
    End Select
End Sub
```

 This procedure begins by assigning values to two variables, ReadOnlyPW and ReadWritePW. By using variables for the passwords, it's easy to change them later because they are in one place at the top of the procedure.

An input box retrieves the user's password and a Select Case statement is used to determine which level of access to give the user. If the user entered the value of ReadOnlyPW in the input box, the first case is run. Then, Sheet1 is protected. With the sheet protected, the user cannot make any changes to the cells. To keep the user from simply unprotecting the sheet, the ReadWritePW password is used for the Password argument of the Protect method. A message box appears to alert the user that read-only privileges have been granted.

If the user entered ReadWritePW in the input box, the second Case block is run; the sheet is unprotected and the user is notified of full read/write permission.

If anything other than one of the two passwords was entered in the input box, the `Visible` property of `Sheet1` is set to `xlVeryHidden`. When set to this value, a sheet can only be made visible again via VBA code—by setting the `Visible` property to `True`. It won't be possible to simply unhide the sheet by choosing F̲ormat, S̲heet, U̲nhide.

A much less obvious use for the Auto_Open procedure is to put Excel on the lookout for events. An example of such an event would be when a particular sheet in the workbook is activated. At this point, you might want to run a procedure automatically. The Auto_Open procedure shouldn't contain the code that will run when these events occur; those procedures will go else-where. Instead, you include an instruction to VBA to run a particular proce-dure when the event occurs. The details on how to do this are discussed in greater detail in the following sections.

Plain English, please!

An Excel **event** is something that happens that Excel can detect. It can be a user action, like a mouse click or keyboard entry, or it can be some state that is reached by the computer, such as a point in time.

TIP   **If you put an Auto_Open procedure into the PERSONAL.XLS file** or into another file that loads automatically when Excel is started, you can write code that will run every time Excel starts up.

`Auto_Close` is analogous to `Auto_Open`. The code contained in `Auto_Close` runs automatically when a workbook is closed. You could use this procedure as a place to prompt the user to make a backup copy of the current file onto a floppy disk.

Procedures that run when a certain event occurs

There are some pretty sophisticated alarm systems on the market. They can be hooked up to motion detectors or sensors on your windows, and can automatically call the police when one of these devices is triggered. In a similar way, VBA can detect certain events and run procedures when the events are detected.

When you open a workbook, VBA automatically runs the Auto_Open procedure for that book (if it exists). However, for most events, there is no automatic procedure. You need to write an ordinary procedure and tell VBA in advance that you want this procedure to be run if a certain event occurs.

If you have a home alarm system, it won't do any detecting unless it is turned on. You "turn on" Excel's alarm system by running a special line of code that tells Excel to be on the lookout for an event. This statement doesn't run a macro, but it tells Excel which macro to run if and when the event occurs.

Thus, there are two different procedures involved in this kind of situation. There's the procedure that contains the instructions to be on the lookout for the event (this is like turning on the alarm), and there's the procedure that takes place if and when the event occurs (like calling the police when the alarm is triggered).

How to make Excel look for an event

There are a number of different properties and methods that allow you to associate a procedure with an event. For example, each worksheet has an OnSheetActivate property. You set this property to the procedure you want to run when the sheet is activated. So if you wanted to run a procedure called ShowDialog whenever your Quarterly Earnings worksheet was selected, you could run the following line of code:

```
Worksheets("Quarterly Earnings").OnSheetActivate = "ShowDialog"
```

When you run this line of code, it doesn't run the procedure ShowDialog. Instead, it sets things up so that if and when you activate the Quarterly Earnings worksheet, the ShowDialog procedure will run.

To learn about properties and methods, see Chapter 11, "How VBA Refers to Things in Excel."

How you associate a procedure with a particular event varies from event to event. Some events, like activating a sheet, can be detected by setting the property of a particular object. Other events require using a method and providing the procedure as one of the arguments. The following sections discuss several different kinds of events that can be detected and the kind of code required to detect them.

Usually, the Auto_Open procedure is used to set the properties and methods for the events you want detected. That way, as soon as the workbook is opened, Excel is on the lookout for these special events and will respond as necessary. However, you can put this code in any procedure you like. Just remember that until you run this procedure, the alarm system is turned off and the events will not trigger their macros.

Catch the bug

I put this line into my Auto_Open procedure so that when the Quarterly Earnings worksheet is activated, my dialog box called ShowDialog will appear:

```
Worksheets("Quarterly Earnings").OnSheetActivate _
= Sheets("dlgQuart").Show
```

But, the dialog box is displayed as soon as I open the workbook, even though this sheet isn't active. What's wrong?

Answer: The OnSheetActivate property of the worksheet needs to be set to the name of a procedure. For example:

```
Worksheets("Quarterly Earnings").OnSheetActivate = "ShowDia"
```

Then the ShowDia macro will have a line in it that shows the dialog box:

```
Sheets("dlgQuart").Show
```

These two lines cannot be combined into one.

Activating and deactivating sheets

Excel can detect when a sheet is activated or deactivated. By setting the OnSheetActivate or OnSheetDeactivate properties of a sheet to a macro, you can automatically run procedures when various sheets become active.

```
Sub Auto_Open()
    Worksheets("Data Entry Sheet").OnSheetActivate= "ShowMyToolbar"
    Worksheets("Data Entry Sheet").OnSheetDeactivate = "HideMyToolbar"
End Sub
```

Because this procedure is named `Auto_Open`, it will run automatically when the workbook is opened. `ShowMyToolbar` and `HideMyToolbar` are the names of macros that are located elsewhere in this module. The second line of this procedure sets the OnSheetActivate property of the worksheet called `Data Entry Sheet` to the `ShowMyToolbar` macro. Thus, when this worksheet is activated, the `ShowMyToolbar` macro will run. The OnSheetDeactivate property is similarly set to the HideMyToolbar macro.

The Application object also has an OnSheetActivate property. This property applies to any sheet in any workbook. However, if a sheet has its own OnSheetActivate property set to another macro, then this one will take precedence and the one set for the Application object will not run. For example, suppose these two lines are in the Auto_Open procedure of a workbook and no other code exists to set OnSheetActivate properties:

```
Sheets("sheet1").OnSheetActivate = "ShowMe"
Application.OnSheetActivate = "Beeper"
```

The first line sets the OnSheetActivate property of `Sheet1` to the `ShowMe` macro. The second line causes the `Beeper` macro to run when any sheet is activated. So, whenever `Sheet1` is activated, the `ShowMe` macro will run, and whenever any other sheet is selected, the `Beeper` macro will run and the `ShowMe` macro will not.

Q&A ***I wrote a macro that brings up a sheet, but the OnSheetActivate procedure doesn't run. What's going on?***

OnSheetActivate and OnSheetDeactivate only detect the event if it's caused by direct user action. If you activate a sheet using VBA code, the event will not be detected.

Changing windows (changing workbooks)

The activation and deactivation of sheets is useful when you want to make changes within a workbook, but sometimes you'll want to run code when the user switches from one workbook to another. Each open workbook resides in a different window, and the action associated with selecting a window is called OnWindow.

This statement runs a module called CheckPassword whenever the PERSONAL.XLS window is selected.

```
Windows("Personal.xls").OnWindow = "CheckPassword"
```

To learn how to write code for displaying menus, see Chapter 16, "Using VBA to Work with Your Menus."

The Application object also has an OnWindow property. If you set this to a macro, that macro will run whenever any window is selected (unless another macro has already been associated with that particular window). The OnWindow property works for workbooks in much the same way that the OnSheetActivate property works for sheets.

Time-related events

Every second that elapses on your computer's clock is a new event. Excel can keep an eye out for one of these events—in other words, it can keep an eye on the clock.

How can I use this in the real world?

Customized menus are saved in a workbook, but when that workbook is opened, they can affect all open workbooks. You can write a procedure that will look at the current workbook and display the appropriate menus for that workbook. This procedure can be triggered by an OnWindow event.

You can include a statement in the Auto_Open procedure to run a macro called WindowSwitch whenever an OnWindow event is detected. The WindowSwitch procedure will look at the name of the window that was selected and display the appropriate menus.

With OnTime, you can respond to many different kinds of time-related events, and do any of the following:

- Run a macro at a particular time on a particular day

- Run a macro at the same time every day

- Wait for a certain amount of time to elapse and then run a macro

- Specify an interval of time so that if Excel is run any time during that interval, a macro will run

When supplying the *earliestTime* and *latestTime* arguments, you need to use valid time values. The Now function supplies the current time, which will be the time that the function is called. TimeValue is a function that will turn text strings into valid time values. This line of code uses Now and TimeValue to schedule a procedure. The WakeMeUp macro will run 15 minutes after this statement runs.

```
Application.OnTime earliestTime:=Now + TimeValue("00:15:00"),_
Procedure:="WakeMeUp"
```

Other actions Excel can detect

There are many other kinds of events that Excel can detect. Most buttons, menu items, and graphic objects have an OnAction property that can be set.

Speaking of *OnTime*

OnTime is a method of the Application object. The syntax for OnTime is

```
Application.OnTime earliestTime, procedure, latestTime, schedule
```

Two of the arguments of this method are required: *earliestTime* and *procedure*. *earliestTime* is a time value used to schedule when the OnTime event will occur. When the event occurs, the macro specified in *procedure* will be run. If Excel isn't running or isn't able to perform this macro at *earliestTime* (because another macro is running, for example), then the macro will be run at the next available opportunity unless the time is later than *latestTime*.

The *schedule* argument takes a True or False value. The default is True, and False is only used to cancel an existing scheduled OnTime event.

Which action will trigger the event depends on the object in question. For buttons, it's a click. For menu items, the event occurs when the item is selected. You can set the OnAction properties of these items through VBA code, but most of these objects will also allow you to specify a macro in other ways. For example, if you use the right button to click on a dialog control, you can choose Assign Macro from the pop-up menu and then select the desired macro from a list.

To learn how to use Excel's online help, see Chapter 6, "VBA Information Online."

Menus, toolbars, and dialog controls can all have macros assigned to them without using VBA code. The chapters on each of these objects have instructions on how to assign macros without using code. However, you can also use the OnAction property of these objects and of many other objects to assign macros. You can find a complete list of objects that have the OnAction property by looking up **OnAction** in the Index page of Excel's online help.

Excel also detects errors. If an error occurs in a VBA program, Excel will display one of the famously incomprehensible dialog boxes like the one shown in figure 22.1. By now, you may have a good idea of what most of them mean, but other users will probably be intimidated by them. You can create code to deal with errors in a friendlier way. This is discussed in greater detail in the next chapter.

Fig. 22.1
By writing procedures to handle errors, you can bypass error messages like this.

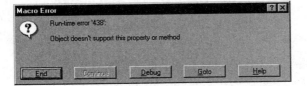

There are a few other events that Excel can detect. For example, the Application object also has an OnUndo method that will allow you to change the text of the Undo menu item and lets you run a custom procedure when this menu item is selected. This can be useful if you want to provide the capability of undoing an entire macro. Look in Excel's online help under the Events topic and then find the Making Procedures Run Automatically subtopic to learn about the other events that Excel can detect.

How can I turn off the event detection?

You might set things up so that an event triggers a reaction. Later, you may want to change things and no longer have the event trigger this reaction. There are two situations that might occur: you might want the event to run a different procedure from the one you originally defined, or you might want to turn off the event detection altogether.

For most events, automatic detection involves setting an "On" property to the name of the procedure you want to run. If you want to change this, you merely change the value of this property. Each property can only have one value at a time. As soon as you assign the new procedure, the old one will no longer be triggered.

If you don't want anything at all to happen when an event occurs, you can set the value of the On property to an empty string: quotation marks with nothing in them. That way, nothing will happen when the event occurs. For example, this statement prevents any events by being triggered when Sheet1 is deactivated.

```
Worksheets("Sheet1").OnSheetDeactivate = ""
```

 TIP **It doesn't matter if the OnWindow property was already set to an** empty string. You can run this line multiple times without generating an error.

You can create a general purpose procedure that turns off all of the event detecting that's going on. This might be useful if you need to make changes to your programming within the workbook and don't want to have all the backup and password features you've designed for other users to get in your way.

Summary

In this chapter, you learned how to create macros that will run automatically when certain events occur. In particular, you learned how to associate macros with the selection of worksheets and workbooks, and how to run a macro when a specified amount of time has elapsed or when a time is reached. You also learned about the XLSTART directory which stores workbooks that are opened every time Excel starts up.

Review questions

1 What happens when you put a workbook in the XLSTART directory?

2 Name three kinds of events that Excel can detect.

3 How can you make Excel run a particular macro every time it starts up?

4 If you set the OnSheetActivate property of a worksheet to a macro, and then activate that sheet through VBA code, what will happen?

5 What would you do to make a dialog box appear when a workbook is activated?

6 How could you make a toolbar appear only when a particular worksheet was active?

Exercises

1 Create a visible workbook that opens automatically each time you run Excel.

2 Make a message box that says Hasta la vista, Baby every time you quit Excel. (Hint: use the Auto_Close procedure of PERSONAL.XLS.)

3 In a new workbook, write a procedure that will display a message box saying This is sheet 1 whenever you click on Sheet1. Add another procedure that will beep whenever you switch from Sheet1 to another sheet.

4 Set up a lunch alarm that will display a message box at noon each day.

5 Write a macro that will get rid of all the OnSheetActivate and OnSheetDeactivate procedures in a workbook. (Hint: use a For Each statement to affect all sheets in the workbook.)

23

Making Your Programming User-Friendly

● **In this chapter:**

- Put your behind-the-scenes sheets where the user can't get to them

- How can I make Excel look like my own application?

- Get rid of Excel's error messages

- Make the work environment easy to understand and use

How about hiding the worksheets, changing the menus, and replacing the interface entirely with your own dialog boxes? . . . .

Excel is a spreadsheet. It has worksheets with rows and gridlines, and menus and toolbars that you're familiar with. You can put your information into the worksheets and customize the menus a bit. You can even add a few buttons and dialog boxes here and there. It's still recognizable as Excel, though.

How about hiding the worksheets, changing the menus entirely, and replacing the interface entirely with your own dialog boxes? Now you've got something else altogether: a spreadsheet application. You're creating your own program that works on top of Excel.

There are, of course, many steps in between small customizations of Excel and full-fledged applications. As your VBA efforts become more and more application-like, you need to focus more attention on how the user will be interacting with your program. If you're replacing the Excel environment—even in part—by one of your own, you need to make it a place that works for the user. While adding functionality, you need to make sure that things work smoothly and are easy to understand.

Keeping things out of sight

"Out of sight, out of mind" and "Ignorance is bliss" are two apt phrases when considering how to make workbooks and Excel applications user-friendly. The Windows 95 environment encourages users to explore in order to learn more about how to use programs. What if they explore their way right into your module sheets and start changing code? All of a sudden, the walls come tumbling down and things don't work anymore.

To learn about add-ins, see Chapter 21, "Integrate Your Program with Excel."

The solution to this problem is to keep the user blissfully ignorant of what's going on behind the scenes. One way to achieve this is with an add-in. Add-ins have their limitations, though. To change them, you need to convert the original workbook to an add-in all over again. Sometimes, skillfully tucking away sheets and workbooks where they won't be found is more appropriate.

Keeping sheets completely hidden

You're probably already familiar with hiding sheets. You can do this with VBA code or with menu commands:

- To hide a worksheet or a dialog sheet with menu commands, choose F_o_rmat, _S_heet, _H_ide

- To hide a module sheet with menu commands, choose _E_dit, _S_heet, _H_ide

- To hide any kind of sheet with VBA code, set the Visible property of the sheet to False

The problem with hiding sheets is that it's pretty easy to unhide them. A user can unhide and easily display the sheet that was hidden. So if you really want to keep a sheet from prying eyes, you can set the hide property of a sheet to the value xlVeryHidden.

This can only be done with VBA code, like the following:

```
Sheets("Sheet1").Visible = xlVeryHidden
```

When you run a line of code like this, the sheet becomes invisible. Moreover, it cannot be made visible again unless you run the following statement:

```
Sheets("Sheet1").Visible = True
```

In other words, the sheet cannot be displayed via the menus. This effectively protects these sheets from harm by non-programming users. The sheets are not write-protected in any way, so you can still make changes to or get information from these sheets while they are hidden.

How can I use this in the real world?

All of your variables automatically lose their values when the workbook containing those variables is closed. You can store values in a worksheet whose Visible property is set to xlVeryHidden. They can only be affected there by VBA code.

To reinstate the value of the variables, you can write an Auto_Open procedure that assigns the value of a cell on this sheet to the appropriate variable.

By the way, this is one of the things you can do with an xlVeryHidden sheet that you can't do with an add-in.

To learn more about Auto_Open procedures, see Chapter 22, "Making Code Run Automatically."

Once a workbook has been designed, there's generally no need for the user to ever see module sheets or dialog sheets. Thus, it's a great idea to set their Visible property to xlVeryHidden to keep them out of the way.

> **TIP** You can still show a dialog box even if the Visible property of the dialog sheet is set to xlVeryHidden.

Can I make it look like Excel isn't there?

You can set the Visible property of a window to False. This has the effect of hiding a workbook. Although the workbook is hidden, you can still access its cells and show its dialog boxes. By hiding the workbook yourself, the user may not even know that a spreadsheet is present. You can guide the user through data entry or via your own dialog boxes, menus, and toolbars. In essence, you'll have your own application, with the interface designed to your specifications. Behind the flashy front end, however, is the full horse-power of Excel. It's the best of both worlds: the control of writing your own application with the functionality of a first-class spreadsheet backing it up.

Take a look at the program in figure 23.1. This is just plain old Excel running with a few modifications. The caption of the Application object has been changed, a new menu bar and custom toolbar have been added, and a dialog box is being displayed. Except for the little Excel icon in the top left corner, you would never know that this is actually a spreadsheet!

Looks like a new application

Fig. 23.1
Is this a spreadsheet or what? The user need never know.

All new menus

No sheets in sight

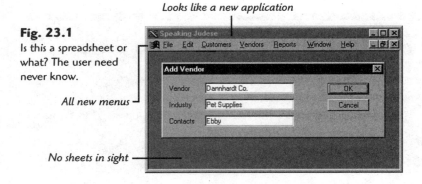

Keep your program from crashing

Here's a sure recipe for losing points with your coworkers: Customize Excel in such a way that frequent errors are generated; make sure that Excel's hard-to-understand messages are displayed; leave your coworkers frustrated, confused, and unproductive.

Mistakes are made and programs crash; it comes with the territory when you're working with computers. It's possible, however, to put error-handling procedures into your programs so that if your programs can't run, they can at least provide useful information to the user. This sounds like pretty sophisticated programming, but, actually, the programming required to deal with errors is not difficult at all. The real art lies in discovering what kind of errors can happen and planning for them.

What is a runtime error?

To learn more about syntax errors and how they're displayed, see Chapter 2, "Module Sheets: The Home of Macros and VBA."

VBA errors come in several different varieties. **Syntax errors** are ones that show up as soon as you type in the code. They are violations of the rules of VBA and will turn red as soon as you type them into your module sheet.

A second kind of error is one that the editor does not catch. A **runtime error** is one that isn't detected in the module sheet but causes your program to crash when you try to run it. This type of error can be further broken down into two categories: ones that show up every time you run a program, and ones that only show up under special circumstances. For an example of an error that will always occur, this statement will always produce an error message when it is run.

```
Sheets.Activate
```

Activate isn't a method of the Sheets collection. Running this statement produces an error message to that effect.

It's pretty easy to find and patch up errors like this one. You try your program once and if it doesn't work, you fix it. The more insidious type of error is the one that doesn't always show up when you run a program. These are like those engine noises that magically vanish when you bring your car to the shop. For example, the following procedure really has nothing inherently wrong with it, but can still crash under certain conditions.

```
Sub MightCauseErrors()
    x = Sheets("Sheet1").Range("a1").Value
    y = 45
    z = x + y
    MsgBox z
End Sub
```

This macro assigns the value of cell A1 in Sheet1 to the variable x. A second variable, y, is created and assigned the value 45. x and y are added together and assigned to z, whose value is displayed in a message box.

Although this procedure will work just fine under normal circumstances, it can crash for two different reasons. First, if Sheet1 is renamed or deleted, an error message will appear announcing that the Sheets method of the Application class failed. That's VBA's fancy way of saying, "I can't find Sheet1."

To learn about type mismatch errors, see Chapter 7, "Putting Together Lines of VBA Code."

If Sheet1 does indeed exist, but has a word in cell A1, like "Artichoke," then this procedure will cause a type mismatch error when it tries to add 45 to Artichoke.

Theoretically, you can take measures to keep this kind of error from occurring. You might protect the workbook to keep the sheet from being deleted or renamed. You could also lock the cell to keep its contents from being changed, or write VBA code that checks to make sure that the value entered into the cell is of the right data type.

Do your best to write code that will prevent errors. However, the next section shows you that not all errors can be prevented. In this case, you'll want to write code to intercept these errors and handle them gracefully.

Not all errors can be prevented

Although there's a great deal you can do to circumvent errors, some just can't be avoided. This procedure is designed to run automatically if the user hasn't saved in the last ten minutes. Under normal circumstances it will work fine. Can you think of when it might cause an error?

```
Sub SaveMe()
    Answer = MsgBox("It's been 10 minutes since you saved. Save again?", vbYesNo)
    If Answer = vbYes Then
        For Each bk In Workbooks
            bk.Save
        Next bk
    End If
End Sub
```

The SaveMe procedure displays a message box with Yes and No buttons, asking whether or not the user would like to save again. If the user clicks the Yes button, then a For Each structure cycles through each open workbook and saves it.

This procedure can cause a runtime error when the location of a file is unavailable. For example, you may have loaded one of the workbooks from a floppy disk and then ejected that disk. In that case, an error message of: `Cannot Access 'A'` will appear. A similar situation would occur if the workbook was located on a network drive that subsequently was disconnected.

Not only is this an error that is virtually impossible to prevent, it's one that you might never encounter while developing your programs. The moral of the story is to expect the unexpected and to realize that sometimes you can't create a completely error-proof program.

Intercepting errors

Because you can't keep errors from happening, you need to do something to make them less devastating. This means you need to create special VBA code that will detect and react to errors when they occur.

An error is an event that can trigger error-handling code. Just like other kinds of events, such as clicking buttons or selecting menu items, Excel detects errors and can run associated code.

The way that you tell VBA to be on the lookout for errors is with an On Error statement. Putting a statement that starts with On Error at the beginning of a procedure will keep VBA on the lookout throughout the course of the procedure. If an error does occur, what you put on that line after the words On Error tells VBA what to do.

There are two options for dealing with errors. One is to ignore the line that caused the error and go on to the next statement. The other is to send VBA to a different part of the procedure whose job it is to deal with errors.

Instructing VBA to ignore errors

Some errors aren't so bad. If they occur, you just want to pass them by and get on with the rest of the program. By running the statement

```
On Error Resume Next
```

in a procedure, VBA will just skip the statement that caused the error and go on to the next one. Here's a procedure that performs an action on each cell in a range and skips the cells where it would normally cause an error.

```
Sub MultiplyRange()
    On Error Resume Next
    For Each cel In Sheets("Sheet1").Range("A1:D20")
        cel.Value = cel.Value * 2
    Next cel
End Sub
```

As soon as VBA runs the On Error line, it's ready to intercept errors. The For Each structure goes through each cell in the range A1:D20 and tries to multiply its value by 2. When the value of the cell is numeric to start with, it will succeed and replace the cell value with the result of this multiplication. If it encounters something in the cell that is not a number, it will just skip that cell. Without the On Error line, it would crash at this point with a type mismatch error.

Instructing VBA to ignore errors in this way lasts as long as the procedure is running. In other procedures, errors must be handled separately.

Running special code when VBA encounters an error

Most of the time, you don't want to ignore an error entirely. Instead, you want to deal with it. This might mean stopping the program and informing the user of the problem. Or, you might want to perform some alternate action. To do this, you need to use a GoTo statement.

Speaking of *GoTo*

The syntax of GoTo for error-handling is

```
On Error GoTo line
```

where *line* is an identifier for the line to which VBA should go when the error is encountered. VBA will recognize this line by the identifier *line* followed by a colon (:).

TIP **If you've ever programmed in BASIC, you may recognize the GoTo** statement. Don't use it for anything but errors. Nowadays, that's just about the only accepted use.

Dealing with errors in this fashion consists of two parts. You must run the On Error line and also create a place for VBA to jump to when it encounters an error. This all goes within the same procedure. The code that handles the error begins the identifier specified in the On Error line.

```
Sub HandleError()
    On Error GoTo explain
    y = InputBox("Input a number")
    z = y + 4
    MsgBox z
    Exit Sub

explain:
    MsgBox "An error occurred"
End Sub
```

code The first statement of this procedure sets the trap for any subsequent errors. If an error is encountered, VBA will jump down to explain: and continue from there.

An input box is displayed, and its return value is assigned to y. Depending on what is entered, this could be a numeric or text expression. On the next line, y is added to 4. If the value of y is a number then the next two lines run normally and the procedure ends without ever running the explain: code. If, however, the value assigned to y was not a number, an error occurs and the program jumps down to the explain: line. This line does nothing except indicate where the program should go. VBA continues and displays the message box that says An error occurred.

Q&A *Why is there* Exit Sub *in the middle of the program?*

If no error is generated in the course of the program, you don't want the message box saying that an error occurred. Without Exit Sub, the procedure would run from beginning to end, including this line. Notice that if an error occurs, VBA jumps right over this line to explain:, completely ignoring it.

Whenever you create error-handling code, you want to make sure that it doesn't run unless an error actually occurred.

Recognizing what kind of error has occurred

Errors can happen for a variety of reasons. When Excel encounters an error, it associates a number with it. You can use this number to identify what kind of error occurred and take relevant action. You may have already noticed these numbers on error messages. Figure 23.2 shows the type mismatch error, which is error number 13.

Fig. 23.2
Learn from your mistakes. If you cause an error, you can use the opportunity to check out the number associated with that error.

As soon as an error occurs, the value of a variable called Err is set to the value associated with that kind of error. This procedure causes a type mismatch error that sets the value of Err to 13.

```
Sub ShowErrorNumber()
    On Error GoTo ShowErr
    y = "artichoke"
    z = y + 4
    Exit Sub

ShowErr:
    MsgBox "The error number is:" & Err
End Sub
```

The line On Error GoTo ShowErr instructs VBA to skip down to the part of the program labeled ShowErr: if it encounters an error. Two lines later, VBA tries to add a number and a word. This causes a type mismatch error which has the value of 13. VBA now skips down to ShowErr: and displays a message box like the one in figure 23.3.

Fig. 23.3
Instead of the normal error message, VBA can display one that you supply.

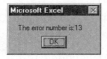

If no error had been generated, VBA would exit this procedure on the line above ShowErr:, and the error-handling code would not have run.

To learn how to use the online help system, see Chapter 6, "VBA Information Online."

You can find out the number associated with a type of error by looking at the error message that Excel automatically generates when you don't use an On Error statement. You can also find a complete list of various errors and descriptions about what causes them in the online help. Look up Error Numbers in the Index page of the Help Topics dialog box.

Identifying what kind of error has occurred lets you have contingency plans for different kinds of errors. For example, the MightCauseErrors procedure used earlier in this chapter could cause an error because it couldn't find a particular worksheet or because of a type mismatch. This procedure uses the value of Err to figure out which of these errors has occurred.

```
Sub DealWithErrors()
    On Error GoTo ErrorHandler
    x = Sheets("Sheet1").Range("a1").Value
    y = 45
    z = x + y
    MsgBox z

ErrorHandler:
    If Err = 13 Then
        MsgBox "You need to put a number in cell A1 of Sheet1."
    ElseIf Err = 1004 Then
        MsgBox "Sheet1 is missing. Find Sheet1 then try again."
    Else
        MsgBox "An unidentified error has occurred."
    End If
End Sub
```

I started with the MightCauseError program and added a line to look for errors. This goes at the top so that any errors encountered will send VBA to the ErrorHandler part of the procedure.

The rest of the program is designed to handle the two possible errors that might occur. If a non-numeric value is in cell A1 of Sheet1, then error number 13 is generated. If Sheet1 is missing, then error number 1004 is generated. The If and ElseIf lines look for these two particular values and display an appropriate message box so the user knows what went wrong.

There's no problem that your error-handling code can't fix. For example, in the DealWithErrors program you could have prompted the user to type a new value for cell A1 into an input box. Then, you could replace the value in cell A1 with this value and also use it for the value of the variable x.

Resuming the program where it left off

Sometimes, you'll want to deal with an error and then get back to the procedure that was running when the error occurred. This can be done with a Resume Next statement. Earlier in the chapter I talked about using this statement as part of

```
On Error Resume Next
```

but by putting it near the bottom of the procedure with the error-handling code, you can also include other error-handling techniques. Here's a modification of the MultiplyRange program you saw earlier in this chapter. Each time it encounters a cell whose value it cannot change, it tells the user which row and column the cell was located in and then resumes the procedure on the next cell.

```
Sub NewMultiplyRange()
    On Error GoTo ErrorHandler
    For Each cel In Sheets("Sheet1").Range("A1:D20")
        cel.Value = cel.Value * 2
    Next cel
    Exit Sub

ErrorHandler:
    MsgBox "Could not change cell in row " & cel.Row _
    & " column " & cel.Column
    Resume Next
End Sub
```

If no errors are encountered, this program works just like the MultiplyRange procedure from earlier in this chapter. Each cell in the range A1:D20 on Sheet1 will have its value multiplied by two. If an error is encountered, the program jumps down to the ErrorHandler part of the program. Here it displays a message box telling the user which cell caused the problem. After this message box is displayed, VBA returns to the For Each structure and goes on to the next cell in the range.

Summary

This chapter discussed some of the issues involved with making your programs more user-friendly. By fine-tuning the environment so that the user only sees the parts he will interact with, you can make the program less intimidating and also protect your code and other customizations from harm.

A major portion of this chapter was devoted to the subject of runtime errors. To keep your programs from crashing, you need to write error-handling code that will intercept errors as they happen and run code that deals with the problem. Dealing with the problem can range from ignoring it, to explaining to the user what has happened, to actually fixing the problem on the spot.

No matter what your level of programming expertise or involvement with VBA is, keep in mind why you're making these changes to Excel. The goal is to make the users of your programs (including yourself!) more productive. Throughout this book, you've learned to extend Excel's functionality by customizing the environment and automating tasks. Putting these changes together into a well-designed, understandable package will mark you as a good designer. You can write brilliant code with amazing functionality, but it is all for naught if no one uses or understands it. Making your programs user-friendly puts the finishing touch on all of your VBA work.

Review questions

1 What's the difference between a syntax error and a runtime error?

2 Why would you set the Visible property of a worksheet to `xlVeryHidden` instead of `False`?

3 If a program of yours causes a runtime error and you haven't written any error-handling code, what happens?

4 Can you fix the problem that caused the error while a procedure is running? If so, how?

5 What advantages can be gained by hiding sheets from the user?

Exercises

1 Change the `SaveMe` procedure so that if an error is generated, a dialog box appears and instructs the user to insert a disk before trying the macro again.

2 If you try to divide a number by 0, it will cause an error. Find out the error number associated with this error. (Hint: check the online help.)

3 Change the `Visible` property of a module sheet to `xlVeryHidden`. Make sure that it is really impossible to make the sheet visible again without resorting to VBA code.

4 The NewMultiplyRange procedure doesn't contain any error-handling code to deal with an error caused by the absence of Sheet1. Add to the error handling portion of the program so that a message box will alert the user that the sheet can't be found and so the macro was not run.

Answers to the Quizzes

Chapter 1

1 A macro is a list of instructions that Excel automatically carries out .

2 VBA, or Visual Basic for Applications, is a programming language that comes with Excel.

3 By recording a macro with the macro recorder, you are actually writing a VBA program behind the scenes without typing any code yourself.

4 You can run a macro by choosing Tools, Macro, and double-clicking your macro from the list; by typing a shortcut key that you've associated with your macro; or by adding your macro to the Tools menu and selecting it from there.

5 Which cells a macro runs in is affected by whether the macro recorder was started before or after the initial cell was selected and whether or not Use Relative References was selected.

Chapter 2

1 A module sheet is a special Excel sheet for storing macros and other kinds of VBA programs. The format of these programs is VBA programming code.

2 A syntax error is a mistake in code that breaks some rule of the VBA programming language.

3 The first line of a macro is always Sub *MacroName* ( ). *MacroName* can be replaced with different names. The last line of a macro is always End Sub.

4 Red text means there is a syntax error on that line, green text indicates a comment, and blue text indicates a VBA restricted keyword.

5 The Visual Basic toolbar has shortcuts for inserting a module, running and recording macros, and stopping the macro recorder, along with several shortcuts for debugging features.

Chapter 3

1 The macro recorder often includes extraneous code. You'll want to delete this code to make the macro easier to read, to make it more efficient, and to ensure that it runs properly.

2 Before deleting a line of code, change it into a comment and try running the macro. If the macro works properly with the line as a comment, then it's safe to delete it.

3 Macros can call other macros that are in different module sheets as long as they are in the same workbook. You can also call macros in other workbooks by using the name of the workbook followed by an exclamation point.

4 Add to an existing macro by positioning your cursor where you want the additions to be inserted. Then select Tools, Record Macro, Mark Position for Recording. Start the recorder by selecting Tools, Record Macro, Record at Mark.

Chapter 4

1 The two types of VBA procedures are functions and subroutines.

2 A variable is a named placeholder for a value.

3 A function returns a value.

4 Excel has built-in functions, like SUM or AVERAGE, which can be entered into worksheet formulas. VBA has built-in functions, like Sqr, which can be used in VBA programs.

5 Breaking your code into small, self-contained procedures lets you use them for a variety of purposes, and makes your code more manageable for editing and debugging.

6 In the parentheses in the first line of a function, you list variables for the values that the function will receive. The number of variables you list here is the number of values that the function will expect.

Chapter 5

1 A control structure is code that affects which part of a VBA program runs or how many times it runs.

2 An If/Then statement tests a condition to see if it is true. If it is, then code within the If/Then is run; otherwise, it is skipped.

3 A loop allows code to be run over and over until a specified number of repetitions have occurred or a condition has been met.

4 The For/Next loop repeats code a certain number of times. A Do While loop repeats code based on whether a condition is true or not.

5 The With statement saves typing and makes a procedure run faster when several properties of a single object are being affected.

6 The And and Or operators allow you to test more than one condition in an If/Then statement.

Chapter 6

1 Choose the Contents page of the Help Topics dialog box. Select the Microsoft Excel Visual Basic Reference, open it, and select Statements to get an alphabetized list of Excel VBA statements.

2 Choose the Index page of the Help Topics dialog box and type **loop** into the text box.

3 With your cursor positioned anywhere in or immediately after the keyword, press F1 to bring up the appropriate help page.

4 In an Example page, the red text is a necessary part of the syntax, and any black text can be replaced with text appropriate to your program.

5 Rectangular brackets indicate optional parts of the syntax. Their contents may be left out.

Chapter 7

1 A statement is a line of code that issues an instruction to VBA. Statements can stand alone on a line.

2 No. Expressions can be used in creating statements, but an expression alone cannot be an instruction to VBA.

3 The concatenation operator (&) combines text strings.

4 A logical operator allows you to combine two True/False expressions into one.

5 `x = Cos(Angle)`

6 Yes, because one of the two expressions is true, it will beep.

Chapter 8

1 An argument is a value required by a procedure for it to run.

2 When you write a statement that instructs a procedure to run, you call the procedure.

3 Functions have a return value; subroutines don't.

4 Functions that change cell contents or formatting can't be used in worksheet formulas.

5 By preceding the name of a built-in worksheet function with `Application.`, you can use it as if it were a VBA function. For example,

```
Result = Application.Max(5, 6, 7, -1)
```

would assign the return value of the MAX function to `Result`.

6 To exit a subroutine prematurely, use the Exit Sub statement.

7 Use the As keyword to specify a data type for an argument. This function has two arguments; x requires an integer be passed to it and y requires a string.

```
Function TwoArgs(x As Integer, y As String)
```

Chapter 9

1 Explicitly declaring a variable means writing a line of code whose sole purpose is to instruct VBA to create a variable.

2 A local variable is one declared and used within a procedure. Outside that procedure, VBA will forget its existence.

3 Declare a variable that expects a whole number by using As Integer in the declaration. For example:

```
Dim PaulKle As Integer
```

4 Type the words **Option Explicit** at the top of your module sheet to tell VBA to force you to declare your variables, or choose Tools, Options to display the Options dialog box. Select the Module General tab and mark the Require Variable Declaration check box. Then any new module sheets you create will already have the words Option Explicit at the top.

5 The String data type is used for text.

6 By declaring a variable with Static instead of Dim, it will remember its value even after its procedure has stopped running.

7 Use module-wide or public variables when you need a variable to be used in more than one procedure.

Chapter 10

1 The two types of Do loops are Do While and Do Until.

2 By using ElseIf and Else clauses, you can consider several different cases with an If/Then statement.

3 A For Each loop lets you work with each object in a collection or each item in an array.

4 Exit a For statement with the Exit For statement. Exit a Do loop with the Exit Do statement.

5 By putting the condition to be tested at the end of the loop, you ensure that the loop will be run at least once.

6 An If/Then statement can test multiple conditions for true or false. When any one of them is found to be true, its corresponding code is run. A Select Case statement takes one expression and evaluates it. Based on the value, it runs the case that is associated with that value.

Chapter 11

1 A property is a setting or attribute of an object.

2 A method is something that can be done to an object.

3 To find out what an object is called, you can look through the alphabetical listing of objects in the online Excel help files, use the Object Browser, use the Object Model, or record code with the Macro Recorder, and then view that code in a module.

4 The Object Browser can tell you what properties and methods are associated with an object and provide links to the help files for them. It can also help you find procedures you've written or give you a list of all VBA constants.

5 `Workbooks("Budget.xls")` specifies this file as an object.

Chapter 12

1 Individual cells and groups of cells are both range objects.

2 Both the Range and Cells methods can be used to return a reference to an individual cell.

3 You can select an entire row by using the Rows method.

4 The Cells method allows you to specify a cell using variables for its row and column coordinates.

5 Name a range by selecting it and the choosing Insert, Name, Define and typing a name for the range in the Define Name dialog box. Alternately, you can select the range and then type a name for it in the Name box (located on left side of the Formula bar.)

6 `ActiveCell.Offset(0, 4)` refers to the cell that is four cells to the right of the active cell.

Chapter 13

1 An array is a device in VBA that lets you store a list of values and refer to them by number. An array element is a single item on the list. The index number of an array element is the number that specifies which item of the array it is.

2 There are 16 elements in this array. They are numbered from 0 to 15.

3 When you don't know how many items will be in an array, or if you want to change the number of items in an array, declare it as a dynamic array.

4 This statement changes the size of LabData to 500 elements and deletes all of the information that was previously in the array.

5 To transfer a range of spreadsheet cells into VBA, create a two-dimensional array. The first dimension can correspond to the rows, and the second to the columns of the range. By using a loop and the Cells method, you can write a loop that goes through each row and column, copying the value from each cell to the appropriate array element.

Chapter 14

1 The Debug window is a window where you can access all of VBA's debugging tools.

2 The three panes of the Debug window are the Immediate, Watch, and Code panes.

3 By typing a line of code into the Immediate pane and pressing Enter, the code will be run.

4 You can check the value of an expression while a procedure is running by entering Break mode and using a print command in the Immediate pane or by adding a watch to the expression and viewing its value in the Watch pane.

5 If you're stepping through a procedure that calls another procedure which you don't want to step through, use the Step Over command.

6 You can tell your program to enter Break mode by setting a breakpoint or by using a Stop command.

Chapter 15

1 An accelerator key is an underlined letter in a menu item that enables you to select it with the keyboard.

2 No. Excel's built-in menus can be hidden but never permanently deleted.

3 In the Menu Bars box of the Menu Editor, you select which category of menus you want to change. To work on the menus for your module sheets, select Visual Basic Module from the list of menu bar categories.

4 Macros (Sub procedures that don't take values) are the only kind of VBA code you can attach to a menu item, although they can be created by writing VBA code as well as with the macro recorder.

5 The new workbook will reflect the menu changes in the other workbook as long as the other workbook is open.

Chapter 16

1 If the macro is associated with a menu item, it will not run properly in certain circumstances. The menu item should be grayed out at these times to prevent the user from selecting it.

2 The statement

```
MenuBars(xlWorksheet).Menus("View").MenuItems("MyBar").Checked _
= True
```

will put a check mark next to the My Bar item on the View menu.

3 File is a text string representing the name of the menu and requires quotation marks. By contrast, xlWorksheet is a named constant that represents a number associated with the toolbar and thus requires no quotation marks.

4 If you don't delete the menu somewhere, then every time you open the workbook you'll automatically get an unwanted extra copy of the menu.

5 Using the Reset method on a menu bar will restore all of its menus and menu items to the original versions supplied in Excel. Any customizations you have made will be deleted.

Chapter 17

1 A floating toolbar is one that is not anchored to a side of the screen but floats over the worksheet. It can be repositioned by dragging it.

2 To make a custom toolbar button do something, you attach a macro to it.

3 Changes to toolbars are saved even if you don't save the workbook when you quit. What's more, they apply to all workbooks you open, not just the one that was active when you changed the toolbar.

4 By attaching a toolbar to a workbook, you can distribute copies of your toolbar.

5 Excel's online help has a topic that lists all toolbar buttons and their ID numbers.

6 By writing procedures that display a toolbar when a workbook's window is activated and hide it when it is deactivated, you can limit a toolbar to only appear in that workbook.

Chapter 18

1 There are four icons that can be displayed in a message box: Exclamation, Question, Information, and Critical.

2 By using a message box as a function, you can react to the button that the user selects.

3 When you use MsgBox as a function, you must enclose its arguments in parentheses. Also, the MsgBox function does not comprise an entire line of code on its own. It must be used as an expression in a statement, such as assigning its return value to a variable.

4 The linefeed character, `chr(13)`, will cause a new line to start in displayed text.

5 The constant for the Save As dialog box is `xlDialogSaveAs`.

Chapter 19

1 Command buttons are used to run macros.

2 To select a dialog control, hold down the Ctrl key and click on it, or move the pointer over the dialog control and click the right mouse button.

3 Using dialog controls on a worksheet gives the user easier ways to enter data, restricts the kind of data that can be entered, and allows you to protect the contents of cells while still allowing data entry.

4 Check boxes are independent. Each one controls a separate setting that can be turned on or off. Option buttons come in groups. Only one option button in a group can be selected at a time.

5 You can assign a procedure to a dialog control by choosing Assign Macro on the pop-up menu for the control.

6 By protecting the worksheet, no locked cells can be directly modified by the user.

Chapter 20

1 A dialog sheet contains a dialog frame. The dialog frame is what actually gets displayed as the dialog box. The sheet is only used when designing the dialog box.

2 By referring to the dialog sheet and using the Show method, you can run a dialog box.

3 You can display a dialog box when a menu item is selected, when a button is pressed, or when Excel first starts up.

4 If you link a control in a dialog box directly to a worksheet cell, you will not be able to use the Cancel button to abandon the changes you made.

5 There is a procedure associated with the dialog frame that is run whenever the dialog box appears. By putting statements in this procedure that initialize your dialog controls, you can specify how your controls should look when the dialog box appears.

6 There is a procedure associated with the OK button of a dialog box. By using this procedure for all the code that implements selections made in the dialog box, these changes will only be run if the OK button is selected.

Chapter 21

1 Add-in files are ones with an XLA, XLL, or XLT extension.

2 In the Add-Ins dialog box, a check mark appears next to the names of the installed add-ins.

3 Once you've converted a workbook to an add-in, you can no longer make any changes to it.

4 If it is stored in PERSONAL.XLS, it will appear in the Function Wizard as `Personal.XLS!MyFunction`. If it is part of an add-in, it will appear simply as `MyFunction`.

Chapter 22

1 Any workbook in the XLSTART directory will automatically open when the Excel program is run.

2 Excel can detect when a sheet is activated, when a certain time is reached, when a window is selected, when an error occurs, when a dialog control is used, and many other actions.

3 The Auto_Open procedure of the PERSONAL.XLS workbook (or any other workbook in the XLSTART directory) will run every time Excel is opened. If you call a macro from this procedure, it will be run every time Excel starts up.

4 Activating a sheet through VBA code will not trigger the OnSheetActivate event, and the macro will not run.

5 Create a macro that shows the dialog box. Then, in the Auto_Open procedure of the workbook, set the OnWindow property of the workbook to the name of the macro.

6 Create two macros: one that shows the toolbar and one that hides it. By setting the OnSheetActivate and OnSheetDeactivate properties of the worksheet to these macros, the toolbar will appear and disappear as the worksheet is activated and deactivated.

Chapter 23

1 A syntax error is a violation of the rules of VBA. These are detected by VBA before you run your program. A runtime error is one that only becomes apparent when the program runs.

2 If the Visible property of worksheet is set to False, the user can unhide the worksheet via the menus. When Visible is set to xlVeryHidden, the worksheet can only be displayed via VBA code.

3 If your program causes a runtime error and you haven't written any error-handling code, the program will crash and display an error message.

4 Yes. You can write error handling code that performs actions to correct the problem and then returns to where it left off when the error was encountered.

5 By hiding sheets from the user, you can make your programs easier to use and protect programming and other data from being inadvertently changed.

Help Index

The Excel and VBA environment

If you have this problem...	You'll find help here...
The VBA help files aren't on your computer	pp. 94–95
You're sick of the syntax error messages that keep appearing	pp. 29 and 36–37
Some lines of code are running off the edge of the screen	p. 30
The Visual Basic toolbar disappears whenever you switch to a worksheet	p. 39

Macros

If you have this problem...	You'll find help here...
The macro recorder won't stop recording a macro	p. 10
You can't find a macro you recorded	pp. 46–49
The Personal Macro Workbook is missing	p. 33
Your macro isn't running in the right cells	pp. 15–18
The macro you recorded isn't available in other workbooks	pp. 32–35

Functions and procedures

If you have this problem...	You'll find help here...
A function or procedure doesn't appear in the Macro dialog box	pp. 47–48
Your procedure still doesn't appear in the Macro dialog box	pp. 130–131
You get a #VALUE! error with your user-defined worksheet function	pp. 133–134
There's no User Defined category in the Function Wizard	p. 62
You don't want to see PERSONAL.XLS in front of procedure names	p. 358

Objects, properties, and methods

If you have this problem...	You'll find help here...
You can see an object in Excel but you don't know what VBA calls it	p. 191
You know the name of an object but you don't know how to use it	pp. 102 and 200–202
You need to see which objects belong in which containers	pp. 108–109
Methods have too many arguments to deal with	pp. 194–197

Menus, toolbars, and dialog boxes

If you have this problem...	You'll find help here...
You've deleted a menu item and you need to get it back	pp. 263–264
The Menu Editor keeps adding blank spaces where you don't want them	p. 261
You can't get to the Menu Editor because you deleted its menu item	p. 278
Menus from one workbook are leaking over into another	pp. 278–279
You moved to another computer and lost your custom toolbars	pp. 298–299
You keep deleting a custom toolbar but you can't get rid of it	p. 300
The text in your message box is too long to fit on one line	pp. 315–316
You can't select controls that you've put on a worksheet	pp. 321–322
Selecting one option button deselects another one that's not related to it	pp. 327–328

Error messages

If you get this error message...	You'll find help here...
Type Mismatch	pp. 121–123
Any message saying a method failed	pp. 199–200
Argument Not Optional	pp. 131–132 and 194–197

continues

If you get this error message...	You'll find help here...
Subscript out of Range	p. 224
Wrong Number of Arguments	pp. 131–132
Reference is not Valid	pp. 344–345

Index

Complete and Return this Card
for a *FREE* Computer Book Catalog

Thank you for purchasing this book! You have purchased a superior computer book written expressly for your needs. To continue to provide the kind of up-to-date, pertinent coverage you've come to expect from us, we need to hear from you. Please take a minute to complete and return this self-addressed, postage-paid form. In return, we'll send you a free catalog of all our computer books on topics ranging from word processing to programming and the internet.

r. ☐   Mrs. ☐   Ms. ☐   Dr. ☐

ame (first) ☐☐☐☐☐☐☐☐☐☐☐☐ (M.I.) ☐   (last) ☐☐☐☐☐☐☐☐☐☐☐☐☐☐☐

ddress ☐☐☐☐☐☐☐☐☐☐☐☐☐☐☐☐☐☐☐☐☐☐☐☐☐☐☐☐☐☐

☐☐☐☐☐☐☐☐☐☐☐☐☐☐☐☐☐☐☐☐☐☐☐☐☐☐☐☐☐☐

ity ☐☐☐☐☐☐☐☐☐☐☐☐☐   State ☐☐   Zip ☐☐☐☐☐ ☐☐☐☐

one ☐☐☐ ☐☐☐ ☐☐☐☐   Fax ☐☐☐ ☐☐☐ ☐☐☐☐

ompany Name ☐☐☐☐☐☐☐☐☐☐☐☐☐☐☐☐☐☐☐☐☐☐☐☐☐☐

-mail address ☐☐☐☐☐☐☐☐☐☐☐☐☐☐☐☐☐☐☐☐☐☐☐☐☐☐

Please check at least (3) influencing factors for purchasing this book.

ont or back cover information on book .... ☐
pecial approach to the content .... ☐
ompleteness of content .... ☐
uthor's reputation .... ☐
ublisher's reputation .... ☐
ook cover design or layout .... ☐
dex or table of contents of book .... ☐
ice of book .... ☐
pecial effects, graphics, illustrations .... ☐
ther (Please specify): _____ ☐

How did you first learn about this book?

w in Macmillan Computer Publishing catalog .... ☐
ecommended by store personnel .... ☐
w the book on bookshelf at store .... ☐
ecommended by ____ end .... ☐
eceived advertisement in the mail .... ☐
w an advertisement in: _____ ☐
ead book review in: _____ ☐
ther (Please specify): _____ ☐

How many computer books have you purchased in the last six months?

his book only .... ☐   3 to 5 books...................... ☐
books .... ☐   More than 5 .... ☐

4. Where did you purchase this book?

Bookstore .... ☐
Computer Store .... ☐
Consumer Electronics Store .... ☐
Department Store .... ☐
Office Club .... ☐
Warehouse Club .... ☐
Mail Order .... ☐
Direct from Publisher .... ☐
Internet site .... ☐
Other (Please specify): _____ ☐

5. How long have you been using a computer?

☐ Less than 6 months   ☐ 6 months to a year
☐ 1 to 3 years   ☐ More than 3 years

6. What is your level of experience with personal computers and with the subject of this book?

	With PCs	With subject of book
New	☐	☐
Casual	☐	☐
Accomplished	☐	☐
Expert	☐	☐

Source Code ISBN: 07897-0325-4

7. Which of the following best describes your job title?

- Administrative Assistant ☐
- Coordinator ☐
- Manager/Supervisor ☐
- Director ☐
- Vice President ☐
- President/CEO/COO ☐
- Lawyer/Doctor/Medical Professional ☐
- Teacher/Educator/Trainer ☐
- Engineer/Technician ☐
- Consultant ☐
- Not employed/Student/Retired ☐
- Other (Please specify): _____ ☐

8. Which of the following best describes the area of the company your job title falls under?

- Accounting ☐
- Engineering ☐
- Manufacturing ☐
- Operations ☐
- Marketing ☐
- Sales ☐
- Other (Please specify): _____ ☐

Comments: _____
_____
_____

9. What is your age?

- Under 20 ☐
- 21-29 ☐
- 30-39 ☐
- 40-49 ☐
- 50-59 ☐
- 60-over ☐

10. Are you:

- Male ☐
- Female ☐

11. Which computer publications do you read regularly? (Please list)

_____
_____
_____
_____
_____
_____
_____
_____
_____
_____

Fold here and scotch-tape to mail

The VBA programming environment

Insert a module sheet into your workbook and you can start writing VBA programs or editing your recorded macros

Breakpoints are brown

You can put comments on
the same line as code

Comments are green

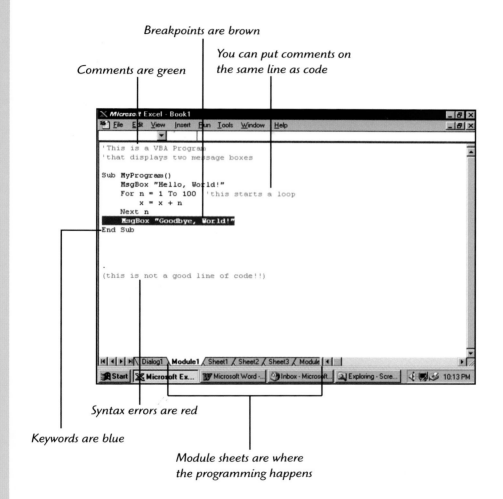

Syntax errors are red

Keywords are blue

Module sheets are where
the programming happens

Module sheet shortcuts

Shortcut	Visual Basic toolbar button	Action
F5	▶	Run a macro
		Insert a module sheet
F2		Open the Object Browser
Ctrl+G		Display the Debug window
F9		Add or remove a breakpoint
F8		Step into a macro

The Debug window

A place to try out programming and to help fix problems in your code

Keep an eye on variables and expressions in the Watch pane

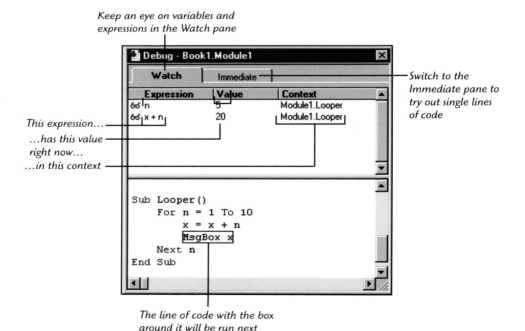

Switch to the Immediate pane to try out single lines of code

This expression…

…has this value right now…

…in this context

The line of code with the box around it will be run next

Common objects in Excel

Half the trick is figuring out what everything is called

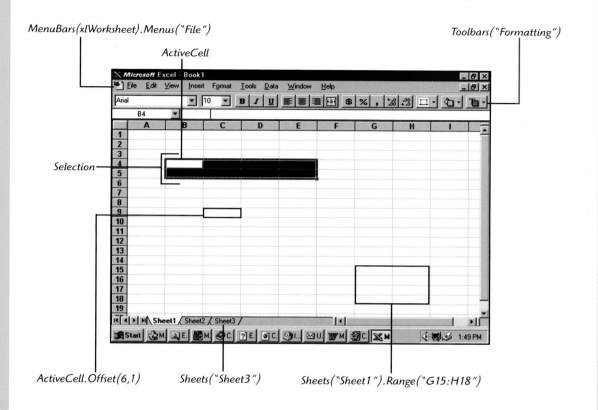

MenuBars(xlWorksheet).Menus("File")

ActiveCell

Toolbars("Formatting")

Selection

ActiveCell.Offset(6,1)

Sheets("Sheet3")

Sheets("Sheet1").Range("G15:H18")

Object	Some useful properties and methods
Range	Activate, Clear, Copy, Delete, Font, Name, Style, Value
Worksheet	Copy, Delete, Move, Name, Protect, Type, Visible
Worksheets	Add, Copy, Count, Delete, Visible
Workbook	Close, NewWindow, Save, SaveAs, Protect

Help with objects

- In a module sheet, press F2 to see the Object Browser

- In the Online Help Index, look up Object Model to see the Object Model

Using Excel Visual Basic for Applications

Record a macro

Create complicated programs without writing a single line of code yourself

To make a menu item for the macro, check this box...

Use one word to name your macro

Record New Macro ? ✕

Macro Name:
Splendid

Description:
Macro recorded 10/31/95 by David Moretsky. Calculates win/loss averages of NBA teams.

OK

Cancel

Options >>

Put a description here of what it does

Assign to

☑ Menu Item on Tools Menu:
Splendid Sonics

☑ Shortcut Key:
Ctrl+Shift+ S

To create a shortcut key, check this box...

...and type a name here

...and type the shortcut letter here

Store in
○ Personal Macro Workbook
◉ This Workbook
○ New Workbook

Language
◉ Visual Basic
○ MS Excel 4.0 Macro

Put your macro in the Personal Macro Workbook if you want it to be available from all workbooks, or...

...store it in the current workbook if that's where it will be used

1 Choose Tools, Record Macro, Record New Macro to bring up the Record New Macro dialog box.

2 Click on the Options button for more options.

3 Enter your choices and click on OK to start the macro recorder.

4 Perform the actions you wish to record.

5 Click the Stop button to stop the macro recorder.

6 Replay your macro later by selecting Tools, Macro and choosing your macro from the list.

 ® 201 W. 103rd Street • Indianapolis, IN 46290 • (317) 581-3500
Copyright© 1995 Que Corporation